CARMELITE AND POET
ST. JOHN OF THE CROSS

THE MACMILLAN COMPANY
NEW YORK · BOSTON · CHICAGO
DALLAS · ATLANTA · SAN FRANCISCO

MACMILLAN AND CO., LIMITED
LONDON · BOMBAY · CALCUTTA
MADRAS · MELBOURNE

THE MACMILLAN COMPANY
OF CANADA, LIMITED
TORONTO

CARMELITE AND POET

A Framed Portrait of

ST. JOHN OF THE CROSS

[Juan]

With His Poems in Spanish

By

ROBERT SENCOURT, pseud.

[George, Robert Esmonde Gordon]

NEW YORK

THE MACMILLAN COMPANY

1944

Nihil obstat
ARTHUR J. SCANLAN, S. T. D.

Imprimatur
✠ FRANCIS J. SPELLMAN
Archbishop, New York

February 18, 1944

2 3 5 0 5

Copyright, 1944, by
ROBERT SENCOURT

———

FIRST PRINTING.

A WARTIME BOOK
THIS COMPLETE EDITION IS PRODUCED
IN FULL COMPLIANCE WITH THE GOVERN-
MENT'S REGULATIONS FOR CONSERVING
PAPER AND OTHER ESSENTIAL MATERIALS

PRINTED IN THE UNITED STATES OF AMERICA
AMERICAN BOOK—STRATFORD PRESS, INC., NEW YORK

Hawarden,
March 25, 1943.

DEAR EVAN,

Not only as the President of the Catholic Poetry Society have you spread an interest in the literature of the Church, but by a special intuition you understand the minds which commune with and through the unseen. Here is one of the most brilliant of them, a man who gives us both the soul of poetry and the poetry of the soul. And though you are at the War Office, and we are both far from that Roman air in which we met twenty-one years ago, we know still how little can be seen or done, unless we have windows to let in the air and light of heaven.

Yours ever,
ROBERT.

To the VISCOUNT TREDEGAR,
13 *South Audley Street,*
W.1.

THE writings of St. John of the Cross will always be unintelligible to whoever does not understand that in them he is occupied wholly with the things of the spirit, with the relations of the soul to God, to which all else is entirely subordinate. By the greater part of those who would claim to be believers these, summed up as "religion," are, on the contrary, regarded mainly as a support to practical life—rather, that is, as a means to something else than as an end in themselves. For such, reality resides first in the world of things that come within the perception of their senses and their intellectual faculties: physical and metaphysical facts. God is, of course, "real" also: but however sincerely they may acknowledge Him as the source and controlling force of all that they know, actually for them He remains a somewhat shadowy form amongst the well-defined figures that fill their experience: for, not being *immediately* perceived, He has not that quality of reality which their thought adjudges to the objects that are so apprehensible.

The standpoint of St. John of the Cross is almost the exact antithesis of this. For him God is quite literally "The All": created objects, together with the activities that they provoke, are *poco mas que nada* —"little more than nothing": God is not revealed in or by things, but they in and by Him, for their reality is only a participation of His: we may (indeed we must) use them as first steps with which to raise ourselves up to Him, but they can serve us for but a little way, and we begin really to ascend only when their support is gone—

> *By the secret ladder, disguised*
> *(O happy lot!)*
> *In darkness and concealment,*
> *My house being now at rest.*

No one who has meditated the implications of the title "Creator," proper only to an infinite, eternal Being from whose free choice all existence issues as it were drop by drop in each instant of time: or has noted how, necessarily, such a Being must be independent of all the bounds and limitations that do not so much restrict as actually supply the framework of our thought: but must concede that the outlook of St. John of the Cross is a strictly logical one, even while at the same time it seem to him strange and difficult. It should therefore be easy to understand that one who sees God and the world as our Saint does will speak of them in a way which must be largely incomprehensible to those who cannot, at least speculatively, appreciate his postulates. Hence the common complaint that his works are esoteric, enigmatic, disturbing. He states, in fact, in the Prologue to the first Book of the *Ascent of Mount Carmel,* that he is addressing himself not indiscriminately to every manner of person, but designedly to those "who by the grace of God are on the pathway of this Mount": but one ventures to interpret this as including those also by whom, though it be from afar, the slopes of this mystic Hill are yet discernible. Among such, indeed, it ought not to be too much to say that all practising Christians should be numbered, for the content of the three volumes—the Ascent, the Dark Night, the Living Flame—amounts in essence to no more than a development and application of those words spoken by Our Lord on the eve of His Passion—the key-words of His universal teaching—that it is Eternal Life to know the only true God and Jesus Christ whom He has sent. For knowledge of God, rightly understood, is union with Him: and our progress towards this is, the Saint tells us, by faith, adding that "there is no progress but in the following of Christ." It is when he traces the path of this progress, analyses this faith, details the course of this following, that he undoubtedly does make severe, though not unreasonable, demand upon our understanding. But this is because by their very nature these things (beyond their first elementary beginnings) simply will not go into common words. He teaches, but we can never possess the complete key to his doctrine except at the price of being such as he was himself. Well, we cannot deny that this *is* the goal: and our inveterate defeatism in this matter does not dispense us from recognizing it as such, and should not disqualify us for aspiring at least to a growth in perception of the lofty principles that lead up to it. No one who is not grossly insensitive to what is fine and true and noble, however remote-seeming, can fail to be the better for the glimpse of the wonderful world of reality which he will catch in the writings of the Saint: God *must* in consequence mean something different and be something more to him, and the supernatural *must* establish itself more easily and habitually as the true

plane of his thought and action. And just as the study of a perfect
piece of painting or sculpture or music will for ever afterwards sharpen
our perception of what is good and true in art and our reaction to what
is inferior, so even such a distant Pisgah view of the Holy Land will
make us for ever after see the most common things of the spiritual
life no less than the rarest, with a bright delicacy of vision that never
could we otherwise have attained, though it should be our humble lot
to finish our days in the dim land of Moab.

It is here that the outstanding merit of Mr. Sencourt's study of St.
John of the Cross is *specially* manifest. By linking up his teaching with
the material as well as the spiritual circumstances and influences of
his life—his character, his nationality, his upbringing, his historical
setting, his social and religious contacts—the author goes very far
towards bringing both the personality and the science of the Saint
out of the rarefied and inaccessible region in which so many have been
content to leave him, and exhibiting him as a real person speaking
intelligibly about real things: a saint for all time, yet also a man of his
own time, proposing a sublime and almost ineffable doctrine, yet without going either beyond or aside from the plain teaching of the Scriptures and of the Christian Church. No excuse is available for those
who are disposed to regard study of the works of St. John of the Cross
as something unusual or freakish or as necessarily implying the
possession of special gifts and graces, for all that the Saint has to tell
us is how most perfectly to pursue the ideal set before us by Christ
Himself, that we should be "perfect even as our heavenly Father is
perfect," meaning that no one of us His followers has ever the right to
content himself with whatever spiritual height he may attain. One
learns from him that advance towards the knowledge of God (as
distinct from knowledge *about* Him) can never be made in the spirit
of a scholar investigating a complex intellectual problem, since the
special knowledge at which one aims eludes the categories of ordinary
thought and experience, for it deals with propositions and principles
which transcend both. His primary preoccupation is to free our conceptions of God and our methods of approach to Him from the
hindrances occasioned by the machinery of the reasoning faculty,
the imagination, and the sensitive will, so to prepare the soul for the
acquisition of that habit of passivity which will be used by God as the
vehicle of His communication of Himself not to our "powers" but to

our *selves*—substance to substance, as it were. The "Nights" of which the Saint speaks so terrifyingly are the means by which this freedom is reached through the sacrifice of all in order to possess The All, leaving the soul anxiously, agonizingly, still and void, like an empty vessel waiting helplessly to be filled. Yet the darkness of these Nights is in fact lit by that "luminous faith" of the mystic world which is by contrast with what we were before accustomed to call light what the gift of sight to a man born blind would be by contrast with his former means of contact with his surroundings: there is no place for it among the data of our past experience: for a time we can find no name and no use for it: hence the often long and painful duration of our pupillage. It is only as with ever more complete interior surrender to God of all the best that we have hitherto called our own, integrated by a corresponding advance in ascetical practice (for the level of a man's prayer is the level of his life), that everything that we had renounced is at last recovered and possessed more truly than ever before, because all that we have is now not ours *and* God's, but ours *because* God's.

Mr. Sencourt's very able study of the great Mystical Doctor will do much to encourage the many spiritually minded persons who find themselves at once attracted by his renown and repelled by what seems to them, on a cursory acquaintance, his obscurity and severity; for by its means they will be brought to realize that, for all their dark problems and hard sayings, the writings of St. John of the Cross are the work not of a mere visionary or sentimentalist; on the contrary of a man of trained mind and much practical experience, responsive to the influences of times and places and persons and acquainted with human infirmity in all its phases. It may come to them as a surprise to discover for themselves that not in spite of, but because of the sublimity of his doctrine, it has a message for all those who acknowledge that their destiny with regard to God is "to know Him, to love Him, and to serve Him in this world, and to be happy with Him for ever after in the next."

R. H. J. Steuart, S.J.

CONTENTS

INDEX TO POEMS IN SPANISH

LIST OF ILLUSTRATIONS

I am much indebted for help in finding these illustrations to the Duke of Alba, to the Revd. R. Trevor Davies, and to Miss Rose M. Fenn.

CARMELITE AND POET
ST. JOHN OF THE CROSS

THERE are several reasons for greeting the centenary of St. John of the Cross with a study which seeks to show how his work and his life are one, and frames him in his time and his Spain. He needs the frame to explain him, and none from any country has added it except when, for an absorbing hour at Cambridge in 1933, Professor Allison Peers read out a Rede lecture which was afterwards published.

My chief object has been to offer an explanation of not only a mystic whom many Catholics have found hard to understand, but also of a poet who has long since taken his place among the greatest poets of mysticism and passion. His sign was the Cross, but this is not a record of mere austerity: St. John of the Cross did not live alone: his was a genius complementary to that of his greatest friend, Santa Teresa, and I have sought to show how, at every turn, his story fits into hers, as into that of Spanish poetry and Carmelite mysticism.

This story of a mystic and a poet, furthermore, involves incidents so dramatic that Catholics have hesitated to tell it.

In a thoroughly documented work, Père Bruno established the facts of the saint's life in relation to the sources; but there was much that he did not explain. Since he wrote, moreover, a number of important studies have appeared; the *Introducción a la Historia de la Literatura Mística* of Professor Sainz Rodríguez, *L'Influence des Pays Bays sur les Mystiques Espagnols,* by Père Groult, and another study by a Viennese, Fr. Wessely. I have sought also to incorporate the results of three capital works of foreign scholarship: *Les Sources de Sainte Thérèse* by M. Etchegoyen; *St. John de la Croix et la Problème de la Connaissance Mystique* by M. Baruzi; the third and quite the most essential, *San Juan de la Cruz* by Fray Crisógono, a brilliant Carmelite of Ávila.

Besides these I have used a masterly life of Santa Teresa which Mrs. Cunninghame Graham, after her long work on original documents, published in 1893, and the monumental edition of the Saint's letters by Fray Silverio. Always supporting me also was Professor Allison Peers' admirable translation of the complete works, including the poems, of St. John.

It was in *The Criterion* in 1931 that, after making friends with Fray

Crisógono in Ávila, I first wrote on St. John of the Cross. Part of that article is here reproduced. Many a time, before and afterwards, I have sought an opportunity to make England better acquainted both with St. John and with the work of Fray Crisógono. Now I am able to do so with the help of Professor Allison Peers, of a Spanish Benedictine scholar, Dom Román Ríos, O.S.B., and of Don Alberto Jimenez, whom I first knew as head of the Residencia de Estudiantes in Madrid.

This work is not inapposite to wartime.

Though his poetry and his style have the abundance, and the surprise and the beauty of the period when Renaissance becomes baroque, St. John was absorbed in dealing with tribulations, in self-renunciation, and in regenerating the world through the powers of grace and the spirit. In the stress of catastrophe one does well to recall a genius whose way of life was that of the soul, and of the cross.

There is yet another reason why one should return at this time to him. Mr. Aldous Huxley has drawn to him the interest of many through a painting of the Secretary of Richelieu who first made popular the expression, *Eminence Grise*. It would be out of place here to repeat what I have already written for the *Hibbert Journal* on the vagueness and the inaccuracies of *Grey Eminence*. It will be sufficient to repeat it is misleading especially on four points: (1) on the place of St. John of the Cross in the history of mysticism; (2) in stating that his mysticism is impersonal; (3) in separating his mystical life from the sacrifice and suffering implied in the Cross from which he took his name; (4) in ignoring the foremost place which the dogmas of the Incarnation and the Trinity take in his writings.

Lastly, Mr. Huxley so much admires those excitable libertarians of Spain's spiritual life, the "alumbrados" or illuminists, whose lawless individualism was censured by the Church, that he has confused their flashlights with the "dark night" of the Dionysian tradition. This art—the passive contemplation of adoring calm—is not unknown to English literature. It was finely pictured by Wordsworth, who shared with St. John of the Cross a delight in wild nature, as well as a devotion to charity and duty. As Mr. Huxley speaks slightingly of Wordsworth, I have sought to show how, in spite of some sharp distinctions, he and St. John of the Cross sing in harmony the quality of receptivity and the place of Nature in the spiritual life.

As Mr. Huxley, disregarding his own dictum, "to over-simplify is fatal," has ignored the complexity of the Spanish Renaissance, one may ask what called forth at the period of the Spanish Renaissance a mysticism so heroic and what accounts for its magnificent expression? Professor Allison Peers sees in this question four factors involved— historical, social, religious, literary. One method of approach, he says, would be "to attempt to solve each part of the problem separately: to account for the suddenness of the mystical eruption by the exalta- tion due to the Reconquest, and perhaps also of the intellectual stimulus of the Renaissance; for the length of the period during which mysticism flourished, by the impetus given to it, in what otherwise might have been the highest point in its career, by the Carmelite saints; for its fervour, by the emotion engendered in them and in others, by the Reformation and the Counter-Reformation, and by the intensity normally and particularly observable in Spanish religious experience; for the richness of its content, by the combined influence of the Fathers, the Northern mystics and the Neoplatonists; for the nature and the slow pace of the decline, by the strong influence of the Carmelite School." [1] And finally he concludes that "nothing approaching a similar conjunction of circumstances ever occurred again." [2]

Professor Sainz Rodríguez in his Introduction to the *History of Mystical Literature of Spain* not only explained how San Juan is the complement to Santa Teresa, but he relates how the whole mystical movement is related to theology, to neoplatonism, to chivalry, and to literature. It is because, as the mystic returns from the ineffable, he seeks to relate it to human life as a whole that he seizes associations evoking love and joy, to relate what he has learned intuitively of the ineffable in his transient and expectant mood. [3]

Then is Mr. Huxley mistaken in connecting the Carmelites with the Buddhist mysticism? Not entirely—but the connection is remote. The story of Spanish mysticism certainly would not be complete with- out a reference to the Arabic mysticism which at times flourished in Spain. The names of Algazel and Abenarabi remind us that a kindred experience had influenced the Middle Ages, and through Leon Hebreo

---

[1] *Hispanic Review*, Vol. X, 1942, pp. 29-30.
[2] *Ibid.*, p. 30.
[3] Sainz Rodríguez, *Introducción*, pp. 56-59.

it affected the Platonism of the Florentine Renaissance, which in turn affected the poets and the men of culture of the sixteenth century in Spain as well as in Italy. Professor Sainz Rodríguez gives, in fact, the scheme of relations between the mystical schools (see below).

Here in a single diagram [4] we have a conspectus of the great field of study in which Mr. Huxley boldly though blindly gropes, and which rises to its most eminent height in the two Carmelites of Spain's Golden Age, Santa Teresa and St. John of the Cross. This book attempts to follow the track upward. But it will not be understood unless it is clearly recognized from the outset that the Catholic Church has always regarded her position as unique: that her mystics draw a distinction between, on the one hand, the value of contemplation and mysticism as a gift superadded to Divine revelation and supernatural Grace for the purpose of the completion of the life of the Church in the body of Christ—between these and, on the other, experiences which in themselves seem akin but which are separate both in their past, their present, and the future from the life of the Church in grace. These experiences are judged by Catholic authorities not in themselves but in their effects: their effects not only towards the supernatural perfection in Christ of the persons enjoying, or suffering, them, but in their relation to the life of the Church as a whole—the Church which always unites in her life theological precision, unselfish work, and even common sense, with the elevations of interior prayer.

Here is the scheme:

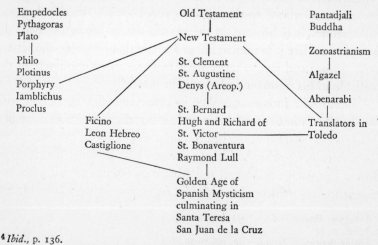

Empedocles	Old Testament	Pantadjali
Pythagoras	|	Buddha
Plato	New Testament	|
|	|	Zoroastrianism
Philo	St. Clement	|
Plotinus	St. Augustine	Algazel
Porphyry	Denys (Areop.)	|
Iamblichus		Abenarabi
Proclus	St. Bernard	
Ficino	Hugh and Richard of	Translators in
Leon Hebreo	St. Victor————	Toledo
Castiglione	St. Bonaventura	
	Raymond Lull	
	|	
	Golden Age of	
	Spanish Mysticism	
	culminating in	
	Santa Teresa	
	San Juan de la Cruz	

There are frequent references to the following works:

Ford: *Handbook to Spain,* by Richard Ford. 1st edn., 1845.

Cunninghame Graham: *Life of Santa Teresa,* by Gabriela Cunninghame Graham. 2 vols., 1893.

Bruno: *Life of St. John of the Cross,* by P. Bruno. English edn., 1932.

Zimmermann in Bruno: A conclusive essay in the 1932 translation by Benedict Zimmermann.

Crisógono: *San Juan de la Cruz. Su obra científica y su obra Literária,* by Fray Crisógono de Jesús Sacramentado. 1929.

Baruzi: *St. Jean de la Croix et la Problème de la Connaissance Mystique,* by Jean Baruzi, 1924.

Stanbrook. Life: *A Life of St. John of the Cross,* by the Benedictines of Stanbrook, assisted by Benedict Zimmermann.

Allison Peers: *Translation of the Works of St. John of the Cross,* by E. Allison Peers. 3 vols., 1934–35.

Among these are:

D.N.: "Dark Night of the Soul."
M.C.: "Ascent of Mount Carmel."
C.E.: "Cántico Espiritual, or Song of the Spirit."
"The Living Flame of Love."

Besides a brilliant and penetrating study of St. John of the Cross in *The Philosophy of Mysticism,* by Mr. E. I. Watkin, useful studies have recently been made by Dom Bede Frost (Hodder and Stoughton, 1937), Father Gabriel (Thos. Baker, 1942) and Professor Allison Peers (S.C.M., 1943). The two former are called *St. John of the Cross,* the last, *Spirit of Flame.*

I should like to say in conclusion how grateful I am for help in reading the proofs to my friend Mr. F. J. E. Raby, C.B., F.B.A., Litt.D.

R. S.

We can make patience a noble fortitude
And thinke not how unkindly we are us'de.
Man (like to Cassia) is prov'd best, being bruised.[1]

I

THERE are periods in history, there are periods in certain lives when the combinations of character and fate press hard, as the clouds congregate their might of electricity and moisture before they discharge the storm. Life appears to move both into the cloud and into the night. We cannot foretell the future, we find ourselves stripped of many comforts; life, if not gloomy, at least is stern. Such periods of bruising and dark night, whether in national events or in personal affliction, link us with a Spaniard born four hundred years ago, who went through great sufferings of body and soul before he gave to Spain and literature the finest love-lyrics ever written in Castilian. He was a Carmelite Friar, and has long since been proclaimed a Saint: we know him generally as St. John of the Cross. But his poems are Spanish poems: his story is a Spanish story: and as we trace how the two make one life, we do better to recover the Spanish atmosphere, and grow accustomed to the Spanish name by which he signed all his letters, the name Fray Juan de la Cruz: [2] he grew up into a boy in Castile with the name of Juan de Yepes y Álvarez.

2

Words finely picked and skilfully interwoven in the deliberate pattern of verse to speak the speech of rapture: these mark the poet who summons his imagery to tell the hidden things within him. We hardly expect this, do we? from a man mewed in a rigid monkish life. Yet the two who stand together as the lyric poets of Spain both lived the strict life of friars; they were contemporaries and died within a

---

[1] Webster, *Duchess of Malfi*, III, 5, 86-88.
[2] The Spanish J has the sound of ch in loch; z the sound of th in the; the u in Cruz the sound of u in bull. Pronounce therefore Hwahn de la Cruth.

year of one another. One is Juan de la Cruz, the other Luis de León. Both combined their religion with their lyric art, so that their mysticism is the very stuff of their excellence as poets. Juan, indeed, worked out the doctrine of self-renunciation with the extremest thoroughness, and it is as a symbol of his abnegation that he explains his best-known poem. This poem, and the elaborate mystical explanation of it, are each known as *The Dark Night of the Soul*.

But he was no poet of tragedies or of storm. His, on the contrary, are the songs of joy. This lyric of the dark night tells of lover meeting lover to be united in bliss: it was explained a second time as the Ascent of Mount Carmel; and here, though the asceticism is uncompromising, it has a core of rapture, a love of beauty which recalls, as the title itself suggests, the views over the Mediterranean and the plains of Esdraelon and Acre as we look across them from the beauty of high hills.

It could be no accident that made these two masters of the Lyric both friars and contemporaries in Old Castile. There was something evidently in the way their strict ruled life was combined with their people, their place, and their century that occasioned this peculiar turn to their genius. Each was a son of Castile, and duly born into his time. Every feature of the Spain around them is significant. For this was not only Spain, the country of strong character, but Spain at her meridian, when her golden age was beginning, and her nationalism extreme.

3

Juan was born, the son of Francisco de Yepes and Catalina Álvarez his peasant wife, about four hundred years ago, in 1542. It will take us a little time to see exactly what that means. In 1542, it was exactly fifty years since Columbus had discovered that two continents were strung together to stop his western voyage to India. Since then, the wealth of the Americas, like that of the Indies, came back to Europe through Iberian ports. For while he sailed westward, Portuguese navigators, not less distinguished—Vasco da Gama and Magalhaes—crossed the Equator to the Cape of Good Hope and Cape Horn. It was an age of excitement and excess, soon to be reflected in Elizabethan England: [3] but Spain, because her navigators were early

[3] Hakluyt's *Voyages,* Vol. XII, pp. 92, 93.

on the seas, because her ports were filled with their traffic, and finally because her sovereigns were lords of most of the Continent, felt the effect earlier and felt it more.[4]

For Charles V was not merely King of Spain; as a Habsburg he inherited also the Netherlands, and the Holy Roman Empire. After he defeated Francis I at Pavia he was almost the Emperor of Europe, and the Pope endowed him with the Americas.

For him and his people, practical objects were to be connected with those of the Catholic Church. To construct ships and to furnish palaces was one task; to build convents and churches another. On the one side there was a rush for gold and silver; on the other, every sacrifice was made to christianize the newly discovered continents, which, indeed, heard the Gospel before they knew the masterpieces of Cervantes.

4

In Spain, therefore, there were two immensely strong currents: those of the Spanish nation, and those of the Spanish Church. It is by launching out into the mingling currents that we take history at the flood of its events and of its men.

For the Spaniards are not as the other peoples of Europe. Among many characteristics, they have always been markedly intractable: no people are stronger individualists, or less willing to pull together.

And the Spanish nature often presented peculiar dangers. Undisciplined and individual, they became, after reconquering the Moors and conquering the Americas, yet more arbitrary, vainer and prouder. Robust and handsome, they found that the new wealth enriched their blood, made their hearts hotter. Less than ever were they inclined to serve others, or bear the burden of the day. And the need to discipline the American natives to work, the need to assert their national and religious unity against foreign influences from the past, each added to what was long their character—a capacity for occasional cruelty. Among their "regions" or provinces they had made war for centuries. And this habit of warlike expeditions, which they called guerillas,—little wars—made them love the mimicry of combat, above all in the bull-fight, with its flashing costumes, its agile movements, its skill, its drama of blood and death, and its sense of agility

[4] *Ibid.,* pp. 17, 18.

meeting bestial savagery and overcoming it. They had no industry but their sport, and that was the great game of war.

Now, therefore, we can see a little more of the meaning of saying that Juan de la Cruz was born a Spaniard in 1542. His life and work were to be a strong reaction to the peculiarities of the Renaissance Spain.

5

And we need also to have as clear an idea as we can of the country which nourished him. In four hundred years it is little changed. It is a great plateau set between three and four thousand feet above the sea, with few trees, few streams, and its features two wild sierras to the south and east. That on the east cuts it off from Madrid, it is the Sierra de Guadarrama, in a fold of which the King was soon to be building his great palace of the Escorial. On the south the Sierra de Gredos above richly wooded valleys rose majestic and abrupt to the height of ten thousand feet, with sharp peaks of rock in the sky to the Picos de Almanzor, and beneath these streams flowing down wooded valleys, the Alberche eastward to join the Tagus, the Tormes westward beyond Salamanca to the Douro. On this high plateau, the year shows its extremes; from early autumn to late spring the winds are icy, and the country is made most winterly by storms and by occasional falls of snow. After a hurrying spring, summer bursts on it with torrid sun, which draws out the growth of wheat. For those boundless plains are in spring green, in summer golden with grain, with waves endless as those of the sea and vast as the great arc of sky above. In this country the weather is so merciless, the conditions so hard that they kill all but the hardiest. Even the sheep cannot survive the winter, but over great broad tracks—*cañadas*—millions of them are driven backwards and forwards with the seasons.[5] Of the human survivors there are two types. The robust and exuberant, easy, friendly, magnetic; the solemn and reserved, supporting their hardships austerely. But in each the eyes are alive: for they know the mysteries of life and of death. Each knows what dignity it is to be a man and a Castilian; each savours both earth and eternity: and for each the blood is a power, the soul a flame. Each combines shrewdness with idealism.

[5] Cf. R. Trevor Davies, *Golden Century of Spain*, pp. 18-20.

"The two Castiles," says Ford, "are the largest provinces in Spain and contain some of the oldest and most interesting cities. The mountains are highly picturesque, abounding in curious botany and geology, and their Swiss-like valleys are watered by trout streams; they present a perfect contrast to the parameras, tierras de campo y Secanos, the plains and tablelands which are bounded only by the horizon, silent, treeless, songless and without hedges, enclosures or landmarks. The Castilians have a singular antipathy to trees, and like Orientals they seldom plant any except those which bear fruit, or give shade for their *alamedas*. Political instability adds to the austerity of an unwatered wildness: for who, asks the Spaniard, has seen tomorrow? Where in other countries the birds sing, here one sees the air swept only by the eagle or the vulture. Only the bee is busy among the wild flowers or poppy or cornflowers, over the hedgeless, treeless tracts of cornfield. Silent, sad and lonely is the face on which the stranger will too often gaze." [6]

Castile and its people are one.

But if the land is bare, and shows few features but the mountains, the air is keen with the rareness of mountain land; through it the eye sees with a dazzling clearness, and the breast is raised to have the fill of it. Such was the native air of Juan de la Cruz.

6

Here men live not on the fat and flesh-pots of good cooks, but on the finer food in air and light. These brighten the eyes and enrich the chemistry of the blood. Heat, cold, and light all combine to teach the Castilian intensity. He is as much raised among common men in the knightliness of life as the ground he treads is high above the sea. He feels that no matter how hard his life, he must maintain the standards not merely of a man, but, as he understands them, of a Christian. For his ideal is soldierly, with something within to preserve from marauding Goth or subtle Moor. Observers now, and still more observers in the sixteenth century, noticed the sensitiveness of the Castilian in all to do with honour. They would die rather than suffer a stain, said the Florentine, Guicciardini, in 1513. "They think it beneath them to become merchants, for they all affect the honours of persons of quality and would rather go soldiering even with poor prospects, or take service with some great noble and put up with a thousand discomforts." [7]

The Venetian Contarini noted in 1525 that they made a cult of honour which inclined them to the military career. He noticed their reserve, their discipline, their envy. For these Christians rose from their knees to be God's warriors.

Though Italians do not usually like the Spaniards, whose virility made them contemptuous, and whose national qualities could give them the air of swashbucklers, yet even an Italian could praise them for their hardiness, their self-respect, and their piety.

"They concern themselves," said an Italian Professor at Salamanca, Lucio Marineo, in 1535, "about religious matters and the salvation of their souls with quite as much diligence and care as about the riches and amusements of the world. Indeed, the Spaniards of the present day are very religious and display great reverence for the worship of God; the priests are very solicitous for the spiritual welfare of the people, over and above celebrating mass and observing the canonical hours, and interest their flocks with sermons and good example. And laymen—not only noblemen and educated men but also the common people and the uneducated—are very obedient to the commandments of Christ and the Church." [8]

Romantic, and rather high-flown, with a taste for sumptuousness, the Spaniards, by seeking too much, often obtain too little. They are, indeed, people not only of volcanic energy, but stayers. Yet their strenuousness stops short at what strikes them as dull, and "Drudgery they will do none at all." [9] Their acuteness they show in the sharp brevity of their proverbs. Insight they have and rapid vision, but fail to think things co-ordinately out or preserve with solid will.[10] At the heart of their eloquence and nobility is a surge of unquiet; for ever with them in that age as still to-day is "the harsh, turbulent, sternly original character of the race which has never allowed them to rest,

[7] H. D. Sedgwick, *Ignatius Loyola*, p. 7.
[8] *Ibid.*, p. 6.
[9] Sir R. Wynn. *A brief relation of what was observed by the Prince's servants.* 1623.
[10] Azorin, *La Voluntad.*

but kept them perpetually at strife." [11] Apt to take umbrage at their shadows, they were not made for smooth success. The valiant, the high-sounding, the heroic, the exciting: these entice men to embark on great projects, and Spain would die but that somewhere among the poor the patience and the hardihood survived.

Such, then, was the Spain, religious, powerful, virile, generous, with a sense of nobility current through all the people, as though all were knights, with the ceremonious formality of Islam and Africa affecting their manners and their speech, yet with spontaneity, vitality, energy and ease, into which Juan de Yepes came when he was born in 1542. He belonged to it with every fibre of a peculiarly sensitive, intense, and ardent nature.

[11] Ricardo Léon, *Acalá de los Zegríes,* quoted in Aubrey Bell, *The Magic of Spain,* p. 23. Barcelona, 1902.

*With zeal to win souls, with highest charity and insuperable cour-
age, in spite of innumerable contradictions, travails, voyages, hardships and dangers, they spread in the Orient the gospel of Christ our
Lord and made His Name known and loved and reverenced with
urgent and apostolic preaching, confirmed with many miracles, and
shedding of their blood in martyrdoms; and in Europe with teaching
of sane and excellent doctrine, truly Christian, with virtue, religion,
culture and administration, with reading and frequenting the Sacraments, they conserved and led to perfection the man of religion, and
reformed the erring with their example, and with their exercises of
piety and penitence they made the priests more numerous, more
practical and more illumined.*[1]

I

THE village of Fontiveros, his birthplace, is almost at the centre
of the base of the equilateral triangle made by the roads between
Ávila, Salamanca, and Medina del Campo, the central plateau
of Old Castile.

Lying in a fold of the plain, this village enjoys a spring and green
grass amidst the yellowing plain of stone and barrenness. Here the
villagers lived, as they live still, the simplest life. Many have fowls,
and therefore eggs; they eat polenta, they have some bread: but their
lives are simplicity itself. For months, the cold winds chill and harden
them, and penury is their close companion. Cold, hungry, amid the
humblest tasks, little Juan de Yepes and two elder brothers lived with
a widowed mother, who, in the intervals of cooking, working and
cleaning, tried to earn money by some weaving. But there was so little
to earn, and therefore so little to eat, that while the boy was still
young his mother, who had tried in vain to get help from her dead
husband's relations in the neighbourhood of Toledo, took him for a
short time to Arévalo on her way to Medina del Campo, "the City
of the Plain," where merchants dealt in wares from many places in
streets round a market-place sheltered by a feudal castle.[2]

[1] Cabrera, *Istoria del Rey Felipe II*, Book VI, ch. v, relating to the Jesuits.
[2] Bruno, pp. 3, 6.

2

The Medina of to-day, though it still has an Eastern tang, is very different from the populous city which then drew to its fair the merchants and traders of Western Europe. For its fairs were then famous. In them the cloths and tapestries of Flanders, with ware and French papers and French trinkets, were exchanged for the silks and spices of Valencia, the sugar of Seville, the saddles and morocco leather of Córdoba, the steel of Toledo, the cloths of Cuenca and Ciudad Real. It was a town of 50,000 people, and it was said that fifty-three thousand million maravedis changed hands at one of its fairs: a maravedi, it is true, being but a farthing. After the fair the streets would grow quieter: the ragged labourers came in on ragged donkeys from the dusty roads, bearing their loads of wheat beneath the faded bricks, the Renaissance architecture, the embossed escutcheons. Here one became aware of both the traffic and the history of Spain.[3]

3

In Medina the starving mother with her three children found some work, and therefore some nourishment. Her youngest son began by serving in a hospital for men suffering from tumours. This still allowed him some time to go to school, and with an apt brain and quick perception, he became the docile pupil of a new company of men vowed to religion; they were known already as the Society of Jesus, and they stamped his young mind with their character, while at the same time it reacted in marked contrast to their methods.

4

Everything about this striking company was a reminder that their founder was a Spaniard and an officer.

He kept all through the habits of mind of his first vocation. He had the soldier's temper, practical, courageous, and disciplined. He set out to fashion a company, then a regiment, then an army which would employ the heroic Spanish virtue to overcome the dramatic Spanish faults—the faults of individualism, selfishness, pride, and

[3] G. Cunninghame Graham, *Santa Teresa*, I, 326; II, 250.

vainglory. Thus he won souls back from worldliness and hell to the love and service of his Saviour: bound by no close monastic observance, no attachments to a house, they were to be men who could go anywhere and do anything that the Church required. Loyola would have every man ask himself three practical questions: What have I done for Christ? What am I doing for Christ? What can I do for Christ?

This converted officer stands out like the Cid, eminent as a towering peak in Spanish history. No one has better sketched his remarkable outlines than our own vivid Protestant historian. "In his early life," wrote Macaulay, "he had been the very prototype of the hero of Cervantes. The single study of the young Hidalgo had been chivalrous romance; and his existence had been one gorgeous daydream of princesses rescued and infidels subdued. He had chosen a Dulcinea, 'no countess, no duchess,' these are his own words, but of a higher station, and he flattered himself with the hope of laying at her feet the keys of Moorish castles, and the jewelled turbans of Asiatic kings. When on the bed of pain, religion coloured all his chivalry, his designs were far more practical without being less romantic. He would still be a soldier; still be a knight errant; but the soldier and knight errant of the Spouse of Christ. He would smite the Great Red Dragon. He would be the champion of the Woman clothed with the Sun. He would break the charm under which false prophets held the souls of men in bondage. His restless spirit led him to the Syrian desert and to the chapel of the Holy Sepulchre. Thence he wandered back to the farthest West, and astonished the convents of Spain and the schools of France by his penances and vigils. The same lively imagination which had been employed in picturing the tumult of unreal battles and the charms of unreal queens now peopled his solitude with saints and angels. The Holy Virgin descended to commune with him. He saw the Saviour face to face with the eye of flesh." [4] Indeed, it was his gift and his method to use the senses and the imagination as a means of commune with the unseen and with the mysteries of faith. He met human nature on its own ground, and won it to his purpose with all the resources of the intellect, all the eagerness of the will, all the fervour of feeling and romance. And the world ceded to his ardour. "Poor, obscure, without a patron,

---

[4] Macaulay, *Essay on Ranke's History of the Popes.*

without recommendations, he entered the city where now two princely temples, rich with painting and with many coloured marbles commemorate his great services to the Church; where his form stands sculptured in massive silver; where his bones, enshrined amidst jewels, are placed beneath the Altar of God." [5]

He was indeed a mystic, who, kneeling once to pray on the steps outside the Church of San Domenico in Rome, had seen the very essence of God, the Trinity in Unity, and wept aloud in joy and wonder. But what with his military training, his travels, and his Basque shrewdness, he was also a man of the world who knew how to lead his followers, how to be all things to all men that he might save some. His society advanced like a cohort to regain for the Church the allegiance of those that count. Nothing was beyond their interest: no soul was too worldly to help: no zeal too arduous for their heroism. "Some," says Macaulay, "described those men as the most rigid, others as the most indulgent of spiritual directors. And both descriptions were correct. The truly devout listened with awe to the high and saintly morality of the Jesuit. The gay cavalier who had run his rival through the body, the frail beauty who had forgotten her marriage vows, found in the Jesuit an easy, well-bred man of the world, tolerant of the little irregularities of people of fashion. The Confessor was strict or lax according to the temper of his penitent. His object was to drive no person out of the pale of the Church." [6]

5

Such was the order which set out over the Protestant North, and Catholic Spain, to use every faculty and taste of men for the glory of Christ crucified and the increase of Holy Church. Macaulay pays his tribute to the Spanish valiance of their combat: their vehemence, their discipline, their self-denial, their fearlessness, their intense and stubborn devotion to the end in view: he recalls the distrust and hatred which they aroused among their enemies. But he points out the brilliant success of their campaign. He traces them out to the shores of the Spice Islands, to the Observatories of China, to the deep mines of Peru, to the hovels of Connaught, and the manor houses of

[5] *Op. cit.*
[6] Macaulay, *op. cit.*

GLORIA IN EXCELSIS. HIGH MASS AT SAN ISIDRO, IN MADRID

Showing the majesty of Spanish art and worship in the period of St. John of the Cross

Cheshire. Their enterprise led them "to make converts where neither avarice nor curiosity had tempted any of their countrymen to enter"; they "preached and disputed in tongues of which no other native of the West understood a word"; they laboured not only in the pulpits and confessionals but in the Universities, the hospitals, the libraries. With the most elastic and generous ingenuity, they made friends with literature, with science, with adventure, with exploration, with fashion, with philosophy and with romance.

Stamped with the enterprise, the energy, the idealism, the shrewdness, the excitement, and the dauntlessness of Spain, and of Spain above all at the inception of her golden age, such was the Society which the impoverished but brilliant little boy from Fontiveros met, and by whom he was taught in the intervals of his humble service in the tumour hospital of Medina del Campo.[7]

He was an eager student. His wondering relations would tell how as a small boy he sat on a pile of wood, reading by the light of a little candle. And he caught from the Jesuits their interest in secular literature, their mingling of individuality with discipline, and their personal enterprise. All were sharpened by courage.[8]

[7] Bruno, pp. 11, 12.
[8] Ibid., p. 13.

I have desired to go
 Where springs not fail,
To fields where flies no sharp and sided hail,
 And a few lilies blow.

And I have asked to be
 Where no storms come
Where the green swell is in the havens dumb
 And out of the swing of the sea.

GERARD MANLEY HOPKINS.

I

YET, brilliant as the Jesuits' Society was, it was an innovation. It left practically undisturbed those great societies of the religious life which withdrew from the world to adore the majesty of God. The gift of contemplation, the sense of a Divine Society, the obligation of worship: these through the ages had called men and women to the hermitage, the desert, and the convent. And this ordered preoccupation with God, this concentration on the study of the Bible was even in that active, surging Spain of navigation, colonization, and battle, the Spain of Charles V and of Philip II, a more insistent thing than the cultured militance of San Ignacio and his Jesuits.

It is curious that Protestants have been so slow to understand the power of the tradition which through the centuries has grouped men together to live the life of holiness. Both men and women have found in those houses, quiet, spaciousness, courtesy, cleanliness, and for the most part good taste, where the normal discipline and energy demanded by affairs could be given to the spiritual life. The principle of that life has been the reading of the Bible and the honour and praise of God: those are houses from which curious and worldly people are excluded; where a wise discipline maintains a high tradition; where the Divine office is a delight; where the mind is set upon divinity, and the heart on the mysteries and love: [1] where each fulfilling

---

[1] Bossuet, *Oraisons Funèbres*, Anne de Gonzague.

his separate function in the community looks to the peace and well-being of the house as a whole; where each could say, "One day within thy courts is better than a thousand." [2]

In such houses the rules of poverty, chastity, and obedience were universal—the three principles which combated as contraries the self-ish faults, the lust of the eyes, the lust of the flesh, and the pride of life. Such, with the motto of Peace, was the order of St. Benedict. Such had arisen (or re-arisen) in the twelfth century the order of Mount Carmel.

It centred on the life of mysticism, which was as remarkable in the Spain of that time as its navigators, its warriors, its colonizers, its sheep-farmers, its architects, or its poets.

2

Indeed, the mystics stand high, if not highest, among the Spanish writers of the sixteenth century. For while on the one side, men wrote of the adventures of the rogue or harlot—and *Lazarillo de Tormes* disputed popularity with *La Celestina* and *Don Juan*—or, like Manrique, developed the theme of nobleness and honour—yet on the other was an intense interest in the spiritual life, an interest which produced one classic after another from the time of Luis de Granada onwards, and were not unconnected with the love of nature, a theme which was developed by Antonio de Guevara, a Bishop who wrote a book on true honour called *The Dial of Princes,* and another on the advantages of the village in comparison with the Court. These were not mysticism, but among the writers on the spiritual life were, after Granada, San Pedro de Alcántara, Francisco de Ossuna, and Juan de Ávila.[3]

Apart from these, the scientific study of theology—asking the portentous question *What is God?*—raised its gaze to the survey of His infinity. When man engaged his intellect on something which the intellect could not attain, he had need for it to be lifted by su-pernal aids, and looked by the intenser light which is faith, faith which, as it deepens, merges into hope and love. This realm of faith

[2] Psalm LXXXI.
[3] For further information on all these, see Professor E. Allison Peers, *Studies of the Spanish Mystics.*

was the realm of the Bible; here, surveyed with all the acuteness of a logical mind, was the Sum of Theology as an Italian son of Santo Domingo had noted it down, and which was being studied afresh in Salamanca not only by the Professors of Theology, but by very acute scholars among the Carmelites themselves. These scholars, adapting the rather disjointed style of San Tommaso di Aquino, with its questions, its string of objections and its string of answers to these, into a more coherent and literary body of work, more like the *Summa Contra Gentiles* of their master, were to prepare in imposing volumes a whole course of theology dealing with the supreme verities of the Christian religion as they had been understood by the greatest thinkers and scholars of the Church.

3

The Carmelites did not take the Dominican masters as absolute and final: they had their own metaphysicians in the English friar, John Bacon, who lived from 1290 to 1356, and his contemporary Michele di Bologna. By a prescription of 1510, every Carmelite house had to contain a copy of John Bacon's works.[4]

The chief distinction between the teaching of San Tommaso and that of John Bacon was that while the former taught that the intellect perceived a "universal" as the reality, the latter insists that each singular thing has a subsistent reality. The truth of a thing, according to Bacon, is not an abstraction: it is the underlying reality of every individual which exists, and therefore every single thing God has created is directly related to His grandeur. The differences of philosophy are perhaps explained by differences of psychology and approach: if not, the argument is indeed exhausting, for neither side has ever proved its case in such a way as to carry general conviction.

4

Anchorites and holy men through the ages sought out in the caves and solitudes of Carmel to give themselves more wholly as sons of the prophets to a life of quiet and solitude with God. But it is not until 1155 that the name of the order appears in authentic documents;

---

[4] Crisógono, I.

and then it is connected not merely with the tradition of the Old Testament, but with a particular veneration of the Blessed Virgin, under the title of Our Lady of Mount Carmel. The order spread first up the Syrian coast to Acre, Tyre, and Tripoli; then to Jerusalem: afterwards to Europe.[5]

The object of this order was that its members should live in their cells or near them, meditating day and night on the law of the Lord and His word. Their houses, therefore, were often built in lonely places: the religious had long and severe fasts: they celebrated the offices with special care: they gave up much further time to communion with God in meditation and contemplation—in a word, it was their object to be masters of the spiritual life.

5

The Carmelite life envisages God's love for individual men meeting their own efforts. On the one side the friar should offer to God a heart holy and free from all actual sin: he should toil and sacrifice himself, grace being his helper. But in return for this, he is to receive something beyond all human effort, something beyond what men may ever merit, something which came from the overflowing love in the soul of Jesus, an experience in the spirit of the strength of the Divine presence. Those, then, are the two ends which the Carmelite has in view, that he might say with the psalmist: "In a desert and pathless land where no water is, there have I looked for thee in holiness that I might behold thy power and beauty." [6]

Often alone, nearly always at prayer, fasting for long hours, awake at night in vigil, the Carmelites lived indeed austerely; yet in the sixteenth century in Spain literally thousands crowded into their houses: and these were centres of culture, almost of society, where educated people shared not only in the things of taste but exchanged with one another many a shrewd comment both on what was going on in the world and on what was going on in the convent.

For in those days the religious orders in Spain comprised a quarter of the population; they had vast possessions and influence, and they present a picture not merely of religious life but of the Spain of their

[5] *Catholic Encyclopædia*, III, 354.
[6] Psalm LXII, 3 (Vulgate). Here, as in other references to the Psalms, the Coverdale and authorized versions of the Psalms are one more in number: here, *e.g.*, LXIII, 3.

time; many a drama occurred in the conflict between the two atmospheres, that of Spain and that of monasticism: as, in the hearts of men and women, between the impulses of grace and those of rude will.

6

A man entering a monastery or convent found himself in most friendly and excellent company. For is not the Spaniard the most delightful person to know? And above all the Spaniard of Castile. Every Castilian feels himself a noble, and is indeed an honest, right good fellow, being well-bred rather than polite, but, once attached, sincere. What attachment, what confidence is more complete than that of friendship? For even in religious houses there are personal predilections, personal antipathies. "The Castilian," says Ford, "is simple and with few wants, or vices; he lives and dies where he was born after the fashion and ignorance of his ancestors, and although a creature of routine and uneducated, he is shrewd and intelligent in his limited scope. He may have a hard life, but he faces it with spirit; the peasants among themselves are as full of amusement as children, and full of raillery, mother-wit and practical joking." [7] For education to them is not reading and writing (though they can count if required), but the manners and the taste which shows a knowledge of the world.

"They have, it is true," Ford goes on, "no book conversation but reason rather from instinct; and what they say has a game flavour, albeit sometimes rather strong; but they are neither tame rabbits nor house-fed lambs; a want of the gentle, the tender and the conceding marks the character of the Oriental and Castilian; bred and born among difficulties, obstacles and privations, under a fierce sun, and on a hard soil, the wild weed of strong, rank nature grows up harsh and unyielding. Here *man* is to be seen in his unsophisticated, untamed state, in all his native force; for here everything is personal, and the very antithesis of our social, corporate, fusing political combinations; as there is no homogeneity, so there is no amalgamation, no compromise, no concession." [8] It is plain that much had to be done before such laymen as these would live harmoniously together in the

[7] Ford, 1845, I, 151.
[8] Ford, 1845, II, 718.

social life of discipline. Yet the common person of Castile finely understood the art of living: even though proud, obstinate, and uncommercial, he was true to his God and his King: there in Castile was the soundest stuff of Spain, strong in life and virility. Of these robust individualists, in the sixteenth century, many naturally went adventuring over sea; of those that remained in Spain, no less than a quarter, as we have just seen, found a vocation in religion, and formed the populace of convents and monasteries.

7

It was nothing extraordinary, therefore, for a gifted young man like Juan de Yepes to enter a religious house. What were the other choices? For an ardent mind of keenest intellectual ability and delicate perceptiveness of all that was exquisite and beautiful, many courses were open. There were devout and ardent laymen in the Spanish Church then as there are now. Would not perhaps the freedom of the layman's life best accord with the gifts of the scholar and poet? Or if not, what of all the variety of culture, of adventure, of enterprise in the new Company of Jesus? Among the members of that company was a fervent *esprit de corps*. They longed that the ardent souls of those they influenced should share in their exalted enterprise. Yet neither the life of variety nor the wide choices of the layman appealed to him. He looked for that support, that security, that corporate life, that strictness of rule, that tradition and garden of mysticism which a religious order offers to the priest and theologian. He found it not in the wide, cultured, liturgical system of Saint Benedict, nor yet in the generous simplicity of the Franciscans, nor yet in the ordered dignity of the Canons Regular of St. Augustine. He looked for something more directly mystical, more silent, more secluded, stricter: the voice by which the Holy Spirit speaks to the heart called him to offer his life in the order of Mount Carmel.

8

Very small and light, of frail build, though tempered by hardship, Juan had already a peculiar personal attraction. Those that looked at him loved him. Possibly he feared that he would meet with opposition from his family: certainly he knew that Alfonso Álvarez de Toledo, the master of the hospital where he served, had a great regard for him, and believed that he would make an excellent chaplain for the patients; [9] whatever the source of his fears, he waited till all the house was quiet, and then he fled from the hospital secretly in the dark and chill of the night, by a ladder, or secret stair; passing beneath the stars with that indescribable elation with which youth sets out on a high venture, he came finally to the door of the Carmelite house to begin the life in which he felt he would reach the supreme felicity. Through the years, that adventure returned to him to open the floodgates of his enthusiasm: that was the entrance into the dim, youthful rapture which fills the heart with its music; no lover passing through the night to serenade his mistress, no bridegroom exploring in the mysteries of the night the sacredness of nuptial rapture, felt himself more one with the very heart of love and joy than this young Spaniard, whose every longing was alight with love, and who found that night had turned to day in the burning heat and light which filled his heart. That "fortune blest" was to remain the symbol of all he treasured in the life of his new sacrifice.

9

After several months as a novice, he was accounted worthy himself to be admitted as a vowed member of the order. Wearing black shoes and a dark cloak, but with his head already shaven except where longer hair was left in the shape of a crown, young Juan de Yepes y Álvarez was formally received into the House of Santa Ana in Medina del Campo in the cold winter air of February 24, 1563, to take the name of Juan de Santo Matía, to be clothed in a white woollen robe, to take his place in the stall nearest the Altar, and to receive the Holy Communion.[10]

He found his new day a busy and exacting one. In all monasteries, then as now, the monks recited the solemn offices of the Church when, in an appropriate setting of prayer, they read long passages from the Bible, especially from the Psalms. Every day they chanted in its traditional form, with the symbolism of light, of water and of

[9] Baruzi, pp. 76, 77.
[10] Bruno, pp. 15, 16.

fire, amidst the perfumed smoke of incense, the solemn office of the Eucharist, in which bread and wine were offered to God, that by making them holy He might change them till by mystery they became to those that received them the very Body, the very Blood, the very soul and power of Christ Himself. Thus, in the worship of God, and the reading of the Word, many hours went by, both by day and night.

But each convent is also a household where there are rooms to clean, meals to cook, serve and eat, provisions to be found. In all these works the novice had plenty to fill his hours, acting with that prompt, cheerful obedience, that punctuality which means discipline in any sort of institution from the regiment to the hospital, the warship to the school. All these works were to be done thoroughly, in a spirit of humility, and wherever possible with silence. Simple, rough meals, barely served, to the sound of reading, rounded out the day, which did, however, permit of a little free time by way of recreation for talk and walk, sometimes a little expedition. In all this life the religious sought to mortify his selfish, and even his natural inclinations, that the impulses of egoism should be drawn out of him and grace should take their place. Every weed must be rooted out for the chosen plants to flourish.

It is a common thing in religious houses for the novice to be an example. He is still unconfirmed in his choice, and he is as anxious to be finally accepted as a lover is during his engagement. During this time the young Juan excelled among the virile novices. In every matter of obedience he was punctilious, and to those who were around him he seemed like an angel.[11] After six months of the novitiate, he took the vows, received the fuller robe called the scapular, and, being confirmed in his new life, he went, in 1564, the journey of fifty miles to Salamanca to study in the Cambridge of Spain those general subjects of culture, centring around Latin and Philosophy, which are called the Arts.

[11] Bruno, p. 25.

> *Ay levantad los ojos*
> *A aquesta celestial eterna esfera*
> *Burlareis los antojos*
> *De aquesa lisonjera*
> *Vida, con quanto teme y quanto espera!*
>
> *Es mas que un breve punto*
> *El bajo y torpe suelo, comparado*
> *A aqueste gran trasunto*
> *Dó vive mejorado*
> *Lo que es, lo que será, lo que ha pasado?*
>
> . . . .
>
> *O campos verdaderos*
> *O prados con verdad frescos y amenos*
> *Riquisimos mineros!*
> *O deleitosos senos*
> *Repuestos valles de mil bienes llenos.*[1]

I

ONE would be utterly mistaken in this young man if one pictured him as a sheer paragon. He was to win fame above most men of his memorable time, and no horse could win in such a race which had not bone, blood and breed as well as a trainer. His nerves were highly strung, he had a nostril which sensed the tangs of Old Castile, his temper was impetuous:

> Nor less to feed voluptuous thought,
> The beauteous forms of nature wrought,
> Fair trees and gorgeous flowers:
> The breezes their own languor lent;
> The stars had feelings, which they sent
> Into those favoured bowers.

Nor in this was the young Carmelite alone. He had a genius akin to that of the most remarkable personage in the University. Luis de

[1] Luis de León, *Noche Serena.*

León had been appointed four years before Professor of Theology. He had been born in 1527 at Belmonte near Cuenca in Don Quixote's province of La Mancha. The people of that province are lovers of adventure, they are energetic, tenacious, and keen. Bold and direct was the character given them by the rough scene around them. For Belmonte was placed on a high, wide plain.

Luis de León, the father of Luis, was a man of wealth, who could settle on his eldest son an income of 4000 ducats. But though this meant the favour and privilege of the world, the young Luis had been marked by religion for her own.

"My desire," he wrote afterwards, "has been since my childhood to serve according to my talents Holy Church."

So, like many members of the noblest families, not to find security from his enemies, nor to escape from work, nor because it answered the claims of dignity and honour, but because the joys and hardships of the convent life answered an inward call,[2] Luis de León became a friar.

Strict as was the Augustinian discipline, yet it offered delightful opportunities of amplitude, leisure, and cultivated society, nor did it exclude its members from the great positions of power which were then open to the clergy. When in 1544 Luis de León became a student in the University of Salamanca, it was in the same rank of universities as Bologna, Paris, and Oxford.

It was particularly noted for the brilliance of its theologians. Francisco de Vitoria, the great authority on international law and justice to subject races, a man of wide and moderate views, had not yet vacated his Chair of Theology, though he had been called away to the Council of Trent.[3] When he died in 1546, the man nominated as his successor was the hardly less brilliant Dominican, Melchior Cano, who, like Luis de León, came from the province of Cuenca. He had for a time been professor at Alcalá. Just as Vitoria had concentrated on Canon Law, so Cano worked out fully, with high originality, the relation of faith to reason in a great Summa called De Locis Theologicis, which was finally published at Salamanca in 1563.[4] Like Vitoria, Cano arrived at founding theology firmly on its

[2] Bell, Luis de León, pp. 84-5, 93.
[3] Sainz Rodríguez, Introducción, pp. 198, 199.
[4] Espasa-Calpe, Vol. XI, pp. 194, 195. Sainz Rodríguez, Introducción, pp. 198, 199. Menéndez y Pelayo, Historia de los Heterodoxos Españoles, Vol. II.

original sources, the Bible and the Fathers of the Church, then relating it to the full activity of the philosophical mind, and finally expressing his conclusions in clear and elegant Latin. In ten separate books, Melchior Cano developed his ten sources: the Bible, Oral Tradition, the Universal Church, the Councils, the Fathers, the Roman Church, the Scholastic theologians, Science, Philosophy, and History. These, with a book first on the relation of authority to reason, and finally on the application of the sources in argument and discussion, show the thoroughness, the subtlety, and the vigour of his mind.

These Catholic theologians, like San Tommaso di Aquino before them, were nourished on the broad intellectual vigour of the Spanish Church. With minds of tireless energy, they followed out the processes of reason till it led upwards to those vistas into eternity which open to the eye of faith.

2

Luis de León had attended the lectures both of Melchior Cano and of his not unworthy successor, Domingo de Soto, who, indeed, championed the claims of Luis as his pupil, till in 1560, as we have seen, Luis himself became a Professor.

One of his special subjects of study was the *Song of Songs,* which he translated into Spanish. In this he followed up the study of Hebrew which had been initiated by Vives; and as he studied this famous classic of mysticism, he saw that behind all the allegorical interpretations which had been given to it, it was indeed a dramatic arrangement, telling a love story, and as a poem was sacred in its beauty.[5]

Vitoria and Cano had been inspiring lecturers, but here was a speaker more personal, more poetical. Bracing, stimulating, lucid, and flashing with humour, his lectures gathered to him a crowd from the thousands of young men who flocked to Salamanca. For ten years he continued to nourish brilliant minds, and to startle dull and conventional ones by his novelty. Here was a Professor to stimulate the keen young Carmelite from Medina!

[5] Bell, *Luis de León,* p. 25.

3

So marked was his originality that he was gradually falling under suspicion. In 1572 he was to be arrested by the Inquisition. Let us glance forward to that ordeal. From a spacious room with a huge window and a large fireplace, with writing-table and book-shelves, he found himself buried in the fœtid air of a dungeon, with no one to look after him, and often no food. For if the Spaniards could glow with radiant vitality, they could be indifferent to suffering and deliberately cruel. Nothing could make his incarceration pleasant; but his gaolers did so far relax as to allow him a knife—with a blunted point—books, and writing-paper. He met his trials bravely, but at times nervous exhaustion would drown him in melancholy, suspicion, and fear.

The special charge against him was that, belittling the authority of the Vulgate, he had made a rather novel translation into Spanish of the *Song of Songs*. To have that fervid poem at the disposal of the people might well provoke scandal. But his doubts as to the correctness of the Vulgate and Septuagint as translations were also made the subject of attack by conventional pedants. So, amid complications and illness and melancholy, the long lists of unjust accusations kept subjecting him to fresh trials through the summers and winters of five terrible years. Finally he was acquitted by order of the Supreme Court at Madrid. A certificate of innocence was handed to him, and he even received five years' arrears of salary: but his translation of the *Song of Songs* was to be withdrawn from the public.[6]

4

He was reinstated in his Chair at Salamanca, and, according to a legend which may well be true, he began his first lecture with the words: "As we were saying yesterday." Then, though not without fresh accusations and interruptions, he continued his lectures, his writing of his treatise on *The Names of Christ,* and his lyrics; these, joined to the freshness of his mind, his chivalrous disposition, and his irrepressible love of life and human nature, made him the hero of such a poet as Lope de Vega and such a writer as Cervantes himself.[7]

[6] See Bell, *op. cit.,* ch. vii, esp. p. 149.
[7] Bell, *op. cit.,* p. 205.

He exemplified, as he vaunted, the miracle of man. "Man in his dar-
ing and persistence will find a new world unknown even to the birds
of the air and utterly hidden from us, and when he has discovered it,
he will overturn its mountains and blast its rocks and penetrate its
rivers, and draw from it incredible riches. Everything can he attain
but wisdom, unless it be given him from heaven." [8] All through his
life, as in those early years when he was first Professor in Salamanca,
the fountains of his inspiration were nature and those revelations of
divine things which combine with the arts of literature to make the
Bible.

5

Of poetry he said both that all its study was the copy of nature so
as to make a speaking picture, and that it is nought but a communication of the manna which is heavenly and divine.[9] It burst from him
spontaneously in the intervals of his reading and writing. But his
style and versification accord so closely to those of his predecessors,
Boscán and Garcilaso de la Vega, that he could not but have studied
them, as he admits he had read Ausias March and the Coplas de
Manrique. He read also Horace and Virgil. He translated Petrarch
and Cambo. Thus, from an intimate acquaintance with certain masters he turned his inspiration to combining his rapturous sense of
communion with nature with his enthusiasm for a new world of
wonders which kept challenging his mind to fresh jousts with danger
and with habit. He had a new personal sense of the wisdom and
spirit of the universe; it became his mission, in the words of Mr.
Aubrey Bell, "to recreate the external world for his soul in the light
of a new psychology and sensibility, to transform in a freshly awakened curiosity and love of beauty the common things, rain, a leaf, a
cloud, into miracles that revealed the glory and presence of God." [10]
His poetry burst from him in a fire of spontaneous fervour: but
behind its apparent simplicity is a tense and complex life. He had
looked closely, thought intensely, and striven hard to make his life
into a unity of gratitude and rapture. He believed that beauty must
be not merely beauty, but the copy of an ideal. It must always have

[8] Bell, *op. cit.*
[9] Bell, *op. cit.*
[10] Bell, *op. cit.*, p. 239.

a spiritual life immanent within it; his scenes from Nature speak of this, with a personal voice, as heart speaks to heart. The stars also speak to him or listen; they throb and glow in the serene night, a resplendent host in which none usurps the place of its neighbour; where each has its own joyousness. The moon, too, "clustered around by all her starry fays," looks around her in the bare heavens with delight; the air echoes to the poet's cries; there is a different character in the quick-moving weight of winter clouds from those which gather suddenly in the summer for thunder, and the lightning which writhes like a snake. At night, running water speaks with a louder voice: there is laughter in the gurgling of the stream, and laughter, too, when, at sunset, the reawakening breeze seems to set the very shadows in flight.[11]

Luis de León loved both flowers and birds. He knows where the nests are, knows that the young crows soon have to do their own foraging, and he delights in the dazzling feathers of the peacock's neck and tail. He would happily watch the doves—indeed, all the little birds that fluttered round him—and listen to their sweet jargon-ing at dawn: and as he watched the birds, he saw the flowers: the rosebuds among their thorns, the carnations opening from their light bud, or the apple-blossom giving its beauteous colours to the spring, which he will later contrast with the reddening apples among their leaves.[12] He shares with Guevara the new delight in nature which he enthusiastically extended to welcome the sierra, and above all the sky. And all these impressions he would merge in a diamond flash, intense and brilliant, like the dew in morning light shining on blades of grass.

By our own Henry Vaughan, the saints were to be recognized as stars.

> They all night
> Like candles shed
> Their leaves, and light
> Us into bed.
> They are (indeed) our pillar fires
> Seen as we go.
> They are that citie's shining spires
> We travel to.

---

[11] Bell, *op. cit.*, p. 232.
[12] Bell, *op. cit.*, p. 233.

Luis de León, looking at the starry sky, had seen beyond the world's fear and flattering hopes a glimpse of another life where all that had been, all that will be, all that now is shall survive, bettered and more beautifully arranged.

> O meadows of bright truth, he cried,
> Fresh, flowery, full of health.
> O mines of richest wealth!
> O haunts of ancient peace where nought annoys,
> O vales remote, filled with a thousand joys! [13]

6

Nor must we forget that he was a writer of prose. He wrote not only on the Book of Job and the Song of Songs, but an essay on The Model Wife, *La Perfecta Casada,* and a medley of thought under the title "The Names of Christ": *"De los Nombres de Cristo."* These books are not free from rhetoric; life and *décor* crowd them, as they crowd the sculpture and the architecture of the period with excessive ornamentation. It was an exuberant age. Magnificence and fervour marked the mind of this Renaissance friar as they mark so many buildings in Spain, both Gothic and baroque. Nature and the classics both lend adornments to the sacred splendour of the Bible. Luis de León knew something of the work of the painter, the sculptor, the alchemist, the architect, the engraver, the lapidary, the silversmith, the astronomer, the musician, the astrologer, the actor, the singer, the dramatist, the fencer, the physician, the husbandman, and the woodman.[14] And it was only in late years, under the influence of the spontaneous *naïveté* of Santa Teresa, that he simplified the exuberance of his style to something more like speech.[15]

7

Such then was the most brilliant teacher in Salamanca when, in 1560, Fray Juan de Santo Matía arrived there from Medina del Campo.

It is plain when we consider the ingenuity, the spontaneity, the

---

[13] Luis de León, *Noche Serena.*
[14] Bell, *op. cit.,* pp. 247-249.
[15] Bell, *op. cit.,* p. 263.

range, and the elaboration of Luis de León that, however strict the life of the friar or the nun, yet a man who entered the religious life could still live and observe intensely even while he gave himself with strictest vigour to living according to the rules of a religious house, cut off apparently from the world to make easier an unimpeded contemplation of the mysteries of religion and of God.

Nor is Luis de León the most striking example of genius in the cloister. Far more generally admired for shrewd penetration, for tireless enterprise, for sparkling generous humour, for character and for charm is the Carmelite nun, Madre Teresa de Jesús, who was the heroine of Luis de León.

Before Fray Juan de Santo Matía met her, however, he had studied for some years at Salamanca.

O had I the wings of a dove,
Far away, far away would I rove.
In the wilderness build me a nest
And remain there for ever at rest.[1]

I

IN the University of Salamanca in 1564, as at Oxford a hundred
years earlier, a young man in a religious house could play a great
part in the intellectual life of the University. The choir offices
finished, he would set off early in the morning with nine or ten young
friars of his order to hear the lectures in the famous courses of study
which Vitoria and his successors had reawakened. To an eager mind,
this revelation of knowledge, bursting with its freshness and magic
from the stores of beauty and wisdom, opens worlds on worlds. There,
as young men do, Fray Juan found his mind unfolding to all that was
congenial in culture, in poetry, in the love of beauty, in the study of
psychology, and in the fusion and completion of them all in those
studies of divinity which Melchior Cano had reorganized to distinguish between, and yet to comprehend, the two worlds of faith and
reason. Here, with culture and beauty, were the most princely kingdoms of the mind.

But with this intense interest in the exciting world of the time,
there was another passion. It was the life of perfection: the life in
which every motion of the will, every thought of the mind should
accord with the impulses of the Holy Spirit. The fruit of the Spirit,
said St. Paul, is love, joy, peace, patience, breadth of sympathy,
kindly feeling, kindly action, faith, good temper, self-control.[2] These
were the virtues these Castilians set out to cultivate; for their hard
training of the mind made a science of the life of love.

The mystic impulse centred in adoring calm as a means to flood
the consciousness not only with the sense of God's presence, but with
a secret power which would melt and transfuse the faculties till they

[1] Psalm LIV, 13, 14 (Vulgate).
[2] Gal. V, 22, 23.

34

became the bond of perfectness, and the human soul grew into the resemblance of the holiness it worshipped. It needed great heat to melt the intractable metal of their natures to the Christian mould; but as they were strong men, so they could accept the task of taming their own passions. Every romance, every detail, every fancy that could distract or could help men in the life of spiritual effort was noticed by this young man of genius who, among his virile and knightly compatriots, had the most refined and ardent intellect of any then alive.

2

In communities those who excel are noticed. The less generous spirits envy, the more generous admire and praise. The religious life was worked out of the material it found; even the suavity and friendliness of the life of charity mingled with some bizarre, some crude excesses. The convents and monasteries of Spain were in urgent need of reform.[3] It is inevitable in such a case as this, where in any case there are many diversities and much rubbing together of personalities, that the young priest, Juan de Santo Matía, should find much that disturbed him. He himself aspired, in his own exalted, uncompromising, Castilian way, to live the strictest life he could: inured to hardships always, he wanted more hardships; used to solitude, he wanted more solitude; accustomed to meals so rough and scanty that it would account for noticeable meagreness of body, he would fast still more rigorously; with an extremely delicate, lively, and active mind, he was sensitive to every kind of distraction, and the whole University of Salamanca was vibrating with distractions. A university is a medley of youthful minds and characters, busy with all the quests that attract youth or occupy older scholars.

How do more? It is a common, if not a universal experience of ardent souls seeking union with Christ to be heroic; heroic certainly in action, and heroic in endurance. When courage and enterprise were the temper of the people and the time, was there no place for such qualities in the religious life? Life, it might be thought, was uncomfortable enough in a country which never mistook comfort for civilization. Food was not only rough, but long fasts were proscribed in order that, not only by the sacrifice of gluttony, but by the pangs of hun-

[3] Merriman, *Rise of the Spanish Empire*, IV, 50.

ger and the lowering of vitality, men should learn to live not so much by the heat of their blood, not so much by the travail of their entrails, as by the breath of their lungs, and by setting their minds on things above. "Cast thy thought upon the Lord, and He will nourish thee," so they read in a Psalm, to which the liturgy of the Church recalled them.[4] But that was not enough. Rest must be curtailed, that the mind, by yet more sacrifice of its comfort, should rise by the definite act of the will to yet more constant and urgent thought of the Redeemer of Men, who wished to establish His kingdom within them. Let them live, as St. Paul said, in Christ! In Christ! Every thought, every impulse must serve Him. So still further would they by acts of willing endurance accompany Him in the redeeming life of pain.

3

The young monk had been scourged: physical chastisement had through the centuries its place in the training of children. More than once the Bible had recommended it. If a childlike discipline was also asked of those who would accompany Christ in the path of humility, they must chasten the nerves of the skin. Three times a week the young friar bared his shoulders to receive from the hebdomadary, the friar who was in charge for the week, stinging blows from thongs or cords.

Does this seem morbid? It could easily be so, were it not offered as a sacrifice in union with Him who had suffered that He might redeem. If it were so, it could have another effect. Intimate, and in its way exquisite, it made the body—not in its pleasures but in its pains, or rather in a pain chosen and accepted, so that it brought its own intensity of experience, a sacrifice of the very nerves themselves; this offering of the bared flesh, this will for endurance offered to the spiritual life, is not merely what the child accepts, but what husband and wife accept of pain in the intimate experiences which complete the cycle of love and life. For even that human union asks for pain and sacrifice. If the heart of flesh is to be engaged in the quest for God, it must find its own equivalents for the cycle of human experience. For the Master of Souls acts in curious ways, both spiritual and physical, to tame the wild heart and passions of that interacting fusion

[4] Psalm LIV, 23 (Vulgate).

of flesh and spirit which makes man. "Despise not thou the chastening of the Lord," said the Apostle, "nor faint when thou art rebuked of him: for whom the Lord loveth he chasteneth, and scourgeth every son whom he receiveth." [5] And the ardent friar, whose perceptions were so exquisite, sought still further to complete this intimacy and ecstasy by sacrifice. He would flee from every comfort, every agreement of the sense, even to accepting unpleasant smells, and to wearing next his skin a vest of reeds. For in these things he found through patience his own means to love and joy. He was making every effort to found his peace not in his own satisfaction, but on some fresh thing that he could offer to His Saviour.

4

Was it wise—or was it a waste? For the majority such things would doubtless be imprudent and excessive. Such might well agree with Keble that there is no need to go out of our way in the hard path upward which leads daily nearer to God.[6] But there are other men at other times who have arrested others' attention, and transformed themselves by self-sacrifice in a more dramatic form. And in this unique, individual Spain, this Spain of extravagance and excess, this Spain of untamed virility, of melodramatic honour, with all the lusts and heats of high vitality, in such a Spain chastity and obedience could combine with humility to make this offering a salutary path to strengthen character and exalt the passions till sacrifice had enriched its flavours to an ecstasy. For the test was to be in the result: the tree was to be known by its fruits. Here was the thorn of rose or blackberry: but further on, beyond the thistles, and growing from quite other roots, were figs and grapes.

5

After four years of study in the pulsing University, among minds active with every kind of interest, but especially medicine, astronomy, law, philosophy, and theology, the young friar, whose soul was romance, was longing for an intenser life. His passions were poetry

5 Heb. XII, 6.
6 Keble, *The Christian Year.*

and nature: his soul had a mysterious affinity with mountains, streams, and woods, and he knew already from the university of those evocations which come with poetry, above all the poetry which Spanish poets, Garcilaso de la Vega and Boscán, were telling them, of the fields, the woods, the stars, and of love. Did not this all point to a change and development in his vocation: to a life of more undisturbed complications, of solitude more rapturous and inspired? Among young men in religious houses the imagination often flies, in a dream, to the idea of something more congenial than the actual order they have entered: they think of something more arduous, more special.

Fray Juan de Santo Matía found his ideal in the silent order whose central home was in the Grande Chartreuse. He would be a Carthusian, and enter not the new Charterhouse, or, as the Spaniards pronounced it, Cartuja de Miraflores, outside Burgos, but would seek rather the company of the stream and the forest in the exquisite retreat of El Paular, beyond Segovia, in a valley of the Guadarrama, above which the blue-grey rock of Peñalara raised its snow-covered peak into the clouds and sapphire of Castilian sky.[7]

Here was indeed a Paradise—the forest of oak and pine, the countless glades, the sward and streamlet, the mountain heights above in all the beauty of one eminent peak, and set there the secluded quiet of a company of contemplatives, each living in his own little apartment, each cultivating his solitary garden, and yet all uniting in the intervals of their long, solitary hours of prayer to worship in a central and imposing temple.

Here he could love and adore, without interruption, here he could commune with the beauties of Nature, here he could feast his mind upon the study of one of the supreme minds of the preceding century, the great Belgian mystic, Denys the Carthusian—a man who then had immense influence in Spain.[8]

6

Denys said that the object and completion of life was to behold God, to behold Him not by the discursive reason, but as the lover

[7] Bruno, p. 54.
[8] Sainz Rodríguez, *Introducción*, pp. 126, 139; Santa Teresa, *vida* ch. xxxviii.

considers the object of his love in one devouring gaze of rapturous interest, when he looks "at her with all his eyes, and young love has a thousand." [9] This may be a deliberate act, or may be an act into which the mind is drawn by powers other than its own. And his supreme object was to lead man to the loving contemplation of the Holy Trinity. This he would attain by the increase of sanctifying graces, strengthening his faith, by seeking the seven gifts of the Holy Ghost, above all the gift of Wisdom, the very act of which is intuitive vision. [10] But only he can behold the Trinity whose spirit is purified; therefore the spiritual man must lay aside every disquiet and disturbance, every movement of the imagination. Man, he said, is raised to the contemplation of the Divinity by something above, that is by the supernatural irradiation of the Divine mind into his mind, [11] and such an irradiation is less often given to the educated than to simple, unlearned men.

He describes the illuminative way as the study or occupation of the mind in contemplating the sublime ways of the Godhead, especially in the contemplation of the most blessed Trinity. [12] The unitive way is much more: it is the striving through ardour of sincerest giving, for the ecstatic fiery love of God; the soul enjoys at once hidden converse with God, a movement leading to God, an experimental knowledge of God through His loving embrace. In the system of Denys the Carthusian there was no hard and fast distinction between active and passive contemplation. For in that irradiation which, as we have just seen, is often given to simple men, the mystic sees that God Himself directs the guided soul, and from His own generosity dispenses extraordinary consolations. If a man will but prepare himself with love and zeal, God will come and meet him, and give Himself to him; He will exalt him to Himself, kissing him, embracing him, and giving Himself to his enjoyment; [13] though thenceforward the blessed soul is in habitual contact with the Sun of Righteousness, this light, nevertheless, glows but for a short time, and then is hidden by a cloud: for it is God who chooses how He shall reveal it. Yet, even so, a man by his own striving can seek to win it back again. The

[9] Meredith, *The Ordeal of Richard Feverel*, ch. xxiii.
[10] *De Contemplatione*, I, 22.
[11] Wessely, *Johannes vom Kreuz*, p. 95.
[12] *De Fonte Lucis.*
[13] *De Fonte Lucis.*

kingdom of heaven suffereth violence, and the violent take it by force.[14]

Denys the Carthusian, in short, made it clear that the Divine experience which he called "mystic theology" is the general object of all souls trying to find God, and this must indicate the direction of all practices of piety and virtue. But there are two ways to reach the final consummation. The first is in the power of man who can make a definite preparation; the other is beyond his provision.[15] For, said Denys, "a man attains in one way to this mystical contemplation of heavenly wisdom, by spurring himself forward and making himself apt for it by the aforesaid abstraction, by recollection and simplification, by worship and meditation, and by the survey of those things which usually aid to prepare and call forth in the heart the ardent love of God, until the apex of the will really catches fire and is really attached to God so that the rim of the intellect is illumined from above towards contemplation. And lastly, as the Divine Denys teaches in word and parable in the first chapter of his mystical theology:

"And do thou, beloved Timotheus, by the most intense eagerness for these objects of mystical contemplation, control all movements of perception and speech, all sensations and all thoughts of all things that are not and that are, that thou mayest be made one with Him who is above all being and all knowledge, keep thyself unknown among men. This is one way: the other by which man attains to contemplation is beyond this effort and preparation, when in a way that he cannot resist, when nature is suspended not by a shock but by a tranquil adaptation, when bountiful mercy descends upon him and he is brilliantly illumined by divine light." [16]

7

If one would be more precise, one can trace out in the mystical life the seven gifts of the Holy Ghost: to bring them to perfection needs heroic courage and will, and these come with fortitude, or "ghostly strength"; and wisdom will give him the taste for all the activities of

[14] Matt. XI, 12.
[15] *Seven Gifts of the Holy Spirit*, quoted by Wessely, p. 98.
[16] Wessely, *op. cit.*, pp. 98, 99.

love. To calm and soothe all motives of his being in harmony and the preparation of peace comes knowledge. Piety or godliness makes him mild and generous, so that his nature is beautified as with God's own mercy. Counsel holds a man to God's commandments and to the very counsels of perfection.[17] Understanding is a supernatural aptitude infused with charity and grace through which the first principles of Christian wisdom are recognized, and the final sensitiveness of veneration is the fear of God. Like Juan, Denys the Carthusian insists that as love makes us like the Holy Ghost, so wisdom makes us like the Son: but contemplation is an immediate working of the Three Divine Persons upon the soul, and reaches its perfection when man seeks not the gifts of the Lover, but the love of the Giver, not anything, even the highest, accorded by God, but God Himself.

Such was the mystical teaching of the celebrated Carthusian. It was founded, like the work of the Carmelites of Salamanca, on Dionysius the Areopagite, on Augustine, and on Aquinas, but it had a certain personal glow and flavour which combined in Fray Juan with his longing for solitude, streams, woods, and mountains. To reach the Paradise of El Paular the young Carmelite thought of yet another venture and escape, yet another expedition in dark night. But his plan was arrested—by his meeting with a woman!

17 *Seven Gifts of the Holy Spirit*, quoted by Wessely, pp. 100, 101.

With holy earnest eyes enshrined
  She bendeth on her knees.
Her voice is heard, above the wind
  Shrill from the northern seas;
The sisters stoop on either hand,
  She smileth mild on each,
And in the wind a choral band
  Comes singing to her speech.

Her hands are tested, palm to palm,
  Then folded as in rest,
Beneath her dawning eyelids calm
  Upon her snow-white breast.
Her snowy garments rustle clear
  As snowflakes rise and mix
And to her neck there presseth near
  A silver crucifix.

Around her gloried form the air
  Is starred with falling snows
That cover all the convent bare
  With symboll'd pure repose.
Above her halo'ed head the sky
  Is studded thick with spheres,
All swimming to one blissful eye
  Whose beam is bright with tears.

She knoweth that the time will come,
  And in the deepened night
Discerneth well her heaven home,
  The morning and the light—
And thro' the shadow and the pain
  A seraph sister voice;
But now she kneeleth once again
  That others may rejoice.[1]

[1] *Santa Teresa*. A poem of George Meredith, first published by R. Sencourt, *Life of Meredith*.

I

For while Fray Juan, on his return from Salamanca, was indulging these dreams and projects, there arrived at Medina del Campo from the new convent of San José at Ávila a person no less than Madre Teresa de Jesús. No sooner had Teresa met him than she changed the whole current of his aims.

Teresa was the most remarkable woman then living in Spain. She was the daughter of a Castilian Hidalgo, Alonso de Cepeda, and his second wife, Beatriz Davila y Ahumáda. She exemplified to the full the ardent vitality which gives a peculiar charm now as then to Spanish girlhood. Her eyes were dark, her eyebrows thick, her brow low and serene, her figure rounded, her complexion high.[2] As a girl she was of high spirits, a charming and amusing talker. She took a great interest in dress, and her delight was in reading romances.[3] We can hardly doubt that she knew the bull-fight. As a little girl, she had herself thought of going to convert the Moors. As her mother had died when she was young, and her father was devout, what more likely than that she should plunge into the current of Castile, and love the Catholic Church? It offered her for mother the very Queen of heaven. It brought her in the mystery of the Mass to the presence of her Saviour, and as she matured in her growing freshness to the shape of womanhood, she felt drawn to offer herself as a nun in the dignity and order of the convent.[4]

2

Devout as he was, her father objected: in such a case parents generally do: but her mind was clear. Her vitality, her love of adventures, her social gifts, her taste for clothes and perfumes, her quick wit, her glowing heart, and her strong character were henceforth to be consecrated to mysticism in the order of Mount Carmel. She passed out of the thick walls of Ávila, with their huge gateways and their round, heavy towers, to look at the open plain: and there, on the hillside, she saw the lines of the Carmelite House of the Incarnation,

[2] Cunninghame Graham, I, 97.
[3] Op. cit., I, 94.
[4] For an admirable account of Santa Teresa see Allison Peers, *Studies of the Spanish Mystics.*

the convent dedicated, like Christmas, to the belief that the King of Glory had come to men, not to convert His godhead into flesh, but to raise their manhood into God—God, the final reality of perfection, the master Being, the Source and Fount of Life and Light and Love, the fullness that filleth all in all.

Yet it was not without a pang that Teresa gave up her amusements and her coloured clothes. "I do not think," she wrote afterwards, "that when I die the wrench will be greater than when I went forth from my father's house; for it seems to me that every bone was rent asunder, and that there was no love of God to take the place of the love of father and kinsmen. The struggle was so great that, if the Lord had not helped me, my own resolution would not have been enough to carry me through." [5] But this wrench was followed by a swift reaction: once she had entered the convent, she found herself extremely happy, even if washing and sweeping.[6] And soon, in the rule of the place, her radiant Spanish nature, with all its individuality, its distinction, its loyalty, its sunny humour, its love of fun and wit, its strong sense, its excellent taste, and its complete freedom from pettiness and foibles, was growing to its spiritual perfection under the guidance of Spanish mystics and the tradition of Mount Carmel: a presence fragrant as the thyme and rosemary in the fields around the convent, very Spanish—*muy española*—in the Castile in which, at Medina del Campo, the boy Juan de Yepes was growing up to a vocation in the same order as Teresa.

3

After she had spent a few years in the convent, Teresa's health gave way, and never again was it to be normal. For months she lay a cripple, and doctors could do nothing for her. She was resigned, she was even cheerful; her talk remained delightful, with never a spiteful remark, never a joke purchased at some one else's cost: but there she was, unable to move, and apparently incurable. "I saw myself so, paralysed and so young," she wrote, "and seeing how I had sped at the hands of earthly doctors, I resolved to have recourse to heavenly

[5] Cunninghame Graham, I, 111.
[6] *Op. cit.*, p. 112.

ones." [7] She asked for Masses to be celebrated, celebrated with great splendour of ceremony to St. Joseph, and she never doubted that his mediation had given her the power to rid herself of her paralysis and rise up and walk. Will and energy had conquered and were to conquer: but she was never again physically robust. Strokes recurred, and fevers, and she was subject to attacks of vomiting. But she never lost her faith in St. Joseph: for years she would ask something on his festival, and it was always granted. "I know not," she wrote, "how one can think on the Queen of Angels at the time when she suffered so much with the Child Jesus, without giving thanks to St. Joseph for his great assistance." [8]

And then, as the years went on, Teresa began to receive extraordinary signs of grace. She not only understood with singular exactness how the normal nun should perfect herself in humility, in charity, in obedience, in self-denial, in all the art and science of adoration, but she herself began to feel that in the way of the senses she was being given another, a finer experience, an experience which was itself a mystery: she would sense a peculiar perfume, as from certain flowers comes

> A music so delicate, soft and intense,
> That it seems like an odour within the sense.[9]

She would see visions which implied through sight a heavenly way of living: once she had a vision of the living Christ: a beauty which she described as a whiteness and resplendence beyond all that we can imagine here, "not a splendour that dazzles, but a soft whiteness infused with radiance, which gives such great delight to the sight which is not tired by it or by the clearness by which we see this beauty so divine, a light so different from that we see on earth that, after it, the clearness of the sun loses all its lustre, and our eyes would nevermore care to open to that of earth. . . . It is a light which knows no dark night; but as it is always light, nothing ever troubles it. In a moment things which the imagination would take long to put together are unfolded to us, for it goes beyond all we can understand here below. So does that Beauty and Light remain stamped on the soul that nothing can drive it from the memory except when the

[7] *Op. cit.*, p. 131.
[8] *Loc. cit.*
[9] Shelley, *The Sensitive Plant.*

Lord wills that she should suffer dryness and great loneliness." [10]

Later, in her most famous vision, she saw an angel, small but very beautiful, and his face so resplendent that she knew he was of the highest order of the heavenly host. In his hand he bore a long dart of gold, its iron tip on fire, like iron heated in the furnace till, red hot, itself sparkles with fire. And with this dart he pierced her heart to her inmost depths: and when he drew it out, he seemed to draw these with it, and she herself was burning with its flame. "The pain," she said, "was so great that it made me give those moans, and so excessive the sweetness caused by this exceeding pain that one cannot desire it to go, nor can the soul content itself with less than God." [11] Rapture was so intense as to be agony, and agony was rapture.

4

Her intense life of the heart, her happy life among her nuns, and the soft resplendence of her visions went, however, with a very practical life: as Teresa shows in her two treatises on contemplation, *The Way of Perfection* and *The Interior Castle,* not to mention her hardly less famous biography.

The charm of this writing is its *naïveté.* Teresa had the knack of words to convey strong personality as though she were speaking, and it is the spontaneity with which she writes which is her charm. Hers is much the same attraction as Bunyan's—the sense of beauty, the pleasantry, the shrewdness, the ease all combine with the influence of the Bible to give the charm and the strong sense of personality. Those who best know Teresa both admire her as a saint and love her as a woman. She is bred from the same blood as Cervantes: she has known the same people among the same landscapes; and while she knows them to the bone, with all their faults, all their virtues, all their taste for honour, she feels at every moment a passion that they should walk, as she does, that path of shining light which shineth more and more unto the perfect day.

[10] Santa Teresa, *Life,* ch. XXVIII, paras 7-8. Dr. Samuel Heaslett, Bishop of South Tokyo, has told me he had an experience of light not unlike this in 1942. See his fascinating narrative *From a Japanese Prison,* p. 60.

[11] *Op. cit.,* XXIX, 17.

5

This it is that makes readers of many tastes and many countries feel at home with her. This, too, made Crashaw write:

> O 'tis not Spanish but heaven she speaks,
> 'Tis heaven that lies in ambush there, and breaks
> From thence into the wondering reader's breast.

She wrote her story several times over: once in her life, once in conferences for her nuns which she called *The Way of Perfection,* once in the history of her Foundations, and lastly in her old age, as we shall see—in a mystical treatise called *The Interior Castle.* But *The Way of Perfection* was the work she had completed after first founding her reform at Ávila: it was a book written for nuns by a nun that they might have full advantage of a particular woman's experience.

She saw she must deal ruthlessly with the Castilian regard for honour: for what honour is accorded, she shrewdly asked, to a man, however gifted, who is poor? [12] She warned her nuns against close friendships, which, she said, "rarely serve to forward the love of God." [13] But what if a nun should feel a particular regard for her director? Why, answered Madre Teresa, if we feel regard for those who benefit our bodies, we may well feel still more for those who benefit our souls, and need think no more about it: and yet there are directors who have their vanities and levities: and in such cases, of course, a nun should be *most* guarded! [14] With an Abelard, it is only too easy to be a Heloise.

An unselfish nature still loves and gives, even if love is not returned, for those that love God love others far more, with a truer and more generous affection. And yet the most demonstrative attachments are better than quarrels or bickering. But let a nun seek rather to rely on the judgment of her superior, do what was required of her, cultivate cheerful obedience, and, in short, learn the art of being unobtrusive in what the British would call team work.

After she had made many a shrewd remark about nuns and their

[12] *Way of Perfection,* II, 5.
[13] *Ibid.,* IV, 4.
[14] *Way of Perfection,* IV, 9.

headaches and their weaknesses,[15] she went on to treat of the communion of the spirit with God. Prayer is living water to the thirsting soul, and it comes with many different colours and flavours. It might be the following of a form of words with heart and mind: it might be a meditation: it might be that direct, intuitive gaze, that speechless colloquy of heart with heart which is known as contemplation. What was required was that the soul should keep company with Jesus, according to the words *"Whither thou goest, I will go,"* and never mind, said Madre Teresa, "if the Jews trample you under foot." [16]

6

For she was always a woman of the world. She never withdrew her heart and mind from heroism: but she could chat easily with mule-drivers, and liked to scent the towels with orange-flower water. Her gift of contemplation never dulled her to the value of practical virtues, and she sang the praise of Martha, who found God "among the pots and pans." She could compare the cloistered life to a game of chess, to show that humility was the winning move. Yet, through all, she had her own special understanding of the art of adoration: and that was to realize that the Divine Majesty could find a home in the soul of Spaniards, and could transform them by His indwelling glory. Let them but contemplate this, and they would image it. Beholding as in a mirror the glory, they would be changed from glory to glory as by the Spirit of the Lord.[17]

But the particular excellence of *The Way of Perfection* was to make "Our Father" intensely significant for the spiritual life. She made that one prayer the gate of every excellence.

Single, familiar phrases, these were enough to open the window on to the splendour and mysteries of the heavenly landscape. *Our Father who art in heaven, hallowed be Thy name:* there was theme enough to show them perfection in all its majesty, and to fill their hearts with desire for the reign of holiness—holiness indwelling. In this way she would take them through the familiar prayer till it had become a revelation of the episodes and effects of contemplation.[18]

[15] *Ibid.,* X, 5.
[16] *Ibid.,* XXVI, 5, 6.
[17] II Cor. III, 18.
[18] *Way of Perfection,* XXVII.

SANTA TERESA DE JESUS, HER HEART PIERCED BY A SERAPH

From a sculpture by Bernini

What, then, was her secret? It was to wait on single phrases till the everlasting gates turned on their hinges, that the King of Glory might come in. She began to explain a mystery: the prayer of quiet or recollection. By this a soul, like a happy lover, could live and feed on a sense of being beloved, could feel a dim rapture that quietened every movement of the nerves, that closed the eyes, that made sounds seem insignificant, while in adoring calm the faculties and powers of the worshipper were rapt into still communion: and a deeper, fuller sense of life united her with the very reality of love. Love was the secret of her life, and she felt compassion even for the devil because he had lost the power to love.[19] But the love of God was a science and a wisdom. Of all this, since she loved vividness and the arts of interest, Teresa was able to speak with great precision.

If the nuns have a heavenly father, why bother about differences of rank? "Strive, my daughters," she said, "to merit God's caress; cast yourselves into His arms," [20] and there the Holy Spirit could tell them more than any words of hers. For where was heaven but in that mansion of their souls where they found God, in the prayer of recollection? In that narrow compass is enclosed He Who fills a thousand worlds with His immensity. Only if Christ is to come with all His court into our hearts, let us see that neither common people nor rubbish will be in their way. And so let there be still veneration prolonged in quiet and trust when the soul says "Hallowed be Thy Name"; let prayer for the good of others mingle with those of our own when we say "Thy kingdom come."

And, she proceeded, know that when you say "Thy will be done!" "you are begging that God's will may be carried out in you, for it is *this* and nothing else you ask for. You need not fear that He will give you riches, or pleasures, or great honours, or any earthly good—His love for you is not so lukewarm—He places a higher value on your gift, and wishes to reward you generously, since He has given you His kingdom even in this life. Would you like to see how He treats those who make this petition unreservedly?" [21] Many an accident, many a hardship, many a tear had come to Madre Teresa on her travels: but she recognized God's hand in each of them, for this,

[19] Marqués de San Juan de Piedras Albas, *Gracián*, p. 14.
[20] *Way of Perfection*, XXVII, 5.
[21] *Ibid.*, XXXII, 6.

she said, was the way He treated His friends. Her whole desire for her nuns was that they should be thorough, and be valiant. Fervent love can suffer much, while tepidity will endure but little. "For my part," wrote Teresa, "I believe our love is the measure of the cross we can bear." [22]

Her words are never merely words: one feels in them the living nun whose example and whose charm called many a man and woman to walk the narrow way of perfection, whose

> bright
> Life brought them first to kiss the light
> That kindles them to stars.[23]

7

And she certainly wrote the most chaste and racy Castilian. Luis de León, himself, in a preface to her works, wrote in 1588:

> "The writings and books of Santa Teresa are documents of rare excellence: in the loftiness of the things which she discusses, in the delicacy and luminousness with which she treats them, in the purity and ease of style, in the happy composition of the words and in an unstudied elegance in the highest degree delightful. I doubt that in our language exists any work to equal them. And therefore whenever I read them, the more I marvel; and in many parts of them it seems that I am not listening to the imaginations of men; and I doubt not that the Holy Spirit spoke through her." [24]

Luis de León, as we have seen, was also in his way a hero: but he was a learned theologian. Teresa was not that: she was a mystic rising to supreme powers both as a woman and as a nun by the greatness and valiancy of heart with which she gave herself to the Carmelite life.

[22] *Way of Perfection*, XXXII, 6.
[23] Crashaw, *A Hymn to the Name and Honour of the Admirable Saint Teresa* (written while he was still in the Church of England).
[24] G. Cunninghame Graham, *Santa Teresa*, I, 71.

Jesu, heart's light,
Jesu, maid's son,
What was the feast followed the night
Thou hadst glory of this nun?
Feast of the one woman without stain
For so conceived, so to conceive thee is done,
But here was heart-throe, birth of a brain,
Word, that heard and kept thee and uttered thee outright.[1]

"She had a tall and well-formed figure, a white complexion, dark curly hair, round dark eyes, a delicately formed nose; charm, cheerfulness, and high breeding marked her manners and attested her place in society; and in dress she was immaculate; she ate sparingly: to a gift of prophecy she had clear understanding and a powerful mind, shrewd and mature, as shown in the books she wrote, with counsels how to attain perfection. Lastly she was illumined and favoured by frequent visions and communications of Jesus Christ." [2]

I

EVEN before Juan de Yepes had joined the Carmelites, Madre Teresa de Jesús had already been hard at work in effecting a reform in her order. Her generous soul had been much moved by the pictures put before her by a friar who had returned from the palms and millions of the Malabar coast. She had therefore established at Ávila another convent, that of San José, where nuns might live a stricter life, that their piety might win from God more mercy for those distant hordes who, among all the splendours of India, had never heard of Christ.

A reform of the order was certainly required: it also suited the projects of an extremely nationalistic sovereign.

Philip II, though devout, put the State before the Church, and was always glad of any measure which would make the orders more national, more obedient to his authority. He had therefore given his fullest support to Madre Teresa, and she took full advantage of it: but she did not concentrate on the court; she had seized an opportunity to take possession of a dilapidated dwelling in Medina which she had already established as a religious house. She was eagerly looking for men who would help her in her high project when she heard of the young Carmelite friar who was as small and as light as a bird, who led such an exemplary life, and who had shown such brilliant promise in the University of Salamanca. When Fray Juan returned from the University for his vocation, he was quickly summoned to her presence.

He found himself before a nun of fifty-two years of age, whose coarse habit and hemp-soled shoes could not hide the fact that she was a woman of the most striking personality. Her thick, dark eyebrows accentuated the brilliance of her eyes, which pierced into the very souls of men; her skin was fine and clear, and so responsive was her blood to her enthusiasm that when she was moved it glowed to rose; every movement showed that here was a woman of distinction with power to charm and attract; to this she added the peculiar refinement of a holy life. She breathed an air fragrant with the fascination of the Jesus in whose name she lived.

She saw in Juan a figure which, although tiny, was also marked with power, and whose fine personality burnt with the same fire as her own. Both of these eminent Castilians, the young man of twenty-five, the nun who was more than twice his age, drew to one another in the instantaneous friendship of accordant hearts.

She rapidly dissuaded him from El Paular: she showed how his desires could best be fulfilled by joining with her in restoring the crowded order to the primitive loftiness of its conception, that together they might weed a garden where the finest flowers were being choked by rank and wilding growths. She soon saw that the high reputation of this young man was less than he merited, and that he was, in short, the most remarkable personage she had yet met. "I realized," she wrote afterwards, "that he was a saint, and had always been a saint." [3]

[3] Letter of 1577 to Philip II.

"I praised our Lord," wrote Madre Teresa, "and when I spoke to him, he pleased me greatly and he told me how he also intended joining the Carthusians. I told him my intention and fervently implored him to wait until the Lord had given us a monastery, and how great a benefit it would be, if he was to work such a change, to do so in his own order, and how much in this manner he would serve the Lord. He promised me that he would if the delay were not too great." [4]

For he had already what he described afterwards as "a heart of one that had fallen in love." [5]

2

Hungry to get further towards his heart's desire, feeling "like one suspended in the air," [6] and yet magnetized by an irresistible appeal in the new friendship of this nun of genius, Fray Juan waited till the autumn, and then once more, as the heat softened, he took the road over the terra-cotta plain, with the view of faintly outlined hills, with here and there the brick bell-tower of a church rising above the round walls and the red tiles of a rough village, and then again over the bare, bracing solitude of the plain, till he saw once more the sharper outline of the Arapiles, the sweep of the River Tormes, and beyond it in all its splendour the high mass of the old and the new cathedrals of Salamanca; in the cream-coloured outlines, here and there warmed to rose, of the splendid city which set the monuments of greatness around the elaborate relief of the portal to the University where he learnt the science of the ways of God with man. So at the age of twenty-five he brought to an end his study among the acute theologians of Salamanca, the men who in the hard travail of the mind applied now to practical things such as international politics or the life of virtue, at others to the fabric of faith in that Christianized Aristotelianism which added to the most vigorous thinking of the ancients the loftier knowledge, drawn from God's own revelation, which

[4] *Fundaciones*, ch. iii.
[5] C.E. IX, 5; Allison Peers, II, 61.
[6] *Loc. cit.*

they found in the Bible and the fathers of the Church. But he never forgot the training he received there.

In Medina he fell in again with Madre Teresa, who told him that she was shortly going to Valladolid, where she was to found a new house for her sisters, in the hope of rescuing from purgatory the soul of Don Bernardino de Mendoza. In the meanwhile she had found a ramshackle house for him at Duruelo, between Medina and Ávila, and not far from Fontiveros.

3

Madre Teresa de Jesús determined to take the young Carmelite friar with her to Valladolid. Arriving there on August 10, 1568, after a tiresome journey through the night, she heard a Mass with some members of her order. Sleepless, physically exhausted, yet filled with her zeal, she approached the Altar. As she did so, she saw in a vision the soul of Don Bernardino, his face resplendent and joyous, his hands clasped; as he mounted into glory, he thanked her for what she had done for him.[7]

But the gift that brought his soul to glory made the nuns ill with ague. When, five days later, on the Feast of the Assumption, Teresa took possession of the house he had left her, it was only to find that owing to the proximity of the river and its swamps, it was malarious; both Mother Superior and her nuns were infected by the mosquitoes. A kindly providence, however, rescued them from this undesirable bequest. Doña Maria de Mendoza, a sister of the dead benefactor, afterwards gave them a house in a healthier situation in the city itself. There Madre Teresa remained through the winter: in September of that same year, 1568, she had already sent Fray Juan to Ávila on his way to Duruelo.

He had often irritated her in those few weeks of trying business, and she had not suppressed every sign of her vexation. But somehow, his demeanour atoned for all. "He was so good," wrote Teresa, "that I at least could have learnt much more from him than he from me." [8] "We never discovered a solitary imperfection in him: we shall certainly miss him here." [9] "Talk to him, Father, and give him help,"

[7] Cunninghame Graham, I, 357.
[8] *Ibid.*, I, 368.
[9] Bruno, p. 72.

she wrote to a friend at Ávila, Don Francisco de Salcedo. "He is indeed small in stature, but in my opinion he is very great in the sight of God. I find him most fitted for our kind of life; I really do believe that God is calling him to this enterprise. He is still young, but has always practised the most austere penance. The Lord manifestly upholds him with His hand. Nevertheless he really needs all the graces he has received to begin the work all alone and in such a generous spirit. . . ." [10] "I have been greatly encouraged at seeing the spirit with which God animates him and the virtue he has shown on many occasions." [11]

After a short stay in Ávila to pick up a workman, Fray Juan arrived at the village of Duruelo, and began to put in order as a religious house the tumble-down dwelling which Madre Teresa had seen there. She had found it too filthy and bug-ridden to sleep in. The nun who was with her thought it absolutely impossible. "It possessed a tolerable gateway and a room with an alcove and a loft above and a fireplace—this," said Madre Teresa, "was all the edifice our monastery had." [12]

4

To give up the architecture and convents of Valladolid, with all that they told of the glory of the Church both then and in the past; to give up the bracing company of students, companions, directors; to give up the music and ritual of the liturgy, to give up books, and beside a rough-hewn chapel to settle down again in a little village hidden in a fold of the great Castilian plain between Ávila and Peñaranda—such was the experience which inaugurated the new life of a man with a new name. For from henceforward Juan de Yepes y Álvarez was to be known, not as Juan de Santo Matía, but as Juan de la Cruz. "Deny thyself, take up thy cross and follow me." This invitation he answered, and in his favourite treatise, he found it beautifully elaborated.

> In the Cross is safety.
> In the Cross is life.
> In the Cross protection from our foes.
> In the Cross is sweetness poured on us from above.

[10] *Ibid.*, pp. 73, 74.
[11] Cunninghame Graham, I, 365.
[12] *Ibid.*

In the Cross is holiness in perfect beauty.
There is no safety to the Soul,
No hope of life eternal
   Save in the Cross.
Take then your Cross and follow Jesus.[13]

The life at Duruelo was as remote and as austere as any he could have foreseen at El Paular. There was indeed a spring, and the growth that comes from water: not far away was a grove of ilex: but nothing tempered either the heat or the cold of two friars who lived in cells on either side of the little chapel, while some six novices slept together in a dormitory. There was indeed time for solitude and withdrawal from the world: and there he passed a year of his life: a year fixed on far more direct intercourse of his spirit with the transcending Holiness than any he had yet known.

If he had any books with him, they were few. He already set little store on books. To those who have reached this stage of the spiritual life, reading begins to take a secondary place. The soul finds a new activity in resting poised in its act of quiet adoration, in the prayer of recollection so strongly commended by Madre Teresa in *The Way of Perfection*. Even when the mind awakens, it moves in a new way. It discovers new ranges of meaning in phrase after phrase of the Bible. These are now seen to relate to a more interior way of living: they tell the story of the graces of the life of worship. A man hears from God a new and more loving invitation: Seek ye my face; and the heart answers: Thy face, Lord, will I seek.[14] By this new light he begins to see the glory which dazzled Moses and Elijah.

5

This instinct to escape from outward observances, from institutions, from all the practices and associations of piety, from all the materialism of religion, from all those trivialities which fill the doll's house of the Catholic Church with distractions, this served to make life both practical and pure: this was the instinct which in Germany had led to Lutheranism, in Geneva, France and Scotland to Calvinism. In each case, with the advent of the printing-press, men went

[13] *Imitation*, Book II, ch. xii.
[14] Psalm XXVII.

from pictures to words, and found words charged with a life of their
own.

> Visionary power
> Attends the motion of their viewless winds,
> Embodied in the mystery of words:
> There darkness makes abode, and all the host
> Of shadowy things work endless changes,—there
> As in a mansion, like their proper home
> Even forms and substances are circumfused
> By that transparent veil with light divine,
> In flashes, and with glory not their own.[15]

The passion of the time was to get rid of all the machinery and im-
pedimenta which cumbered the Church. Men's souls wanted more
space, more air. Fray Juan knew the need as deeply as any Protestant.
His whole training had strengthened him in it. For hours his exercise had been to recite the psalms, to read the Bible; for hours he
remained in silent prayer; he constantly returned to the words "If a
man wishes to be my disciple, let him deny himself, and take up his
cross and follow me"; [16] and even when he went to the University
and studied theology and philosophy, he found himself occupied,
with the favourite themes of Calvin, with the deep things of thought,
the profound realities which through the ages had occupied the loftiest minds, the meaning of the virtues, the doctrines of grace; the Incarnation of Christ and His redeeming work, the mystery of the
Trinity. He approached all these deep things of God by searching
the Scriptures; were they not, as the inspired Word of God, the
finest revelation? There is, in fact, always in the writings of Fray
Juan de la Cruz the zeal of the extremist Puritan to dig down to the
very roots of the Bible revelation and worship God in spirit and in
truth.

He and Madre Teresa also welcomed the remoteness and poverty
of Duruelo because it enabled him to make a centre of religion among
the lonely peasants of the plain. And there was something about this
little household that attracted the attention of others. Fray Juan was
not alone there. A few weeks after his arrival he had been joined by
another member of the Carmelite Convent at Medina. This was a
man of sixty years of age, no less a personage than the Prior, Fray
Antonio de Heredia. An old friend of Madre Teresa, he, like Fray

[15] Wordsworth, *The Prelude*, Book V, 594-604.
[16] Matt. XVI, 24.

Juan, had been moved by her to make the sacrifice; he had given up the authority of his position and the amenities of his house to face the hardships and meanness of Duruelo. "God," she said, "had inspired him with more valour than he had me, and so he answered that not only there would he dwell, but in a pigsty." [17] These two monks with two others from Medina had begun their regular community life at Duruelo, according to the primitive rigours of the Carmelite order on November 28 when autumn chilled to winter, in 1568.

Three months later they were visited by Teresa, and when she arrived in the early morning she found the former prior busy with the broom. "How is this?" she asked in characteristic fun. "What has become of our dignity?" She observed a community who had found joy in hardship and in servant-work. In those three months, they had got together a number not only of crosses, but of skulls, which at that time were a favourite object of Carmelite piety. In this symbol of the hideousness of corruption, they saw an adjuration to set every affection on things above.

One of the monks had carved a hollowed cross to contain holy water, and he had cut out above it in paper an image of Christ. Everything about the house was to the last degree poor, constricted and austere: but it all gave joy to Madre Teresa, and she was much edified by all she heard of the good done in the neighbourhood.

"They went," she said, "to preach at many of the villages round about which had no religious teaching, for which reason also I was glad the house had been founded in that spot; and since they told me that besides them they had no monastery near, neither was there any other place when it could be had, which was pitiful enough. Already in so short a time, so great was the credit they were held in that it gave me the greatest joy when I heard it. They went as I say to preach a league and a half, and two leagues away, barefoot—for at that time they did not wear *alpargatas* as afterwards they were ordered—and with much snow and cold: and after they had preached and confessed, they returned to the house very late to eat. Their contentment made everything seem little to them. As to food, they

[17] Cunninghame Graham I, 365.

had enough and to spare, for the dwellers of the neighbouring townships provided them with more than they needed, and some gentlemen came to them to confession who lived in those towns, where they already offered them better sites and houses. Among those was Don Luis, lord of the Five Manors." [18]

Don Luis Álvarez de Toledo, this lord of five manors, was a cousin of the Duke of Alba so well known to history. A rich and cultured nobleman, he had brought back from the Low Countries a Flemish Primitive, a finely executed Madonna, which Teresa and many others thought the most beautiful they had seen; and he decided to build in the village of Mancera—a league nearer to the Sierra than Duruelo—a church to house it. With this he wished to associate the company at Duruelo, now increased to fourteen novices, and there on a hill above the valley of the little stream, called the Rio al Mar, he had built the small Carmelite convent of which the young Fray Juan was to take charge. Close at hand were groves and streams, with grass and flowers; in the distance stretched the great spaces of the wheat-field and the plain; above, in all their variety, rose the rocky heights of the Sierra de Gredos. And above this scene, in its endless variety of clouds and colour against the blue, to mark the changes of the day, the sky—not less sublime when it shone with moon and stars. Here the lover of Nature could rejoice even in the entirest simplicity, seeking, as he did so, always to rise above what he enjoyed in thankfulness and praise that he might commune direct with his Creator.

6

Meanwhile the indefatigable Teresa was busy with new projects. Winding over the rough declivities of the Guadarrama, and down through the gorge of the Alberche, she had arrived at Toledo, there to found yet a new convent for her nuns. She had spent two months searching for a house. When the help of powerful friends failed, it seemed to her marvellous when one was found for her by a ragged boy; but of some useful things the poor know more than the rich. [19]

---

[18] *Op. cit.*, 375. *Alpargatas* are the cheapest kind of hemp-soled shoe. The more common name for these friars' shoes nowadays is *sandalias*.

[19] Cunninghame Graham, ch. vii.

She had spent a fortnight of endurance and privations in trying to get this house into order, when a gentleman in boots and spurs appeared at the lattice of the convent.

He came with a message from one of the greatest ladies of Spain, the Princess of Éboli, wife of King Philip's most powerful favourite, the Portuguese, Ruy Gomez da Silva, who had just bought up the entire town of Pastrana in the mountains to the north-east of Madrid, and having put it in excellent order, wished to complete it with a religious foundation. No nun was at that time in higher favour at the Court than Madre Teresa de Jesús. To fetch her the Princess sent her own coach from Madrid.

No sooner had the Reverend Mother arrived there than she found herself making the acquaintance of a remarkable scholar and adventurer, with much experience of the Court. This gifted personage was a Neapolitan who had come to the Court of King Philip with the Prince of Salmeron: after many disappointments he had afterwards spent some time as a hermit on the bank of the Guadalquivir. His name was Ambrosio Mariano Azzaro. For eight years this man of elegance, adventure, and wit, who had delighted equally in words of courtesy and deeds of courage, lived in Andalusia the life of a hermit and a weaver. There he had made friends with an extremely simple-minded peasant, and together they worked and prayed at a hermitage on the outskirts of Seville.

From thence they were summoned to the Court. It was while they were busy with the projects of the King in Madrid that Teresa arrived there at the behest of the Princess of Éboli. She at once saw in the life of the hermit a resemblance to those who lived on Mount Carmel. She saw in the supple mind of Mariano the kind of support of which she was in need. Leaving him behind at Madrid, she now travelled through Alcalá de Henares and Guadalajara into a wild mountain region, where, in that scenery, grandiose and severe, which marks central Spain, she found on an eminence surrounded by orchards and almond trees the ancient town of Pastrana. There Ruy Gomez and the Princess, his wife, had taken over a property developed in earlier years by the knights of Calatrava.

On her arrival, she was welcomed into the palace of its remarkable mistress. Fragile and exquisite in her girlishness, Doña Ana de Mendoza had lost one eye at fencing, and the black patch she wore over it added to the singular appeal of her appearance. Her remaining eye, large and dark, exerted a power that contrasted with her delicate features.[20] She was accustomed to satisfy every whim, and has come down through the years as a mystery. Was there already some dark stain on her character? Had she been the mistress of the King before she was the victim of his malignity? Many questions throw their lights and shadows on this woman who now provided Teresa de Jesús with the means of founding at Pastrana not only a convent for nuns but also a religious house for friars in which Madre Teresa would place her newest recruits, the brilliant Neapolitan Mariano, and his Andalusian companion, whom she found very simple in the things of this world, and who took the name of Fray Juan de la Miseria. To be the Superior of this new community she now summoned from Mancera Fray Juan de la Cruz.

7

Here he could appreciate the charms of Nature and beauty with more enthusiasm than at Mancera. The monastery was built on the summit of a hill, with three valleys radiating from it. On the hills were groves and woods. Further towards the heights were olive groves, and higher still pinewoods; and down through the valleys coursed the streams. Fray Juan, whose sensibilities were so keen, could here enjoy the beauty of the woods and rills as never before. Here he could find a new meaning in the liturgy: "O ye mountains and hills, O ye rivers and streams, bless ye the Lord, praise Him and magnify Him for ever." His mind knew a more rapturous sense of the immanence of God. The Heavens were the work of His fingers, the moon and the stars He had ordained. Yet the very vault of heaven could not give the mystic a more direct communion with the Mind that made them than was to be found in the faculties of a man's own soul: for man, too, was a mystery. "What is man," asked the psalm, "that Thou art mindful of him, and the son of man that Thou visitest him? Thou hast made him a little lower than the angels and crowned him with glory and honour." [21] To the advancing mysticism of the man of prayer, every passage in the Bible glimmered with new meaning

20 Cunninghame Graham, I, 403.
21 Psalm VIII, 5.

and gave a yet richer intensity of adoration to the words: *O Lord our Governor, how excellent is Thy name in all the world!*

8

In Pastrana Fray Juan de la Cruz spent the late autumn of 1570 and at least part of the winter. But early in the following year he was given a new charge: that of a house at the little town of Alcalá de Henares between Guadalajara and Madrid. Here, at the beginning of the century, the famous Jiménez de Cisneros had founded a new university to function according to the use and wont of Paris.[22] The first lectures had been given in 1508. The College of San Ildefonso, as it was called, was a Renaissance building of no great beauty, with a rather bare façade divided into five panels. But the main occupation of the young Carmelite was with his own novices. Those who are advanced in the mystic way can draw men into it by irradiation: "Almost all the religious of this college," says Quiroga, writing some fifty years later, "were great contemplatives." [23] They "tasted in prayer the divine sweetness with which the Holy Spirit favours those who seek their sole consolation in God." [24] The object of the Superior was to instruct their minds in the things of faith, and from this intellectual knowledge to lead the way into the higher activity which comes from the finer faculties of the soul.

While busy with this work of training, the Superior received disquieting news from Pastrana. The man who had been put in charge of the novices there had assumed the name of Angel de San Gabriel. This Angel was himself a neophyte, and he suffered in a peculiar way from the aberrations of the time. Hardship and pain were still sought as a means of perfection; but this Angel of St. Gabriel carried the cult to new extremes. He was a victim of melancholia who released his sense of suffering in frightful applications of the scourge to the bare backs of his novices. They were scourged not only in the monastery, but in the public square, where the derision of young townsmen added to their discomfort. In these cruel orgies some pretended to find perfection; [25] and the lust for cruelty was elaborated: further

[22] Bruno, p. 115.
[23] *Ibid.*, p. 118.
[24] *Ibid.*
[25] Bruno, p. 120.

to gratify their tendencies, they would force the young men to carry logs on their lacerated shoulders.

It was plain that some very morbid elements of the Spanish character were coming out in these men vowed to the religious life. Fray Juan de la Cruz went down to put things in order. He thought it all over, and later made his comments about the spiritual gluttony with which some people for their own pleasure kill themselves (and, he might have added, others) with their penances. This, he said, "was the penance of beasts to which they are attracted exactly like beasts by the desire and pleasure they find in them," and in this way the devil assists them, stirring up in them this gluttony to such an extent that they grow less in virtue, more in vice.[26]

He had hardly had time to return to Alcalá de Henares when he found himself summoned by Madre Teresa de Jesús to her own Ávila to act as director to her own Convent of the Incarnation; a convent to which she had just been named the prioress.

[26] *Dark Night*, I, vii.

Those condescensions to the humours of others, that bearing with the clownish and troublesome actions and ways of our neighbours, those victories over our own humours and passions, those renouncings of our lesser inclinations, that effort against our aversions and repugnances, that heartfelt and sweet acknowledgment of our own imperfections, the continual pains we take to keep our souls in equality, that love of our abjection, that gentle and gracious welcome we give to the contempt and censure of our condition, of our life, of our conversation, of our actions—all these things are more profitable to our souls than we can conceive if heavenly love have the management of them.[1]

I

THE manner of the return of Teresa to her convent is a little drama that carries us far into the ways of the age.[2] Since her departure ten years before, things had gone badly with this ancient house. There were still over a hundred nuns there, but their resources had dwindled away; and they had begun to live an easier and easier life, spending much time in the parlour, and even from time to time receiving visits from gallants in the neighbourhood. Nuns who were interpreting the Carmelite rule in this diverting way had little patience with the example set by Teresa. They thought her reforms far too severe. She was the last person they wanted to have appointed as their Superior.

But a new and austere Pope, Pius V, was reigning in Rome. He had sent to Spain visitors to reform the orders: these visitors had final authority; and it was one of these who decided that Teresa should return to rule her former convent.

To decide was one thing; to effect the decision was another. Recalcitrant nuns summoned to their aid certain armed gentlemen of their following and prepared to resist Teresa's entry by force.

The Provincial and another monk supported the venerable Mother —for she was now approaching sixty years of age. In the choir of the

[1] St. François de Sales, *The Love of God*, Book VII, ch. vi.
[2] Cunninghame Graham, ch. xv.

convent they found a babel. Strident voices rose in dispute: excitement reached a frenzy: the Te Deum begun by some was drowned by the imprecations of others. Turbulent tempers had broken out, and the furious Provincial stood in the midst of a crowd of hysterical and angry women over whom he could exercise no control.

Meanwhile Teresa herself had reached the Altar, and there she knelt at prayer, concealing in her habit a relic of the True Cross. When the pandemonium had reached its height, she rose and began to mediate between the nuns and the Provincial. She told the nuns of her sympathy with their having a prioress forced on them, and a prioress who was so unworthy. She then approached some of the nuns who, in the fury of their excitement, had fainted. In her touch there was something so soothing and so powerful that they recovered consciousness and strength.

Such was the return of Teresa to the unruly crowd of women whom she was to reduce to order. Many remained obstinately defiant: they prepared for fight, if need be with hands and nails. But placing an image of the Virgin in her stall, she told them that not Teresa but Mary was their Prioress. And when she met them in the first chapter, she overpowered them by her tact. "I come only to serve you," she said, "and to administer to your pleasure as far as I am able: and to this end I hope the Lord will greatly help me. For as to the rest any one of you can teach and inform me. For that reason, consider, *Señoras mías,* that what I can do for each one of you, I will do it willingly, even to the shedding of blood, and giving up my life. I am a daughter of this house, and your sister. I know the circumstances and necessities of all, or of the greatest number; there is no reason to dread one who is so entirely yours. Do not fear my rule, for although I have lived till now and ruled, amongst Discalced nuns, by the Lord's mercy, I know well how those who are not should be governed. My desire is that we should all serve the Lord with suavity, and that we should do that little enjoined on us by our rule and constitutions, for the love of that Lord to whom we owe so much. Well do I know how great is our weakness; but although our works do not reach so far, let our desires do so: for the Lord is pitiful and will order it so that, little by little, our works shall rise to our intentions." [3]

[3] Cunninghame Graham, II, 4.

To this accommodating speech, even the most hot-tempered nuns found no answer: Teresa soon showed the other side of her character to a gay young gentleman who spent his afternoons in pursuit of a particular nun. She told him what she thought of him, and said that, if he came again to the convent, she would report him to the King and have his head cut off.[4]

2

But Teresa no longer felt at home in the convent where she had once passed so many happy years: through the following winter she had felt very lonely: she could no longer feel that this was the place of her birth and her childhood. Worst of all, she had no director: no one to talk to at her ease: she must always be circumspect.[5] Such were the occasions, such the difficulties which persuaded her that for her spiritual adviser, and for her nuns, she had better summon as confessor from Alcalá the eager, sensitive, uncompromising mystic now just thirty years of age, whom she had for five years loved and trusted, and whom she had made one of the leading spirits of her reform. So it was that Fray Juan once more travelled round or across the Guadarrama and lived once more in the company of the Paramera de Gredos.

The city of Ávila to which she brought him is little changed since his arrival there in 1572. Then, as now, the solid walls with their eighty towers and the immense bastions of their gates defended a city of several plazas and palaces among hovels running down the hillside towards the Rio Adaja and its mills. Built on the last spur of the Guadarrama, the city looks from the terrace over a sombre upland plain crossed by long, lonely roads. The little river winding among groves of poplars comes to it over the folds of the plain. Seen from afar, the city looks like a regularization of the rock to which it clings; for it is grey and golden in a grey and golden scene of boulders and bare earth. Here and there a Mudejar tower rises to scan the neighbouring road or distant sierra; the narrow, winding, uneven lanes and streets lead either to the gates or against the great gate to that rock which pushes into the city walls to form the Cathe-

[4] *Op. cit.*, p. 4.
[5] *Op. cit.*, p. 174.

dral. For this is a Church of men at arms! Through these streets, which saw the armed cavaliers ride by, the peasant comes still with his donkey or his basket, with his wide black sombrero, with his short coat and his knee-breeches tied in with ribbon at the knee; and still in the summer and autumn the market is coloured with flowers and pears, with gourds, melons, figs and grapes.

"Here," says Mrs. Cunninghame Graham, "the tender gradations of spring and autumn are unknown. Snow, hail and storms of wind and rain sweep over the arid plains from October to June, preceded by a fierce period of African heat. Landscape, town, cathedral, people and climate are alike rigid, grey, fierce, storm-tossed"; [6] for the people are one with scene and climate: hardy, wiry and lean, with bright eyes and fresh complexions, and guarding even in their humanity a hidden power of will and of soul.

Such were the people of whom both Fray Juan and Madre Teresa were come, such were the people of blood and bone whom they sought to win for the praise and contemplation of God Most High.

It was the deepest instinct for the deep things of the Spirit which made Madre Teresa crave a congenial companion. Her genius needed the stimulation of a complementary genius; and the years which the ageing nun and the young friar spent together at Ávila were extremely fruitful in the lives of each.

3

Of Fray Juan in those next five years we hear little: his Mother was proud to think of him directing all those nuns when he himself seemed still so much a boy.[7] Teresa again bore witness to his holiness, and the good he was doing; and she associates him with one of her most intense experiences. She had found that in Holy Communion she received as it were an access of special fervour if the Host she received were large. But one morning—it was November 18, 1572— the octave of St. Martin—after he had walked down the white-and-gold church to the grill, while the nuns knelt one by one to receive Holy Communion, he divided the Host in two, giving half to another nun. But when she returned to her stall, she saw in an ecstasy

[6] Cunninghame Graham, I, 5.
[7] Bruno, p. 26.

Christ Himself appear to her and hail her as His spouse. "My Honour," He said, "is thine, thine mine"; and the day passed for Teresa in a sort of delirium.

Thenceforward she began to live with a new power. She knew by a mysterious sense that she was living in one of the highest mysteries of the life to come, in the vision of the Blessed Trinity; to tell what she experienced, words inevitably failed her: all she could attempt to say was that her soul seemed to be a glass which reflected Christ in the centre of it. "It seemed," she wrote, "as though I saw clearly in every part of my soul as in a mirror, and this same mirror (I know not how) was entirely sculptured in Christ Himself by a communication (that I cannot describe) of exceeding love. I know that this vision did me great good whenever I thought of it, especially after receiving Holy Communion." [8]

This experience was completed later when her sense of God was expressed less by a mirror than by a diamond: "Being once upon a time in prayer, it was represented to me like a flash, although I saw nothing formed, still it was a representation with all clearness, how all things we see are in God, and how all are contained in Him. . . . It seemed to me, I repeat, although I cannot be certain that I saw nothing; (still something must be seen since I am able to give this comparison) but it is in a way so subtle and delicate that either the understanding cannot reach it, or I do not myself understand these visions, for they do not appear imaginary, and in some of them something of this there must be, but rather that as the faculties are suspended, they cannot shape it afterwards in the way the Lord represents it to them, and with which they should enjoy it. Let us say that the Being of God is like a very lustrous diamond, larger than all the world or like a mirror, in the same way as what I said of the soul in a former vision, saving that it is in a manner so transcendental that I cannot express it; and all that we do is seen in the diamond, it being so fashioned that it includes everything within itself because there is nothing but what is contained in this magnitude. It was a fearful thing for me to see in so brief a space so many things together in this clear diamond." [9]

She could not differentiate in the faculties. "As for mind, soul and spirit, it is all one to me," she wrote: [10] but as we shall see she had passed from imaginative to intellectual vision; [11] and she turned to her confessor to compare her experience with his insight: which, as she saw from day to day, was wonderful.

4

"I have found a man after God's heart and my own," said Madre Teresa. Fray Juan was entirely absorbed in the experiences of solitary love, so that every worldly thought seemed deleterious: such a state of mind, however, was not always helpful to a prioress and foundress who, in addition to having to deal with difficult nuns at Ávila, was accustomed to suiting her talk and her ways to men and women living in the world, if it was only to praise the cider they sent her.

"The Lord deliver us," she wrote in her *Vejamen,* "from people who are so elevated in spirituality that they wish at all costs to bring everyone to perfect contemplation." [12] Teresa and Juan were people of very different temperaments, and she was well aware that his gifts were not those of an administrator. She explained with a chuckle that the real fault she found in the sublimities of Fray Juan was that they had nothing to do with the question proposed. But how she loved the innocence and guilelessness which he showed in every glance, and which made him extraordinarily patient and gentle in his dealings with the souls of sinners. [13] Once he had to deal with a young lady who had fallen violently in love with him, and forced her way into his cottage. She left in peace, melted into tears. "Yet," as Santa Teresa attested, "he had the gift of casting out devils from persons possessed." [14] The fact was that Teresa was well aware that though her director lacked her power to deal with very different conditions of men and women, and to manage affairs, his was a soul to ride sublime the heights and depths of love and beauty. She made her little quips at his defects, while she admired outstanding excellences in a person whom she, and many, particularly loved.

[10] *Loc. cit.,* note.
[11] See C. Butler, *Western Mysticism,* p. 49.
[12] Bruno, p. 129.
[13] *Ibid.,* p. 132.
[14] Bruno, p. 136.

This sanctuary of my soul
Unwitting I keep white and whole,
Unlatched and lit if thou shouldst care
To enter and to tarry there.

With parted lips and outstretched hands
And listening ears thy servant stands,—
Call thou early, call thou late,
To thy great service dedicate.[1]

I

ALTHOUGH he may well have known them earlier, he could not have passed this time without becoming acquainted with the classics of mysticism which she had long been recommending to her nuns, the *Conferences* of Cassian, the *Moralia* of St. Gregory the Great, the works of Denys the Carthusian, the *Tercer Abecedario* of Francisco de Ossuna, the *Tratado de la Oración* of San Pedro de Alcántara, the *Libro de la Oración* de Luis de Granada, the *Subida del Monte Sión* de Bernardino de Laredo, and, not least, the *Imitation of Christ,* which was known in Spain by the significant title *Contemptus Mundi;* [2] and which was by far the most important of these works. The others but adapt the lessons it teaches of renunciation, and the rewards of a devout spiritual life.

Nothing that Fray Juan was to write in later years was more uncompromising than the standards of self-renunciation and penance here set before the monk and nun. It began with uncompromising "warnings useful to a spiritual life," insisting on the highest standards of self-renunciation, and Fray Juan, as we shall see, was in turn to reinforce many of these. It then insisted that for joy one must turn to spiritual things: "all His splendour and beauty are from within and in that man delighteth. To one who lives the inner life Christ often comes: sweet is the converse, clear the consolation, great the

[1] C. H. Sorley, *Expectans expectavi.*
[2] Sainz Rodríguez, *Introducción,* p. 239.

peace, and the intimacy wonderful beyond description." Let us therefore put the love of Jesus above all things. "He that to the creature
clings shall fall with what is frail: but he that throws his arms round
Jesus shall grow for ever stronger." He will never leave you. There
is no surer road than the pathway of the Holy Cross. Come unto
Jesus and He will refresh you. "Bless and sanctify my soul," was
the book's concluding prayer, "with blessing from above, that it may
be Thy holy dwelling-place, the home of Thine eternal glory."

Through Teresa Juan came in touch with the Franciscan spirit:
for no one had more influenced her than Francisco de Ossuna, who
was both a profound mystic and a graceful writer. He had a frank
and open delight in creation; he fell in love with all the creatures he
saw. If a man loved,—that for the Son of St. Francis was enough.
Song, joy, and the visible beauties, like flowers and music, urge the
mystic towards the love of God, perhaps without his realising it.[3]
And if we would turn this natural pleasure into heavenly love, and
hear the secret voice which calls us to the love of God, we should
regard created things with eyes as chaste and pure as those of the
faithful bride when she regards the jewels which are given her to
awaken within her a love for him who gave them; she sees in them
more truly the giver than she sees the jewels themselves.[4] Both
Ossuna and Bernardino de Laredo found this doctrine on Hugh and
Richard of St. Victor and on Dionysius, but they also knew St.
Thomas.[5]

Several parallels and common ideas suggest that San Juan had read
at least *The Third Alphabet* of Francisco de Ossuna, who thoroughly
understood the prayer of quiet. "The greater love is," he wrote, "the
less it has need of words and the richer will be the significance with
which the words used are fraught. Because love, if it is true, is unable
to seek the exercise of subtle reasonings, but works great things in
silence." [6] This he often called the way of the *night*.[7] He too taught
that the contemplative must turn away from all things thought or
imagined, and insisted that nature abhors a vacuum. He too had

[3] *Tercer Abecedario*, trat XVI, ch. v, para. 498 b, and ch. ix, para. 500 a.
[4] *Ibid.*, trat XV, p. 500 a.
[5] Etchegoyen, *Sources de Sainte Thérèse*, p. 131.
[6] *Tercer Abecedario*, p. 466 b.
[7] *Ibid.*, pp. 377, 385, 448.

written of the bat blinded by the light and the clear window pane
which lets in more light.[8] And once San Juan, who loved generally
freely to translate from his predecessors, gives a very close echo. On
the letter Y of *The Third Alphabet*, Ossuna leads with *Intimamente
asosiega y acalla in entendimiento.* In *Mount Carmel*, San Juan
writes of *el entendimiento intimamente sosegado y accallado.* This
phrase is not enough to prove that San Juan knew Ossuna, but
joined with many other resemblances, it makes it extremely probable.[9]

Did they know directly of Ruysbroeck? More indirectly than
directly. Ruysbroeck had been the initiator of a whole school of
mysticism of which the great success had been *The Imitation of
Christ*, but mention direct there is none, nor proof.[10] There are, however, many parallels.[11] As for Denys the Carthusian, one of his
works was on the Index, but only in its Spanish translation. And it
did not prevent his general influence spreading through the Carthusian
order or his learning affecting the Carmelites.[12]

2

Whether he first read him now, or when at Alcalá or Salamanca,
Fray Juan also came closely to know that earlier master of the mysteries of the spiritual life, the Syrian (or as some thought Alexan-
drian) mystic who took the name of Dionysius the Areopagite—
though he wrote some five hundred years later than the man of that
name whom St. Paul converted at Athens. This was the writer who
had so strongly influenced Denys the Carthusian. Besides the knowledge of God obtained by philosophical or theological disquisitions,
there is, says this writer, "that most divine knowledge of God which
takes place through ignorance in the union which is above intelligence, when the intellect quitting all things that are and then leaving itself also is united to the super-lucent rays, being illuminated
thence and therein by unsearchable depth of wisdom." [13] These

[8] Fidèle de Ros, *Père François d'Ossuna.*
[9] *Op. cit.*, pp. 625-630. Crisógono, *La escuela mística carmelitana*, ch. III.
[10] See Groult, *Les Mystiques des Pays Bas et la Littérature Espagnole du Seizième Siècle,*
pp. 142-145.
[11] *Op. cit.*, p. 175.
[12] *Op. cit.*, pp. 59-60.
[13] *De Divinis Nominibus*, VII, 3; translation by C. E. Rolt.

super-lucent rays were described as dark by excess of light. "The mind," says Dionysius, "enters into the really mystic darkness of unknowing wherein it renounces all the perception of the understanding, and abides in that which is wholly intangible and invisible, belonging wholly to Him that is beyond all, though being by inactivity of all cognition united in the highest point of Him who is wholly unknowable." [14]

Here was a doctrine which was, because of its profundity, yet more congenial to Fray Juan de la Cruz than the *Abecedarios* of Francisco de Ossuna. Ossuna had written of aridities as the result of some infidelity or neglect which distracted the faculties from the Holy Communion of contemplation. There is no doubt that for the majority of contemplatives Ossuna is right: they too easily forfeit the reward they have gained by accepting distractions, rival interests, rival loves. And then the sacred glow of affective prayer cools, the relish for the things of God is lost, and the surface of the soul's mirror is dulled. Bernardino de Laredo had constantly written in the same sense of the value of affections in orison. Santa Teresa had put in her warning too. In the *Imitation of Christ,* fervour was not distrusted; it was, on the other hand, called "the grace of devotion," which the man of prayer was to receive with thankfulness and with which he was to work with diligence. But here was another method of contemplation. It was to employ a sublime faculty planted in the being of man which gave him an immediate intercourse with the Mind which made him. In this intercourse the details of man's knowledge were lost as details are lost in an access of blinding light. It was in the flash of a trembling glance that St. Augustine had entered into communion with *That Which Is,* with absolute and timeless Being, with the noonday of Reality. If this vision were to be prolonged, he asked, if it were to ravish and absorb him who beheld it in inward joys so that life for ever would be like that one moment of understanding, would not this be "to enter into the joy of the Lord"? Would not this explain the text "We shall not all sleep but we shall all be changed"? [15]

[14] *Mystical Theology,* I, I.
[15] *Confessions,* IX, 25.

3

In the mystical schools of the African coast of the Central Mediterranean, Dionysius had perfected his teaching about the contemplation of the Divine perfection by that faculty of immediacy which is known as the apex, or highest point of the soul, and by a process which Dionysius described as darkness. "In the intent practice of mystic contemplation," directed this writer, "leave behind the senses and operations of the intellect, and all things that the senses or the intellect can perceive, and all things which are not, and all things which are, and strain upwards in unknowing, as far as may be, towards the union with Him who is above all being and knowledge. For by increasing and absolute withdrawal from thyself and all things in purity, abandoning all, and set free from all, thou wilt be borne up to the ray of the divine Darkness that surpasseth all Being . . . and to this Darkness which is beyond light we pray that we may come, and through loss of sight and knowledge may see and know that which transcends sight and knowledge, by the very fact of seeing and knowing; for this is real sight and knowledge." [16]

It is plain that this is for most men an unknown mode of being: the sense of its nature dim and undetermined: in a world so lofty and so hard to realize, man may well have a sense of blank misgiving. And this sense may easily become boredom, blankness, desolation, aridity. In gaining it, one has left the comforts and sights of home to climb high in the mountains along tracts windswept, forbidding and steep.

4

Dionysius saw "the unchangeable mysteries of heavenly truth: hidden in the dazzling obscurity of the secret silence": through "the passive stillness of all his reasoning powers" he is "united to Him who is wholly unknowable": "by a rejection of all knowledge he possesses a knowledge that exceeds his understanding." [17] So in his *Mystical Theology* did Dionysius describe how there was in the being of man a faculty which was supreme: an inward eye which saw in the

---

[16] *Mystic Theology*, I, 1.
[17] *De Divinibus Nominibus*, ch. iv; Rolt, p. 94.

suspension of the lower faculties such glories in the heavens as night discloses through the darkness, when the stars shine out to tell a story denied to the gaudy day.

But if Dionysius thus spoke of the darkness in God, he spoke of God also as Light and Beauty. God, said Dionysius, gave to souls as much light as they could bear, and "ever he constraineth them according to their power of looking upwards." He gave them "one true, pure, coherent knowledge which is described as Beauty and as Love. The super-essential beauty is called Beauty because of that quality which it imparts to all things severally according to their nature, and because it is the Cause of the harmony and splendour in all things, flashing forth upon them all, like light, the beautifying communication of its original Ray.[18] Yet "the Divine knowledge of God, which is received through unknowing, is obtained in that Communion which transcends the mind, when the mind, turning away from all things and then leaving even itself behind, is united to the Dazzling Rays, being from them and in them illumined by the unsearchable depths of wisdom. Nevertheless, as I said, we must draw the Knowledge of Wisdom from all things; for wisdom it is, as saith the Scripture, that hath made all things, and is the Cause of the indissoluble harmony and order of all things, perpetually fitting the end of one part with the beginning of the second, and thus producing the one fair agreement and concord of the whole." [19] By this means Dionysius saw the variety of creation as one order, its music as one song of honour to the Source of the beautiful and the good. "This," said Dionysius, "is the transcendent beginning and transcendent goal of the Universe, for as Holy Scripture saith, Of him and through him and to him are all things, to whom be glory for ever and ever." [20]

5

In this happy sense of a glory enveloping them, and allowing them to share in purest love and beauty, Madre Teresa and Fray Juan shared with one another an interest in verse. The nun wrote her hymns: and the friar too made studies and beginnings which were

[18] *Ibid.*, Rolt, p. 96.
[19] *Ibid.*, Rolt, pp. 152, 153.
[20] *Ibid.*, Rolt, p. 161.

soon to burst forth in overflow in lyric compositions, for which he found the perfect example in the *Song of Songs*. While she told him of her Classics in the spiritual life, we can trace his influence in what she wrote under his guidance after he joined her.

She began to write with greater power: she became aware of his deliberate style, and she had more to relate. After he had encouraged her to study the *Song of Songs*, she began to write as an exposition of it the little treatise she called *Conceptions of the Love of God*. Even though she could not clearly translate into Castilian the Latin words she read, yet they lifted up for her the everlasting doors:

"Let him kiss me with the kisses of his mouth; for thy breasts are better than wine." That, as Teresa read the Latin, was the bold opening of the *Song of Songs*. "I cannot understand this, and I am very glad of it," she began in her shrewd, naïf way, for it is always the Spanish lady, and not a University Professor who is speaking. "For the soul ought not so much to contemplate and honour God in those things that our intellects can master in this life as in those problems we cannot solve . . . for many of these things are not suited for women—nor men either very often. . . ." [21] How well the holy Mother knew her nuns and friars! "You may think that some things in the *Song of Songs* might have been expressed differently," she went on. "Our minds are so evil that this would not surprise me. I have even heard people say that they avoided hearing them. Alas, O God, what most miserable creatures we are; like venomous reptiles that turn all they eat into poison!" [22]

Nevertheless, since this book of the Bible delighted her so much, she would give them some of her personal thoughts on passages which the most learned doctors could not fully explain. It would please and amuse a King if a simple shepherd-lad, who was his favourite, stood amazed at his royal robes and wondered how they were made: and I, said the great mystic, am like that shepherd-boy.

Let him kiss me with the kisses of his mouth. "I own," said Madre Teresa, whose shrewd judgment always kept company with her ecstasies, "that the words have many meanings, yet the soul, intoxicated and inflamed with love, cares for no other meaning, and only desires to utter them, since God does not deprive her of the

---

[21] *Conceptions of the Love of God*, I, 1.
[22] *Ibid.*, 3.

right of so doing. God help me: why should we be so amazed? Is not the reality still more wonderful? Do we not approach the most Blessed Sacrament? I have sometimes wondered whether the Spouse was asking here for the favour which Christ afterwards bestowed on us. At other times I have thought she might have meant the consummated union of God being made Man." [23] So did Madre Teresa develop from the amorous phrases in the *Song of Songs* her conception of the Love of God.

6

The other work she wrote at this time is her masterpiece, *The Interior Castle*, illustrating the mystic way by means of seven apartments [24] or mansions of the soul through which the soul may pass to the fruition of the Godhead in that final state which is known as the mystic marriage, when the soul attains to a final union with God. She begins with an account of the first steps in self-denial: she analyses the prayer of quiet, becoming now able to distinguish it from recollection, as she had not been able to do when she wrote *The Way of Perfection*. She did not scruple to mention in the first mansions the reptiles which disturb the peace of those who live in the yard of the castle. Even here she warns her nuns to think more often of the glory of God than their own sins. In the second mansions they will be tormented with bad thoughts, boredom and aridities, but prayer will preserve them from falling into temptation. In the third mansions the purifying treatment is continued. In the fourth and fifth mansions illuminations bring the soul many consolations. She first distinguishes between the spiritual life as such, and the satisfaction and content naturally brought into the soul by emotion and gratification. The heart is enlarged and set at liberty. She distinguishes between the satisfaction felt in created things when the mind is occupied with those, and a certain direct experience gained by the absorption of the soul in prayer. The soul seems to have an experience of warmth or fragrance: not that such are felt directly, but in a subtle manner the impress comes directly to an inner faculty. These favours may be gained not by seeking, but by a readiness for suffer-

---

[23] *Conceptions of the Love of God*, I, 2.
[24] *Primeras Moradas.* She uses the plural for each of her separate mansions.

ing and self-sacrifice: but they are not subject to a covenant. At such a time the soul will attain the gift of recollection, retreating within itself like a sea-urchin; and it is here Santa Teresa distinguishes between recollection, when the intellect may still be working, and the prayer of quiet when the mind ceases to act. She distinguishes between the languor which comes from exhaustion, and the short rapturous experience.

7

Henceforth Madre Teresa soars into worlds unknown. In the fifth, the sixth, and the seventh mansions she describes the wonders of advanced prayer, and the strong graces that come as the fruit of sacrifice and suffering. In the earlier of these states the soul knows not how, nor whom it loves, nor what it desires. In fact, it has died actually to the world to live more truly than ever in God. And then mightier secrets are disclosed: and Santa Teresa now relates at great length the secrets of the fifth mansion where the soul is as it were affianced to God; here she introduces the famous metaphor of the silkworm. For as the silkworm spins its cocoon, so the soul works itself into grace till it is hid with Christ in God. "He is our home and we can dwell in it by our own power." Then the soul comes forth from its hidden life with all the freedom and joyousness of the butterfly. "Oh, how great God is!" exclaims the saint. "How beautiful is the soul after having been immersed in God's grandeur and united closely to him for but a short time. Indeed I do not think it is ever so long as half an hour." [25]

And now wonders throng upon the soul in the spiritual betrothal which in time lead us to the spiritual marriage, and here, says Santa Teresa, so mysterious is the secret and so sublime the favour that God thus instantaneously bestows upon the soul that it feels a supreme delight; only to be described by saying that Our Lord vouchsafes for the moment to reveal to it His own heavenly glory in a far more subtle way than by any vision or spiritual delight. As far as can be understood, the soul, I mean the spirit of this soul, is made one with God who is Himself a spirit and who has been pleased to show to certain persons how far His love extends, that we may praise

[25] *Mansions*, V, 6.

His greatness. He has thus designed to unite Himself to His creatures. He has bound Himself as firmly as two human beings are
bound in wedlock and will never separate Himself from her.[26]
". . . In spiritual marriage with Our Lord, the soul always remains
in its centre with its God."

The cloud of darkness breaks and a heavenly light shows the wor-
shipping soul the Divine mystery. "By some mysterious manifestation of the truth, the Three Persons of the most Blessed Trinity
reveal themselves, preceded by an illumination which shines on the
spirit like a most dazzling cloud of light. The Three Persons are distinct from one another: a sublime knowledge is interfused into the
soul, imbuing it with a certainty of the truth that the Three are of
one substance, power and knowledge, and are one God. Thus, that
which we hold as a doctrine of faith, the soul now, so to speak, understands by sight, although it beholds the blessed Trinity neither by
the eyes of the body nor of the soul, for this is no imaginary vision.
All the Three Persons here communicate themselves to the soul,
speak to it, and make it understand the words of Our Lord in the
gospel that He and the Father and the Holy Ghost will come and
make their abode with the soul which loves Him. . . . Day by day a
growing astonishment takes possession of the soul, for the Three
Persons of the Blessed Trinity seem never to depart." [27]

The power of grace in these writings of Santa Teresa was very
strong. Many a soul was moved to such an adjuration as that which
Crashaw voiced in *The Flaming Heart:*

> Live here, great heart, and love and die and kill
> And bleed, and wound, and yield and conquer still. . . .
> Let all thy scatter'd shafts of light that play
> Among the leaves of thy large books of day
> Combined against this breast, at once break in
> And take away from me myself and sin. . . .
> Let me so read thy life that I
> Unto all life of mine may die.[28]

But there were many a friar and nun who voiced another view of
Madre Teresa. She was, in fact, shortly to be described as "that restless, roving, disobedient, contumacious female, who under cover of

[26] *Ibid.*, VII, ch. ii, 3.
[27] *The Interior Castle.* Seventh Mansions, ch. i, 9, 10.
[28] Crashaw, *The Flaming Heart.*

devotion invents evil doctrine; leaving the retirement of the cloister to gad about against the order of the Council of Trent." [29]

The person who made this estimate of Santa Teresa in 1578 was a Bishop; he was no other than the Nuncio of the Pope himself. And she herself was aware of it all. "They call me restless and a gad-about," she wrote. "Ah, how few friends there are in time of need!" [30]

[29] Cunninghame Graham, II, 223.
[30] Silverio, *Obras*, VIII, 264, 266.

SANTA TERESA DE JESUS
A polychrome statue by Gregori Hernandez

Jesu lover of my soul
Let me to thy bosom fly
While the nearer waters roll,
While the tempest still is high.

Other refuge have I none,
Hangs my helpless soul on Thee.
Leave ah leave me not alone,
Still support and comfort me! [1]

I

EVEN as she was writing the last chapters of *The Interior Castle,* Madre Teresa de Jesús had an intuition that she was not to be left in peace to enjoy these lofty themes of her contemplation. This world is not the theatre of perfection. Trouble, toil, and pain mark the steep ascent to heaven, even for those who have climbed to a clear sight of the heavenly city. A profound intuition told her that for her and for the young Juan, who had such singular faculties of poetry, of mysticism and innocence, torment was at hand. She saw in a vision what she described as "a great storm of tribulations." Her life at Ávila had not been easy. What the Nuncio was to call "gadding about," the journeys to found new houses, she had found very tiring.

Then the house at Pastrana had been much disturbed by its patroness. When Ruy Gomez da Silva died in 1573, his widowed Princess—having summoned to her the brilliant Italian Carmelite, Mariano Azzaro, whom Madre Teresa had attracted into her order—insisted that he should clothe her in the habit of Teresa's nuns; climbing on to a cart, she drove to their house with her mother, the Princess de Melito, and demanded entrance to the convent at eight o'clock in the morning. There she first insisted on ignoring the courtesies offered to her rank, and finally on receiving many men who came to offer her condolence. Among these were lords "who

[1] Charles Wesley, A.D. 1740.

think not they are lords if they obey laws." And the convent was thrown into disorder. "The Princess a nun!" said Fray Baltasar, the Carmelite. "Then I give up this house for lost." [2]

Appeal was made to Madre Teresa: but nothing could either induce the Princess to live orderly within the convent, or to leave it. After many expostulations, the nuns were constrained to leave Pastrana and the Princess for a new house Teresa had found for them at Segovia. She then journeyed into Andalusia to found fresh convents, one at Seville, and one in the folds of the Sierra Morena on the river Guadalimar at Beas.

2

Meanwhile the Princess of Éboli had driven off to her palace in Madrid, there to become the mistress of the King's new secretary, Antonio Pérez, until the King, discovering all, had her arrested and confined in the Torre de Pinto, near Madrid—and thus she makes her lurid exit from the story of saints and mystics.[3]

There had, of course, been fierce arguments whether or not Teresa herself had not swerved contumaciously from the track. Even as far back as 1565 the Inquisition had been watching her. But Teresa had attracted the attention of the King. Travelling from Valladolid to Madrid, she had left him a message containing information which aroused his curiosity. He sent for her, but she was gone. But believing that she was to play her part in bringing him to heaven, she had asked her nuns to pray for a certain *Gran Señor del Mundo*. Knowing that he was favourably disposed, she had written to him in 1575 to have the Reform made into a separate province, and she had suggested for the Superior a friar named Gracián, who had joined the community at Pastrana and who, when she met him at Beas, had immediately captivated her motherly and discerning heart.

3

Who was Gracián? He was, next to Fray Juan de la Cruz, the most gifted writer among the reformed Carmelites. He belonged to

[2] Cunninghame Graham, II, 27.
[3] Walsh, *Philip II*, pp. 599-600.

a family connected with the Court. His father, Diego Gracián de Alderete, had been a secretary to Charles V; his grandfather, chief armourer of Ferdinand and Isabella; in the train of the Emperor his father had gone to Flanders, where his original name of García had been changed to this unusual and melodious form; he had studied at Louvain under the great Platonist, Luis Vives—afterwards tutor to Queen Mary Tudor. And then he had married Juana Dantisco, the daughter of the Polish Ambassador; she bore him thirteen children; while he pursued his life of culture and bounties. He translated Xenophon and Plutarch: but he never bothered about money or the future. This, his third son, was born at Valladolid in 1545; if the young man inherited no fortune, he was endowed with such a combination of cultivated tastes, a Jesuit's training, a quick and able brain, a singularly appealing personality, that he seemed certain of a happy and high career. What Sir Philip Sidney was to Queen Elizabeth, he might well have been at the rival Court of the Escorial, had religion not been his supreme romance.[4]

In 1569, at the age of twenty-four, overcoming all remonstrances, he was ordained a priest, and was studying in the University of Alcalá when Fray Juan arrived there in 1571.

His future might still have been brilliant, but after preaching for the nuns at Alcalá an eloquent and enthusiastic sermon on the antiquity of the order of Mount Carmel, he embraced in 1572 the vocation to which he owes his heroism, his disgrace, and his fame. While Alcalá was telling with enthusiasm of the lustre of his talents, to which was added a melting charm, he withdrew to Pastrana, and in a short time had become a Carmelite. When in 1575 Teresa met him at her new convent at Beas, she was enchanted: in this grandson of an Ambassador, in this handsome young man, so gifted, so good-looking, so expansive, so well endowed with courtly Spanish graces, she saw among the asperities of Mount Carmel a prince who had moved in crimson velvet. In him she believed she had found one even more suitable for her purposes than either the fine genius of Fray Juan, or the experienced courtier, Mariano Azzaro. Diplomacy and distinction and elevation of personality seemed to combine the gifts

[4] There is a delightful account of Gracián by Professor Allison Peers, *Studies of the Spanish Mystics,* Vol. II; another by the Marqués de San Juan de Piedras Albas (Madrid, 1918). See also Zimmermann in Bruno.

of each in his well-rounded contours. In a short time she was recommending him to the King: she enjoined the prioress at Pastrana to give him the same obedience as to herself: soon after he arrived there he was made Superior at Pastrana, and finally the chief of the whole community of the Reform.[5] This was the man who took the name of Jeronimo de la Madre de Dios: this was he of whom Teresa had thought particularly when she heard of the fierce way the novices at Pastrana were treated by Fray Angel de San Gabriel. When Madre Teresa first met him, "To my eyes, he is perfect," she wrote; "what we must do is to beseech God to give him to us for our Superior. At last I shall be able to take some repose from the management of these houses. For such perfection mingled with such charm I have not seen. May God support and keep him: for I would not for anything have missed seeing him and conversing with him. Julián de Ávila has lost his heart to him. So have they all. He preaches admirably." [6]

We have seen that the reason for Teresa's reform was not merely to win mercy for Indians, not merely to redress the Lutherans, but to cope with scandals in the order. Of these there were many.[7] To live a stricter life was in fact not the only reason why some of the observants passed over to the Reform. Some found it a means to escape merited punishment.[8] Since one of these fugitives from justice had actually been appointed a visitor (or inspector) in Andalusia, the Dominican originally appointed to supervise his inspection called in the help of Gracián when Gracián had been professed only three months. Gracián not only accepted this task, but he used his position to establish the Reform in Andalusia, where the General had forbidden it. Evidently he had an almost excessive endowment of the flair for diplomacy in his family.

The General of the Order, an Italian named Giovanni Rossi, began to suspect that the Reform was defying his authority and slipping from his control. For Gracián had thought it more prudent to tell him nothing. Rossi, whom the Spaniards called Rubeo, had applied

[5] Cunninghame Graham, II, 83.
[6] *Ibid.*, II, 87.
[7] Zimmermann in Bruno, p. 367; cf. Merriman.
[8] *Ibid.*, p. 368.

for information to Teresa, but got no answer, because the letter did not reach her. In these circumstances the General, highly suspicious of silence which looked like evasion, summoned a chapter at Piacenza in 1575 and excommunicated Gracián.

This act of authority Gracián felt able to ignore. In virtue of obtaining authority from a man who had obtained it from the former Nuncio, Ormaneto, he claimed to be the Visitor of Andalusia. He claimed that as Visitor, holding power from the Nuncio, he held authority superior to that of the General, and for this, as even the Nuncio had admitted, he could make out some sort of case.[9] "I made him Commissary for the Visitation of the Province," wrote the Nuncio Ormaneto on February 5, 1577, to the Cardinal Secretary of State, "and so, things being as I have said, it is quite possible that he may call himself Provincial though not nominated by myself. . . . These Discalced fathers are leading a very holy life and are giving the greatest edification, and are enjoying great credit with the people: would that it pleased God that the others were like them." But the Observants had the confidence of neither the people nor the Court.[10]

It was yet before this that, in March, 1576, Rubeo sent as Visitor to Spain Tostado, who had had experience and shown judgment. But the rumour spread that he was to destroy the Reform. Teresa believed it, and took her stand accordingly. Gracián supported Teresa in the campaign for independence.[11] The King was still a firm believer in his favourite nun, and just as the Nuncio was to have his orders annulled by the Court, so already in 1576 Gracián and Teresa stopped the visits of Tostado by securing a royal order. It was then that Gracián had convened a chapter of the Reform at Almodóvar del Campo [12] in the far south of Castile. He spoke of the war declared between one set of good people and another. He reminded them that they had been condemned by the Chapter of the Order, repulsed by their General at Rome, and abandoned by their Cardinal Protector. Even the Pope was against them. All these had been behind Tostado.

"Let us admit," said Gracián, with his fair and conciliatory mind, "that both sides are in the right. Our brethren have a good intention:

9 *Ibid.*, p. 370.
10 *Ibid.*, p. 372.
11 *Ibid.*, p. 375.
12 *Ibid.*, p. 375.

we have a better one. Courage and confidence then. Patience wins all." [13]

Patience wins all. That was a phrase which Teresa had written on her bookmark. But there was less patience than argument. Gracián had directed that the friars should give much time to preaching, and not alone to prayer and contemplation. Fray Juan had disagreed: the discussion was fierce on this subject also.

Meanwhile Teresa had found an opportunity for an audience with the King. He had now in the Escorial completed the monument of his ideals: against the violet bloom of the Sierra, she saw it raise the proportioned length and height of its immense façades. The austere granite spoke not alone of might, majesty, and dominion, for in the dormer windows and the angled roofs there was something of soaring Gothic fancy, and the pyramid above the majestic Roman arches of the church, and above the turret and the campanile, joined with a general indefinable suggestion of the East. As she looked at it through the clear and luminous air of Castile, and saw it one with the rock, the pine, the mountain, she saw that here was a king to whom majesty was sacred. He lived in the press not alone of kingship, but of a spiritual urgency. Above the temple a spire pointed toward the sky, and on the spire rested an orb, and above the orb glittered a golden cross.

When Teresa was admitted to his presence, she had asked for his support in the work of reform; he had answered: "Be at peace: all shall be as you wish." She threw herself at his knees in gratitude. He bade her rise, and making her the most courteous bow, gave her his hand to kiss. So she herself told the story to Doña Iñez Nieto, the wife of the Duke of Alba's secretary. Thenceforward she referred to Philip as "my friend the King." [14]

She needed all his help. The powers against her were strong. The Nuncio, Ormaneto, who had been supporting her, was recalled to Rome, and Sega, the one who came in his place, was at once won

[13] Stanbrook, *Life,* p. 55.
[14] Walsh, *Philip II,* pp. 572, 573. Silverio prints the letter to Doña Iñez Nieto describing his interview with Philip II, which is in the Collection of the Marqués de S. Juan de Piedras Albas. See Silverio, *Obras,* IX, 266-268, but, unlike the Marquis, Silverio is highly doubtful of its authenticity (Vol. VII, p. xcviii). So is Merriman.

It is plain, however, from the tone of Teresa's letters that she had been cordially received in audience by the King. Cf. Bertrand, *Ste Thérèse,* pp. 379 f.; Merriman, *Rise of the Spanish Empire,* IV, 51.

over by the Observants to work against her. At first she had almost
enjoyed the excitement: for it was just another diversion in a comic
world.[15] She soon found, however, that this was not comedy, but
war.

Jerónimo Tostado, the Portuguese Vicar-General of the Carmelites
for Spain and Portugal and a Consultor of the Inquisition, had been
thoroughly persuaded against her. He was determined to prevent her
being re-elected as Prioress; and went to Ávila to manage the election
in a way that many a Spanish politician has since used as a model,
and which caused Teresa to call him "Friar Mary Magdalen." He
threatened with the direst penalties every nun who voted for her. She
herself has left her own account of what followed.[16] "Fifty-five nuns
voted for me," she wrote, "as though they had never been threatened. Each time that one of them gave me her vote, the Provincial
excommunicated her and loaded her with curses; he crushed the voting papers in his fist, beat them with a stick and burnt them; and
so the sisters are excommunicated." [17]

Such was the state of the convent at Ávila in 1577. Fifty-five nuns
supporting their Reverend Mother; a visiting prelate, in highest
authority, cursing them for doing so; services suspended, and all the
time the nun was writing the concluding chapters of *The Interior
Castle,* which relates the joy of a soul fixedly united to God and
firmly upheld by Him to enjoy the favour of highest heaven.

4

Tostado, supported by a certain Maldonado, a Prior from Toledo,
meanwhile persevered: he had come to the conclusion that the nuns
were supported by their fragile-looking director; Tostado asked Fray
Juan to come round to his way of thinking; but Fray Juan would do
nothing of the sort. Very well, then, Tostado would compel him:
Maldonado arrested both him and his companion, carried them off to
his own convent, had them beaten, and locked them up in separate
cells.

In the morning Fray Juan escaped for a moment, rushed back to his cottage to destroy some papers, was recaptured, dressed in the habit worn by his malefactors, and carried off by them to Toledo.

Important as Tostado was, Madre Teresa did not hesitate; in a powerful letter to the King, she complained at once of Maldonado:

"The whole city is scandalised," she wrote. "Everyone is asking how he could have had such audacity. He is not a prelate, and has not showed us the powers in virtue of which he is acting, yet he has dared to rage against the Carmelites of the Reform, who are subject to the Apostolic Commissary, and that in a place close to where Your Majesty is. He and his seem to fear neither justice nor God. As for myself, I am desolated to see our fathers in the hands of those people. They have long been wanting to get hold of them. But I would prefer to see them among the Moors, for they perhaps would take more pity on them.

"As for this barefoot Carmelite Father, this great servant of God, Fray Juan, he is so weakened by all he has endured that I fear for his life. For the love of God, I implore Your Majesty to set him at liberty." [18]

Fray Juan had been carried off after being struck in the face, and with blood flowing from his mouth. While Teresa's letter was going to the Escorial, he was led down the wild gorge into the milder air at El Tiemblo, and so over a rough road to a convent, and a cell in the great city of Toledo, place of the great Cathedral and of the impressive Alcazar which Charles V had lately built in the style of the Escorial.

5

The object of these Carmelite friars was perfectly plain: it was to knock out of the little friar what they would have called his nonsense. It was to terrify him and break his will; and so he was cursed as criminal, and flung into a cell which, as Teresa wrote, was hardly big enough to hold him, tiny as he was. Even in our days, imprisonment has its horrors. They were worse then. From this cell, he was from

[18] Cunninghame Graham, II, 202.

time to time released to come into the refectory to eat bread and
water from the floor. Then his back was again bared and he was
thrashed with the utmost severity. After this he was sent back to his
solitary confinement, where he could barely read, or take exercise, or
speak: so that the pain of vacancy could be added to that of ill-health;
and to exhaustion could be added the dull ache of melancholy.[19]
They well knew, these Spaniards of the time, how to break down
a man's nerves.

We know that it was a cruel age, even in England, where climate
and ease make the national temper mild. Among us, the fire of the
heretic was already giving way to the more fiendish tortures of the
thumbscrew and the wrack. Every refinement that could excruciate
the nerves by gradual dislocation was used to drag people away from
the worship in which, for a thousand years, England had come to the
healing presence of Jesus. In Spain, the pressure was applied on the
other side: this little friar who desired to live so purely in the contemplation of God was to feel what it is to be of a different kind from
the men round about him, even though he believed every syllable
that they believed, and all spent hours of the day in the same prayer.

Of course they found him exasperating: the implied criticism of
reform, the silent arraignment of finer tastes, are very hard for decent
men to bear. Isn't life hard enough? Aren't ordinary people good
enough? And why, these men were friars, supposed to be living
strictly enough, surely, as Carmelites. Why suggest that men were
meant to do more? Why by reform imply the scandals? Why notice
those whose mannerisms, eccentricities, and awkwardnesses betray
their unregenerate self-consciousness?

6

Fray Juan was becoming very well aware of some curious phenomena of the religious temperament: he knew that even in a life
of faith and prayer, many impulses of the unregenerate heart remain,
and burgeon. He knew that some pious people stop short at kindly
actions, that some old priests are domineering, some young ones
affected, many virtuous people self-righteous. He knew that beneath
the scapular a hundred different imperfections, sometimes some in-

[19] Bruno, pp. 169, 170.

sidious vices, can reappear. Temptations are not the less severe because
they are disguised. To a religious temperament, how easy to mistake
antipathies for duties, and pride for zeal! To those who suffer from
austerities, and feel an inner torment, how easy to seek relief by insisting on domination or by giving pain! The intense perceptiveness
of Fray Juan, with its clear insight into the religious mind, was now
to see with the most dramatic clearness the faults which rushed from
a turbulent world into the crowded convents of those days, and
sometimes creep in still. The experiences of Madre Teresa at Ávila,
had they not been enough? But now the friars had found in the intense individuality of the little chaplain there something on which
they must wreak the vengeance of their disordered passions. As from
that constricted cell at Toledo he surveyed men of prayer, he was
to read for eight months the distasteful record of the wickedness in
the hearts of men who thought they were doing good. These men
gave him a quite peculiar insight into what is called the religious life.
For the reactions of fanaticism, like those of patriotism, are not far
from those of vice. Theological precision is other than kindliness, just
as very kindly people often refuse to sacrifice themselves to God.

7

The day after he was brought to Toledo, Fray Juan was brought
before Tostado. He was told to obey: he answered that he was acting
under the authority of the Apostolic Visitor, and of the Nuncio. For
had not Madre Teresa always gone to the fountains of authority? He
had also his own Superior in Gracián. Well, Tostado could make a
powerful case, but he could not convince a young man who joined to
an acute intelligence, buttressed by Santa Teresa, an absolute conviction that he and she were called to do the work of God, and that
signs had proved that they were not deceived. The young friar had
the curious obstinacy which is found in certain refined natures, and
which is the stuff out of which finest courage is made. He refused
absolutely to give up his idea, not only at the first threat, but through
the long months of spring and summer—exhausting fast, of deadly
monotony, of food so foul that he doubted whether it were not poison,
of brutal contempt, and of those frequent kneelings on the floor of
the refectory to receive on his naked skin the sickening blows which

might well have forced even a healthy man to give way. He learnt the whole story of exhaustion: he suffered from an utter sense of desolation: all he said afterwards was in torment—body and soul.[20]

8

Nevertheless he was upborne by the power of an intense will, and the will was infused with a more than human power, the power that comes from the unknown to sustain ideals, the power which Christian theology knows as "the spirit of ghostly strength"—the grace of fortitude. But were there not present other gifts of the Spirit, the spirit of counsel to make clear what he ought to do, the spirit of wisdom which gave him the savour and intuition of heavenly things, the spirit of godliness which consoled his soul with heavenly love, and had he not also those spirits of knowledge and understanding which enable men to see God in all things and all things in God?

It is in this time of heavy and exhausting tribulation that Fray Juan de la Cruz found the powers which command the attention of men of the world, which set up a landmark in the region of culture; it was then he began to compose one of the finest lyrics in Spanish literature.

Then he might say:

> The silence laid invisible hands upon my heart
> And the night knew me.[21]

[20] Bruno, pp. 171, 173, 175.
[21] Laurence Binyon, *The Idols.*

A great poem is a fountain for ever overflowing with the waters of wisdom and delight, and after one person and one age has exhausted all its divine effluence which their peculiar relations enable them to share, another and yet another succeeds, and new relations are ever developed, the source of an unforeseen and unconceived delight.[1]

There are many mysteries contained in poetry which by purpose are written darkly, lest by profane wits it should be abused.[2]

I

FOR suddenly, with the momentum of a masterpiece, the harassed friar proves the quality of his interest and the texture of the mind which for fourteen years had been apparently absorbed in the work of the theologian and the monk. Suddenly, he produces evidence that he was a man of passion pulsing with love and beauty, and that, added to the freedom of an unusual originality, he had the technician's understanding of the fabric of contemporary verse. How much he had actually studied we cannot clearly know: what is plain is that at a time when verses were in fashion, he shows a consummate power in the contemporary style, he takes over a stanza used once or twice by Garcilaso, and proves at once by echoing some of his expressions that he has studied him. With a subtlety and finesse of phrase not less remarkable than the intensity of his passion, he bursts spontaneously into lyric verse. Like the skylark's, his song came native with the warmth, but it sprang from a voice trained in cadences, and still the ages listen.

The original model of his verse was the poem he had commended to Santa Teresa, the *Song of Songs*. Whether he had heard directly or indirectly from Luis de León that this poem was indeed the drama of a personal love, whether he came to it himself as a natural conclusion, or whether he felt that the intimate imagery perfectly suited the passion of his heart, we can never perfectly determine. What is certain is that with a masterly control, he made the inspiration of

[1] Shelley, *Defence of Poetry*. See Prose Works, 1880, vol. III, 129-130.
[2] Sir Philip Sidney, *Defence of Poetrie*.

this ancient poem his own *cri de coeur* to the Heart beating beneath creation, the Heart that was closer than breathing and spoke to his heart in mystical colloquies, completing its discourse in the Bible, in Nature, and in the mysteries of the Faith.

2

By night on my bed, said the Hebrew bride, I sought him whom my soul loveth:

> I sought him but I found him not.
> I said I will rise now and go about the city,
> In the streets and in the broad ways
> I will seek him whom my soul loveth.
> I sought him but I found him not.[3]

Another and a more splendid suitor had come in his place, but again she seemed to hear the voice of her beloved in the night.

> I was asleep but my heart waked.
> It is the voice of the beloved that knocketh.
> Open to me, my sister, my love, my dove, my undefiled:
> For my head is filled with dew,
> My locks with the drops of the night.
>
> I have put off my coat, how shall I put it on?
> I have washed my feet, how shall I defile them?
>
> My beloved put his hand by the hole of the door
> And my heart was moved for him.
>
> I rose up to open to my beloved;
> And my hands dropped with myrrh,
> And my fingers with liquid myrrh,
> Upon the handles of the bolt.
>
> I opened to my beloved,
> But my beloved had withdrawn himself and was gone:
> My soul had failed me when he spake:
> I called him but he gave me no answer.
>
> The watchmen that go about the city found me,
> They smote me, they wounded me;
> The keepers of the walls took away my mantle from me.
>
> I adjure you, O daughters of Jerusalem, if ye find my beloved
> That ye tell him that I am sick of love.[4]

[3] *Song of Songs*, III, 1, 2.
[4] *Ibid.*, V, 2-8.

Such were the famous lines that through the ages had echoed through the souls of mystics, and touched the hearts of lovers and beauty; such was the passage which Fray Juan had so often read and repeated, and which came back to him in his suffering and exhaustion like the visions of the Sierra in the cool, clear air of high Castile, and seemed to carry him

> Far away, far away where the scents of all flowers are sweetest,
> White mountains among.

For it is no uncommon experience for people of delicate feeling to find in hours of intense weakness and intense pain that—as all the lower faculties of the senses and feelings of the body weaken—a vision of past joys, a sense of a sustaining presence, a longing for some exquisite communion with the highest and purest come to solace the spirit wearied by its pain. Lofty and rare are these experiences of a soul to whom the body brings so little, and to which it is attached by so light a cord; such a soul is "a thing enskied and sainted"; such a soul, if it have the gift of words, may weave from the vision and the dream its record of the consolation and distraction; thus in those months of torment, the keen, active mind of the Castilian friar, who was just passing the age [5] when Dante conceived the *Divina Commedia: nel mezzo del cammin di nostra vita,* began to write the lyrics which survive with those of Luis de León as the masterpieces of Castilian lyric:

The Lover cries:

> Beloved, where hast thou fled
>   While here I mourn?
> Stricken and well-nigh dead,
>   Wailing, forlorn.
> I rushed and cried for thee,
>   But thou wert gone.
>
> O shepherds, ye who wind
>   Past folds on high,
> If him ye haply find
>   For whom I sigh,
> Tell how a tender heart,
>   When pierced, may die.

[5] He was actually thirty-six.

Seeking my love, I'll go
By peak and bay,
By forces and frontiers
I'll press my way.
No beasts will rouse my fears,
No bloom delay.

O thicket deep and dene
Made by my love,
O meads of shining green
With flowers above,
Say whensoe'er ye've seen
Him rest or rove.

Nature replies:

These woods with hastening pace
He passed, Divine,
Irradiating grace
So fair, so fine,
That glistening from his face
Our raiments shine.

The Lover again:

Ah who can heal my pain?
See my heart bleed.
And wilt thou not distrain,
To meet my need,
Some messenger who fain
Would bear my bede.

A thousand beauteous hints
They seem to utter.
Can no one clearly say
What 'tis they mutter?
For though I languish, they
Still, still, still stutter.

Life, where thou once didst dwell
Thou dwellest no more,
Thy darts so thick and fell
Make wounds so sore
That life flows fast away,
From the heart's core.

The breast that thou hast pierced
Wilt thou not heal?
Why not enjoy the pleasure
Thou once didst steal?
Wilt thou not hold the treasure
Thou bold didst steal?

Ah wilt thou not redeem
   A heart that dies?
Thou wert my eyes' sole glee
   And yet each cries
To see thee still. And if they not see thee
   What use are eyes?

Ah bring thy presence nigher,
And kill me with thy aspect and thy grace!
Love is ordeal by fire,
Torment too fierce and dire
   To cure but by thy presence and thy face.

O mirror of the stream
   Those eyes engrave
Within thy silvered gleam.
   I always crave
And limn them in my dream.
   They shine: ah save
Me from the transcending beam
   Their dazzling gave.

The answer:

Come back, O dove. The deer
   Stricken, thy flight
Observes and doth appear
   Far up the height.

The Lover voices joy:

The lovely valleys thick with trees,
The strangest Indies on the seas,
The rivers murmuring past the leas,
The amorous whisper of the breeze,
   Sierras, he is all

Of these, and screen and calm of night,
The wings of dawn when poised for flight,
The solitudes which songs endite,
Feasts freshening us for love's delight
   And music at its fall.

O keep the mount for us alone,
Drive off the foxes with a stone.
The grapes and roses both are grown
   Around our happy seat.

Be still, thou ice-blast dead and blind!
Come, breathing love, thou warm south wind,
Blow through my garden suave and kind,
The perfumes from the flowers unbind,
Let rose and jasmine be entwined
   To grace love's rarest treat.

Hold back! provoking, Hebrew maids,
Keep well away from these hedged shades,
And touch them not; where blossom braids
Our verdant shelter in the glades
 And amber scent is sweet.

Hide, love, and silence sounds that tease
Admire, adorn till each agrees
To make the mountains such as please
Thee, like fair companies
 That sail to Indies through the seas
 With her whose sails are fleet.[6]

The art with which the poem was arranged was sovereign and indisputable. The poet had the choice of apt, sounding, and significant words, words of elegant association, and pregnant meaning, words "culled with choicest art":

> *Pastores los que fuerdes*
> *Allá por las majadas al otero,*
> *Si por ventura vierdes*
> *Aquel que yo más quiero.*
> *Decidle que adolezco, peno y muero.*

The richness of suggestion and association in such words as *majadas*, as *adolezco* is matched by the adroit onomatopœia of the line

> *No se que que quedan balbuciendo,*

where the very stutter comes into the verse. He would take from Garcilaso a sophisticated word like *Nemoroso*, and the lines of Garcilaso:

> *Corrientes aquas, puras, cristalinas*
> *Arbolesque os estais mirando en ellos.*

He echoes with water's silvery sound in

> *Cristalina fuente, si en esos tus semblantes plateados* [7]

Then comes the liquid sequence of vowels and consonants:

> *Apartalos amado*
> *Que voy de vuelo.*
> *Vuelve te paloma*
> *Que el ciervo vulnerado*
> *Por el otero asoma*
> *Al aire de tu vuelo, y fresco toma.*

---

[6] Cf. pp. 223-5, 227, stanzas 1-15, 27, 32, 33.
[7] Baruzi, p. 116, stanza 13.

—lines as musical as the opening of Lycidas, and in them the very flight of the dove of which they speak.

This mystic was, in fact, a finished contriver of pattern, evocation, and surprise, who, knowing extremely well the violence of desire, could also distil most subtly the atmosphere of passion and rapture.

3

In the face of a poem of this order—and it was not alone—there comes a lightning flash of insight into what had been going on in the soul of this uncompromising Carmelite. Sometimes there had been spells of blue, unclouded weather when the pictures of beauty mingled with religious reflections, when a delicate and exquisite fancy had passed from theme to theme to give a personal freshness and candour to the quality of his resignation. For here was an individual as avid for freedom and his own way as any other Castilian; and since his religious life meant order and obedience, finding his freedom in his tastes, and his imagery, and then in words. For words are an arm which stretches everywhere to feed the imagination with every variety of fruit. And here plainly was a man of extraordinary originality.

But apart from imagination and originality there were other qualities: a love of freedom and Nature, a share in the country's exploits and the sailors' stories, joined to feelings trembling with tenderness, and spells of violent passion, succeeded by rapture; when there are such qualities in a man, when an imaginative man lives intensely by the heart, he will feel within himself all those returns which human passion and desire bring to the life of love.

Between a love of a human individual and the love of God there are many similarities. The quality of a man's love is much affected by what he loves; but "in the finest part of pure love" there may be often transcendent qualities, even where the object of the passion is human. For elect souls love not only the beloved: they love love.

What, then, is love? It is that attraction which tends to the fusion of two beings: it can lead inward and affect intense natures so ardently that they burn and consume themselves into the very fire of love. Our own Donne tells us that:

> Souls where nothing dwells but love,
> All other thoughts being inmates, there shall prove
> This or a love refined there above
> When bodies to their graves, souls from their graves remove.

Such a power to love as this poet has shown could be absorbed in love of another being, in love of some created thing. Fray Juan knew and could intimately describe the meaning and allurement of entangling fascinations: he could enjoy but too wholly the things he did enjoy: and yet he was a Carmelite: his quest was the All: and so his drama is both a human drama and a mystical romance.

For what did he mean by love? He took his doctrine here, as in so many other things, from his favourite Platonist of the fifth century, "For those who listen aright to the Divine," wrote Dionysius, "the word loving-kindness is used by the sacred writers and the Divine revelation with the same meaning as the word 'love.' It means a power of making one and binding together, and a peculiar commingling in the beautiful and good." [8] Fray Juan rewrote this passage to give his own definition: "The peculiar quality of love is to desire to be united and bound together with the beloved object to attain to perfection in the blessing of love." [9]

4

Now how is the soul to be bound up with, to mingle, to unite with the object of its love? There will first be a process of likeness and assimilation. "Love," said San Juan, "produces a resemblance." [10] In other words, we grow like those we love: we seek to make them like us. But love means much more than this. For even this is but one aspect of a mystery of feeling and passion which moves with desire the strongest energies of being; this Meredith called "a great flood that bears us to the sea." "*Nos passions,*" said Bossuet likewise, "*ont quelque chose d'infini.*" But there are, said Luis de León, two loves, or two ways of love, one of desire, the other of joy. These alternate and interact to make together the unity of love. The first desires this unity, and as much as possible achieves it, while the other

[8] *De Divinis Nominibus,* IV, 12.
[9] Crisógono, I, 336.
[10] *Mount Carmel,* Book I, ch. iv.

possesses it, and delights in its life with it.[11] Our own Donne used much the same words.

This rhythm of desire and joy in the life of the heart is common both to the human lover and to the contemplative. Both are men of passion: both feel within them the surge of something infinite. Both know that this movement of the deepest power within them, a power supreme over the faculties, is leading them to identify their supreme good with one other than themselves. It was the way of the philosopher to call this supreme power the will; by love the will seeks to attain the good; love is the deepest, fullest surge of the strongest motive powers of being towards that which instinct tells them is their end.

Every movement of the heart, said Dante, is towards love. The human heart is incomplete alone. Whether in the order of Nature, or in the realm of mystic contemplation, it cannot attain to peace except in mingling with another being and life: the universe is a system of magnetic attractions:

> Nothing in the world is single,
> All things by a law divine
> In one another's being mingle,
> Why not I with thine? [12]

It is only so that life can continue. God, said San Juan, has handed over to men his power of procreation: it is only so that men and women really and fully live. Is not this the secret of the universe? Is there not in the quality and experience of intense love a disclosure of the final mystery? That was the doctrine of the Catholic Church. *Ubi caritas et amor, ibi Christus.*[13] Between loving-kindness and love, as Dionysius had said, it was unwise to draw sharp distinctions: every phase and aspect of love, as its magnetic attraction drew together separate beings to make them commingle and attain perfection in the blessing of love, revealed some aspect of the love which had created it. If we trace back the origin of the universe, we find it when

S'aperse in nuòve amor l'eterno Amore. [14]

[11] Crisógono, *loc. cit.*
[12] Shelley, *Love's Philosophy.*
[13] Missale Romanum, Office for Maundy Thursday.
[14] Dante, *Paradiso*, XXIX, 18.

All loves of creatures are created love: as created love they reveal of the love which created them some aspect or suggestion:

Wann ich mich lehne an Deinen Brust
Kommt über mir wie Himmelslust.

So it was that as a love poem, the *Song of Songs* opened for the contemplative the doorway into the castle of the soul. Like the enraptured lover, the mystic lives by poising his mind upon one object, and that object is not to be sundered from the love which seeks it. And since love is always love, and is instinct with all the subtle interactions of a universe sustained in love by Love, the mystic naturally turned to the love song he knew best as a model of his own quest of essential love, the love of God.

The *Song of Songs* could not merely be arranged, as Luis de León was teaching, as a human drama. It was marked, had they but known it, by expressions which, when traced back to the original Hebrew, related not only to the psychology, but to the physiology of the natural consummations of love.[15] But, even so, those were in themselves sacred: "Aspiring love had hallowed passions' tide"; and sacred was the deep joy that the poem conveyed: it was "rich, deep, like love in beauty without end." It swarmed with an enchantment which was a consecration!

That men's imagination and feeling were one with their life of sense, Fray Juan could never forget. These movements of the life of the senses were what he called the nymphs of Judaea, and there was a natural communication between the higher and the lower faculties of men. Let the lower remain, however, in their lower place, and words would tell how love would do its perfect work. Such, as he was to explain more fully later, was the significance of the poems he had composed.

5

Rich, therefore, was the revelation of this man's heart that we owe to the torments of the prison cell, where he languished from month to month till the chill of winter was exchanged for the stifling heat

---

[15] I state this on the authority of Professor Wheeler Robinson.

of its summer: it is one of the effects of intense heat to make even the hardest rigour slacken, and at length, as the heat of summer advanced in Toledo, the care of his gaolers relaxed. Cut off, except for what he could read in his Breviary, from participation in the festivals of the Church, their victim was aware that on August 15 was the Festival of the Assumption. When on the eve of this Feast he was visited by Maldonado, he was so absorbed in this idea, and so weak in body, that he did not recognize Maldonado, nor move till Maldonado stirred him with his foot. "What were you thinking about?" asked Maldonado. Fray Juan asked for the consolation of saying Mass. The Prior refused; but that evening Juan had a vision of the Blessed Virgin, and in the vision he was promised a way of escape. A week passed, and then, loosening bolts, he was able to open the door of his cell. Two visiting friars, and one of them no other than Tostado, were sleeping in the hall; but though they heard the staples of the bolt fall, they were soon asleep again; then he passed through to a window, from which he let himself down by a rope he had made of his linen coverlet. This reached some distance towards the ground. From here there was a jump to the rampart below: a little later he had fallen off this on to the steep bank of the Tagus. And from this, following a dog, he jumped once more, this time to find himself in the enclosure between the Carmelites' garden and one belonging to the Franciscans. Yet another wall was before him; before he knew how, he was over it, and shortly after dawn had found refuge with Santa Teresa's nuns at San José, close to the little church, once a mosque, which is known as the Cristo de la Luz.[16]

Here he remained for two months while the furious intrigues that had occasioned his imprisonment, and continued during it, rose to new extremes. Gracián, who had been appointed Head of the Reformed Carmelites, had been deprived of his powers by the Papal Nuncio, and was in hiding. Teresa was forbidden to move from Ávila. And then more dramas and intrigues had taken place.

6

Among the novices at Pastrana in 1572 was a sturdy Catalan who, though he had chosen the name of Juan de Jesús, was always known

16 Bruno, pp. 180-190.

as Roca. He had later been appointed Prior at Mancera. In the spring of 1578, having occasion to proceed thence to Madrid to settle some legal questions, he had naturally visited Teresa on his way through Ávila. There he had entered into the full current of her affairs, and he determined when he got to Madrid to do battle for her, not only with Tostado, but with a new and powerful auxiliary of the Observants, that Monsignor Sega, who at the end of 1577 had arrived in Madrid as Papal Nuncio, to take the place of Ormaneto.

At first the Nuncio had not only refused to listen to Roca, but had confined him in the Convent of the Observants; and then a certain compunction, strengthened perhaps by his assessment of the predilections of the Court, had decided the Nuncio to visit his prisoner. Going to the convent where the Prior of Mancera was imprisoned, he demanded to see him alone.

It was a clash of strong personalities. The Nuncio was an able and experienced Italian who had long since made up his mind. He had given every support to Tostado in his campaign against Madre Teresa and Fray Juan de la Cruz. He it was who now described the Foundress as "that restless, roving, disobedient, contumacious female who under cover of devotion invents evil doctrine; leaving the retirement of the cloister to gad about against the order of the Council of Trent and of her own superiors; teaching as if she were a master against the order of St. Paul, who commanded that women should not teach." But the Nuncio could not cow the Catalan before him. Fray Juan de Jesús was made of hard and heavy metal. Though his father's name was José Bullon, he had received, at his baptism, his mother's name of Roca, and "not without divine intention," says the Chronicler, "because he was a rock of bronze in his resistance to any adverse impulse." This was the man who, converted at Alcalá by the famous sermon of Gracián on the Order of Mount Carmel, had, "thirsting for the invisible," followed him to Pastrana, before he had been transferred to Mancera.

When he heard abuse of Santa Teresa, the Rock of Bronze had at first stood thunderstruck and speechless. He had soon undertaken her defence; and when he finished the opinion of the Nuncio was shaken.[17]

[17] Cunninghame Graham, II, 222-224.

7

Yet at that time the Holy Mother and her company might well have abandoned hope: her friars were after all few, and those few were not only poor, but they had ferocious enemies; she had been driven away and loaded with abuse; their enemies enjoyed that possession which is nine points of the law; and behind them was not only the relentless energy of authority in Maldonado, but now also the new Nuncio himself.[18]

And yet Teresa, as determined and politic in affairs as she was seraphic in the final mansions of her *Interior Castle*, was assured that somehow her cause would prosper.

At this juncture the struggle involved the Court: Teresa was not only sure of the favour of the King, but she had many friends in high places. Among these friends was Don Luis Hurtado de Mendoza, Conde de Tendilla, the Governor of the Alhambra. He had sold his diamond buttons to help the Reform to found a house at Granada. Coming to Madrid, he appealed to the Nuncio at least to listen to the case of his protégés.[19] The Nuncio, who at the moment of his arrival in Barcelona had been met by the Observants and won over to their case, was in an obstinate mood. He lost his temper, and said he would go straight to Chumacero, the Procurator of the Royal Council. Now, the Court, from the King downwards, had the strongest feelings about Spanish independence. They disliked the interference of an Italian in the administration of Spain: they felt that those who followed the Nuncio had been disloyal. "Many there were," says the Chronicler, "and they of the gravest sort, who in public and in secret defended the Descalzos and resented the Nuncio's measures and the conduct of those he chose to execute them." [20] Chumacero had this feeling of national pride as strong as any man; before long, with a typical Spanish gesture, he had rapidly given an order suspending all action against the Reform, by a warrant arresting any action the Nuncio might take, just as he had arrested the orders of Rubeo a year or two before.

Meeting anger with anger, the Nuncio now demanded an audi-

[18] *Ibid.*, I, 232.
[19] *Ibid.*, II, 233.
[20] *Ibid.*

ence with the King. He was introduced into the presence of a man
exquisitely courteous, a quiet, melancholy, religious man of medium
height, who had been married by proxy seventeen years before to his
cousin, Mary Tudor, Queen of England, and was now husband to a
daughter of Catharine de Medici. With his fair complexion, his pale,
heavy cheeks, his large, rounded jaw, his thin line of moustache above
his full lips, his long, straight nose, his faintly blue but very lively
eyes, and his light reddish hair now streaked with grey, he stood
superior and apart in a Venetian dignity. He had long manœuvred
to have in his absolute control Spain and her Americas; uncompromis-
ingly Catholic, and temperamentally devout, he would stop at nothing to strengthen the glory and freedom of Spain; the master of the
Spanish Empire in all its heroism, all its Catholicism and all its
cruelty, he was preparing his armada to defeat the marauding heretics
of England. But to the core he was a Spaniard and a King who would
never allow the Pope a jot more of power in his country than laws
and treaties demanded.

As the Nuncio expressed his sense of outrage to His Majesty,
Philip listened immovable and impenetrable; then he spoke of his
profound veneration for the Papal Envoy, he assured him of his grief
and annoyance at the insult, he promised to reprimand Tendilla;
these courtesies performed, the friend of Santa Teresa fixed with all
his royalty the cold, blue brilliance of his eyes upon the plaintiff: his
manner became yet more icy: in a withering tone he spoke of suspicion being aroused and the need for the protection of true virtue; he
said that the party which the Nuncio appeared to be supporting was
hostile to rigour and perfection.[21]

A letter of remonstrance to the Conde de Tendilla certainly was
sent: a strong reply was in time to be received by the President of the
Council and brought before long to the scrutiny of King Philip.
When Tendilla returned, he made this known to the Nuncio. Envoy
and Pope decided to press no further. All Sega now asked was the dis-
missal of Gracián.

All this time the fight within the Order itself had been continu-
ing; there had been the two stormy chapters at Almodovar; there
had been the first engagement at Ávila, when Tostado had tried to
stop the re-election of Teresa; there had been the capture of Fray

[21] Cunninghame Graham, II, 234.

Juan; there had been the scene with Roca. There had also been the removal and disgrace of Gracián; and though Tendilla had affronted the Nuncio, the Nuncio had not yet decided that it would be more discreet not to counter the King.

At this point, with Gracián still in hiding, the Reform again decided to declare themselves a separate order. It would be a breach of ecclesiastical discipline, but the Court was firm behind them. Old Fray Antonio de Heredia, who had gone from Valladolid to Duruelo with young Fray Juan in 1569, was set up to act as chief, and the reformed held another chapter at Almodovar in October, 1578.[22]

To this from Toledo came Fray Juan. He was still emaciated and ill. "The life Fray Juan has gone through," wrote Teresa, "and that he should have been allowed, being so ill as he is, to go there at once has distressed me deeply. See that they take good care of him at Almodovar. . . . I assure you that if he dies, there will be few left like him."[23]

He went to Almodovar: weak as he was, he was strong against the irregular step which was being taken. But the Chapter, knowing the Court was behind them, decided to press on for independence, to send a delegate to Rome.

[22] Stanbrook, *Life*, 63, 64.
[23] Cunninghame Graham, II, 224.

Are there not, dear Michal,
Two points in the adventure of the diver?
One, when, a beggar, he prepares to plunge,
One, when, a prince, he rises with his pearl?
Festus, I plunge.[1]

1

A<small>T</small> Toledo the waves and storms had gone over Fray Juan de la Cruz, and he arrived in Andalusia exhausted.

"The first time that I saw him," wrote the Carmelite, María de Jesús, "it was in our convent at Beas, when he was about to take up his post as Prior at El Calvario; and not long after his escape from prison. As soon as I saw him, my soul welled up within me. He was suffering then, and had been for some years, from great spiritual trials sent by God—and without alleviation. For the confessors did not understand them. But the confidence that Fray Juan de la Cruz inspired was such that I at once made my confession to his reverence, and set forth the state of my soul. He understood it at once. He confirmed me in my way, and gave me courage to endure what was still remaining." For at Toledo he had been through the worst. "I asked him if he had been in the habit of receiving consolations from God: he told me that that was rare: I believe he told me he had never experienced them. All was in torment, body and soul too." There was nothing then of suffering he did not understand; nothing with which he could not sympathize.

2

But there were many consolations in his stay at lonely Beas with the nuns and their remarkable prioress, Madre Ana de Jesús. Born in Medina del Campo in 1545, she was three years younger than Fray Juan. As soon as she entered the convent of San José at Ávila, she had been high in the favour and estimation of Santa Teresa, and was

[1] Browning, *Paracelsus*, Part I.

herself an advanced mystic. Teresa congratulated her on having such a saint at hand to counsel her as Fray Juan. "In all Castile," she wrote, "there is no director who is so perfect and who communicates so much fervour to aid saints advancing on the road to heaven." [2] Doña Ana soon saw that both Fray Juan and she herself were to be perfected by trials; she had already won his affection and regard. And Teresa was to write to her, "My daughter and my crown! I never tire of thanking God for the favour He granted me in drawing you to us." [3]

After his stay at Beas, Fray Juan climbed up to the hermitage of El Calvario. With a white façade which was dazzling in the sunlight, it stood in a fold of the sierra, and was surrounded by orange-trees, figs, and almonds. It commanded a magnificent view to the great range of the Siniola which filled the horizon. This lonely and majestic scene was made for contemplatives; it was the habit of the superior, as his treatise has suggested, to make his community familiar with the souls of lonely places. When he had found some haven of the stream, or some pleasant place, sheltered by rocks, he would speak to them of spiritual things, and then, when their enthusiasm was awakened, he would scatter them, that each might hold converse alone with God, as he did himself. Every Saturday he would climb up to the pens of the mountain cattle, and leave the shouting stream. There was a more delicious water in a higher spring, near the pine wood; and sometimes he would climb farther still, to the bare Pico Cornicia. For there the view showed both the mountain and the valley, with Beas spread on the slope like a fan, and smoke rising from the chimneys.

In the early summer of 1579 he descended the track from El Calvario to Beas, and then walked down the valley for several leagues to the city of Baeza, where a new university had been founded by Juan de Ávila. Here the friars were to have a little college, such as they had had at Alcalá de Henares. The white streets of the remote town are varied with humble avenues; among the monuments are a Phœnician fountain, a Gothic palace, and a triumphal arch set up by Charles V. But in this atmosphere he did not feel at home: the boisterous, swaggering Andalusians jarred on his Castilian taste; he loved to escape

[2] Bruno, p. 195.
[3] Bruno, p. 196.

to the nuns at Beas, with whom he went to stay once for as long as six weeks. And with them, as we saw, the pleasures of poetry and writing were always encouraged whenever he found leisure to pursue them and was undistracted by intrigue.

3

It was under the encouragement of the nuns at Beas that Fray Juan began to write. The track of El Calvario "put a pen into his hand." So he began the two works which are classic treatises of mysticism: *The Ascent of Mount Carmel* and *The Dark Night of the Soul*. They are based on scholastic philosophy: they reveal a profound study of theology: above all, they are woven out of a deep and wide reading of the Bible.

But they are also the record of a personal reaction. Living as it were hidden and withdrawn, a Platonist, a mystic and a poet—Fray Juan de la Cruz was one actor in a fierce drama of religious history. His country was the Spain of Philip II. His order was the order of Tostado and Maldonado, as well as of Teresa and Gracián. These books, therefore, have in them a touch of subtle polemic.

At the very beginning, *The Ascent of Mount Carmel,* the saint's first treatise on the philosophy of the spiritual life, is already seen to be profound and elaborate: he had applied his scrutiny to its minute particulars. But the guiding principles can be stated more simply: first, he reminds us how different from the infinite and eternal power who creates are all the finite things which are created; [4] how different from the invisible and eternal things are those which are temporal and visible.[5] Secondly, he points out that love, being a movement towards union, makes the lover like what he loves.[6] The conclusion is clear: how different is the love of God from the love of oneself, how different even the love of the invisible and eternal from the visible and transient. Two contraries cannot exist in one person: [7] one cannot be seeking oneself and one's own gratification at the same time as one is moving upwards in the search towards the Highest.

Why, then, does the mystic speak in terms of darkness and light?

[4] M.C. IV, 3.
[5] *Ibid.,* VI, 1.
[6] *Ibid.*
[7] *Ibid.,* IV, 2.

Because the soul comes into the world to learn through the senses: through the senses the soul observes, just as the eyes observe through the medium of light.[8] If, therefore, one is to cease to use the senses, and all those faculties of passion, memory, and imagination which go with them, and which were particularly precious to the poetic genius of the writer, what is left to the soul? It would certainly be in the dark.[9]

But even so it is not lost, nor alone. It still has within itself a certain transcendent quality by which it mirrors the absolute being of God, and can hold communion with Him. Now, the whole teaching of Fray Juan is how to develop gradually this direct and mystical communion: this mysterious converse by which the soul lives as it were in the high and hidden faculties by which God has made it in the image and likeness of his own mystery. Fray Juan insists that in the human soul is a quality, or gift, which is so transcendent that it can absorb into itself by love the qualities of the divine.

4

Then, if so, why is there such a sacramental system as that of the Catholic Church: why is it that the inward and spiritual grace is conveyed by outward and visible signs: why does the Church insist that God has lifted the nature of man into Himself? And, again, has not the Primal Artist left His stamp upon creation? Is not God's transcendence completed in His immanence?

Fray Juan deals with this point very early, and again very late in his discourse: at the beginning he says that, though created things are like crumbs falling from God's table,[10] they are, *in comparison with Him,* wretchedness and ugliness:[11] at the end he pours contempt upon "the pestiferous people," as he calls them, who wanted to do away with images. It is not the image that is wrong: it is our affection for it which obscures the fact that it is only a symbol, and the symbol is meant only to draw us towards the power and love of Him it symbolizes.[12]

[8] *Ibid.,* III, 3.
[9] *Ibid.,* 5, 6.
[10] M.C. I, vi, 3.
[11] *Ibid.,* V, 7.
[12] *Ibid.,* III, xxxv and xxxvi, para. 2.

The whole question is where one places one's affection. Is it on special objects of devotion, as though they were an end in themselves? Is it in music or in natural beauty for what they mean by pleasure to eye and ear? Or can the heart in thankfulness and rapture rise above them to Him who made them? And is it at every turn, therefore, capable of abstracting itself from them to cultivate the habit of that direct and loving communion which unites the lover with his beloved in a gaze of mutual intuition, so that, poised in flight above all acts of reasoning, memory, sensation, and imagination, it floats, as it were, in the air of uncreated being where God is all in all? [13]

5

It is not everyone who knows what this means; and Fray Juan did not write for everyone: he wrote for those who had been called to follow Santa Teresa, to climb barefoot up Mount Carmel, not merely by pleasant and delectable ways, but those who felt such a deep love for the unseen that, being already detached from temporal things, they desired to pass to detachment of spirit [14]—who desired to do so because they were moved to do so by the love burning within them, and consuming their mortal natures with its divine fire. "Can ye drink of the chalice that I shall drink?" So Jesus had asked two of His most ardent disciples, and Santiago, the patron of Spain, was one of them. Their answer had been—"We can!" [15]

That chalice, says Fray Juan, "is to die to our own nature, stripping it and annihilating it, that one may go by this narrow path in all which pertains to sense and soul: that is in understanding, in enjoyment, and in feeling. So that it will not only remain without possession in any of these, but that even in the spirit it will not be embarrassed on the narrow way: where all that is required is denial, as the Saviour teaches, and the cross, which is the staff by which we travel on it, and which makes it light and easy. Wherefore Our Lord said by St. Matthew: 'My yoke is easy and my burden is light.' For if a man is determined to master himself, to bear the cross which is a

[13] *Ibid.*, III, xxv.
[14] *Ibid.*, Prologue 8.
[15] Cf. Allison Peers, *Our Debt to Spain*, p. 16.

sincere determination to find and endure travail in all things for God, so in all of them he will find great ease and pleasantness in walking by this way, stripped of all, desiring nothing. But if he claims to keep something, either of God, or of anything else, as his own property, he is not stripped and denied in all; and so he will neither find, nor ascend, this narrow path towards things above."

6

For chapter on chapter the writer elaborates his teaching about the stilling of desire. He takes text after text from Scripture and applies it to illustrate his argument. He even takes the famous words: "Come unto me all ye that labour and are heavy laden and I will refresh you," to show that since desires torment, load, and weary the soul,[16] the best refreshment is to turn to God.

This teaching is a scientific and philosophic elaboration of that on the Purgative Way in the *Imitation of Christ*. There in the first chapter was written:

> Try to wean your heart from loving what you see,
> And turn to what you cannot see.
> For they who follow where the senses lead will spoil the conscience,
> And lose the grace of God.

In the second chapter:

> But if you would learn something that would profit you
> *Love to be all unknown, and to be held as nothing.*

In the third chapter:

> Truly great is he who has great charity.
> Truly great is he who in himself is small and holds as nought all heights of honour.
> Truly wise is he who deems all earthly things as dung that he may win the prize of Christ.
> Truly learned is he who does the will of God, abandoning that will which is his own.

> Vain is he who puts his trust in man or in created things:
> Shun the noisy world, die unto yourself: suffer contradiction:
> He that has true and perfect charity seeketh Self in nothing.
> Better to live a hidden life.

[16] M.C. VII, 4.

A VIEW OF TOLEDO FROM BELOW THE CARMELITE CONVENT

Such were the austere warnings of the great classic of the spiritual life. Fray Juan repeats them in his thoughts on night and on nothing. But to him there is, as it were, a poetic charm in the idea of darkness, as there is a pleasure in nakedness. The very word "nothing" seems to be ablaze with hidden lights and fires, because it points the contrary way to the fullness of the all: to have nothing of created things should be the preliminary to having everything of the uncreated; to free the window of every pattern or stain is to make it transparent to the full sunlight. Man's nature desires pleasure in everything; how is he to find it? He desires all manner of good things; how is he to obtain them? He desires to know everything; how is he to learn it? And beyond pleasure, possession, knowledge, to satisfy the feelings, the will, the intellect. There is the sum of these in the completed man himself. He desires to have all fullness in himself; to *be* everything; and how can he attain to that? Only by going to the fountain of all being: only by seeking that life which is all in all.

We apply this principle of sacrifice and choice everywhere else: if we choose one thing, we forego another. Every man who attains his ambition makes a sacrifice. What is life except a choice of values? But behind all values there is one primal worth. Behind multiplicity there is unity: behind variety there is order.

> Such is the world's great harmony, that springs
> From order, union, full consent of things.[17]

Creation is but the infinite variety of existences by which the Primal Reality deals with the mystery of nothing; and if we ask Nature what she is doing, she answers:

> And so at the roaring loom of time I ply
> And weave for God the garment thou seest Him by.[18]

Some, therefore, have sought and found a way to the all of still communion with God in contemplation of a created thing. A flower in a crannied wall, the starlike shadow of a daisy on the smooth surface

[17] Pope, *Essay on Man*, III, Sec. 6.
[18] So schaff ich am sausenden Webstuhl der Zeit
   Und wirke der Gottheit lebendiges Kleid.
          Creative Spirit in Faust, I, i.

of a naked stone—these hide within themselves the same secret as every other thing in creation hides: for the one Creator made them. And all exist within His mind.

7

But beside this searching through immanence, there is another way, harder no doubt, but for those that can climb it, the quickest track up Mount Carmel—the way of transcendence. These find the best way to the One who is the Creator of the All, in turning to Him direct, in one act of transcending love. In Him they find not merely the truth and the life, but actually the way. He has established His kingdom within them. If, then, they seek Him within, it is no longer any advantage to look outside. The inner way, being more direct, commands a concentrated gaze; and so all desires of the heart—like every thought of the mind, and every effort of personal will—must embrace that nothingness in which is hidden the secret of the All. As the lover, to consummate love, must cast away all reserve, so to find union with love itself we must come to love naked. To find all, we must seek nothing.

> In order to arrive at having pleasure in everything,
>   Desire to have pleasure in nothing.
> In order to arrive at possessing everything,
>   Desire to possess nothing
>
> In order to arrive at being everything,
>   Desire to be nothing.
> In order to arrive at knowing everything,
>   Desire to know nothing.[19]

An exhilarating freedom of choice and action comes to the man who is glued down by no responsibilities to his own possessions; a similar freedom comes to him who gives up family ties; a yet fuller freedom comes to him who gives up books and seeks the knowledge that comes from every day's encounter. What, then, must be the freedom and flight of heart and mind when each particular thing is given up that we may in pure freedom seek the fullness that filleth all in all? The logic is inexorable.

[19] M.C. I, xiii, 11.

When thou thinkest upon anything
Thou ceasest to cast thyself upon the All,
For in order to pass from the all to the All
Thou hast to deny thyself wholly in all.
And when thou comest to possess it wholly,
Thou must possess it without desiring anything,
For if thou wilt have anything in all,
Thou hast not thy treasure purely in God.[20]

8

In the dark dead of night
With longings all alight
As loves, ah fortune blest!

With longings all alight as love; kindled in love with yearning; such was the mystic's state. His soul was a lantern, or shall we say a vase of alabaster, lit within. The soul then says that, kindled in love with yearnings, it passed through this dark night of sense and came out thence to union with the Beloved.[21] "For in order to conquer all the desires and to deny itself the pleasures which it has in everything and for which its love and affection are wont to enkindle the will that it may enjoy them, there must be another and a greater enkindling by another and a better love, which is that of its Spouse; to the end that, having its pleasure set upon Him and deriving from Him its strength, it should have courage and constancy to deny itself all other things with ease. And not only would it be needful, in order to conquer the strength of the desires of sense, to have Love for its spouse, but also to be enkindled by love and to have longings. For it comes to pass and so it is that *with such passionate longings the heart of flesh is moved and attracted to the things of flesh, that, if the spiritual part is not enkindled with other and greater longings for that which is spiritual, it will not be able to throw off the yoke of nature* or to enter the night of the senses, neither will it have courage to remain in darkness as to all things, depriving itself of desires for them all." [22]

We see, then, the beginning of the mystic's teaching. There is what St. Paul called war in our members: the human side of our

[20] *Ibid.,* 12.
[21] Peers, I, 64; M.C. I, xiv, 2.
[22] *Mount Carmel,* I, xiv, 2.

nature strives against the inspiration of the Spirit within. In strong and passionate natures, the desires have an overwhelming force; they enfold the objects to which they cling with all the tendrils of the spirit. For the layman, circumstances, family, custom are the gradual way by which selfishness is mitigated. For the religious the supreme thing is the consciousness that God loves him and draws him.

Fray Juan de la Cruz did not wait for the enemy to attack the fort: he charged with all his chivalry: and from the beginning, in the deliberate extremes of renunciation had sought to deaden love of self and fight the fight of heroes. But even those had not been enough: in the choice of mortifications he had been his own master, till God had ordered things beyond anything he had asked or thought. Heroic love had been given superhuman trials. What had Santa Teresa written? "I sometimes think that our love for God is the measure of the crosses we can bear."

9

San Juan had passed not only through the night of sensation and passion, but also that of imagination and reason. And the second night was far the darker of the two. In the night of sense there still remains some light, for the understanding and the reason remain and are not blinded. But the spiritual night, which is faith, deprives the soul of everything, both as to understanding and to sense.[23] In this second night, even the highest human faculties fail: all that is left is a grace, a likeness to the Divine mind given by God Himself; and this light is faith.

The mystic takes two familiar texts: "Eye hath not seen nor ear heard, nor hath it entered into the heart of man to conceive what God hath prepared for them that love him," [24] and he applies it to the life of faith. The conclusion is not to be escaped.[25] In the supernatural realm of faith a man must cease to lean upon anything that he feels, experiences, imagines, or understands. One must, therefore, live by modes of being wholly other than one's own: the only way to march on this road is to leave all roads one knows, or, to express it

[23] M.C. II, ii, 2.
[24] Isa. LXIV, 4; I Cor. II, 9.
[25] M.C. IV, 4.

better, "it is to pass on the goal and to leave one's way, and to enter upon that which has no way, which is God." [26]

The second text which the mystic takes is: "Which were born not of the blood, nor of the will of the flesh, nor of the will of man, but of God." [27] He then expounds it in these words: "He gave power to be the sons of God, that is to be transformed into God, only to those who are born not of blood, that is of natural constitution and temperament, neither of the will of the flesh—that is the free will of natural capacity and ability, still less of the will of man wherein is included every way and manner of judging and comprehending with the understanding. He gave power to none of these to become sons of God, but only to those that are born of God—that is to those who being born again through grace, and dying first of all to everything that is of the old man, are raised above themselves to the supernatural, and receive from God this re-birth and adoption which transcends all that can be imagined"; for, as St. John himself says elsewhere: "Unless a man is born again of water and of the Spirit, he cannot enter the kingdom of God. This signifies: He that is not born again in the Holy Spirit will not be able to see this Kingdom of God which is the state of perfection; and to be born again in the Holy Spirit in this life is to have a soul most like to God in purity, having in itself no admixture of imperfection, so that pure transformation can be wrought in all through participation—although not essentially." [28] It is plain that Fray Juan, with his experience of imprisonment at Toledo, had come to a time when all the consolations of poetry had left him, when, in exhaustion and depression, his mind was a blank, when he was bereft of every human consolation, and yet there had remained a confidence in and a clinging to God.

10

After spending some time in elaborating his points in connection with texts from the Bible, the writer goes on to one of the most practical points of his spiritual direction. This is the necessity for souls to move from that discourse of intellect and imagination which

[26] *Ibid.,* II, iv, 5.
[27] St. John I, 13.
[28] Book II, v, 5.

is known as meditation as soon as God gives them the higher faculty
of concentration—or contemplation, as He calls it—when, by a
happy repose and quiet, they enter into the more direct communion
which is the essence of mysticism.

Above all—and here he reacts against the favoured exercises of
San Ignacio de Loyola—he warns his readers against the use of imagination in connection with the life of Christ: such excesses, he
says, are only for beginners, who should give them up as soon as
they are able.[29] Some, indeed, must first nourish their affection for
God on emotion and imagination. But no one, because he has to
begin on the lower rungs to climb a ladder, must ever imagine that
if he clings to the lower rungs, he will mount to space at the top of
the ladder.[30] And so, he says, "many spiritual men err who, having
exercised themselves in attaining to God through images, and forms,
and meditations, which are suitable for beginners, find God desiring
them to gather good more spiritual, inward and invisible, taking from
them the taste and juice [31] of discursive meditation, but they do not
decide, or dare, or feel able to rid themselves of those material modes
to which they are accustomed, and so they still make every effort to
hold on to them, desiring to advance by formal consideration and
meditation. And they toil much at this and find little or no juice:
firstly, dryness and fatigue and disquiet of the soul increase, the more
they toil for that first juice: for now the soul delights no longer in
that food, as we said, which was so much a matter of feeling, and
does not consist in working with the imagination, but in resting the
soul and leaving it in its quiet and repose: and this is more spiritual.
For the more the soul relies upon the spirit, the more it ceases from
occupying its faculties in particular acts, because it is more given to
an action more general and pure, and so the faculties which were on
the march towards that where the soul had arrived cease their activity:
just as our feet stop when the journey is done, because if there were
nothing but marching, there would be no arrival; and if all were
means, when and where would we enjoy the term and end of them
all?" [32]

[29] M.C. II, xii, 5.
[30] *El termino y estancia de la subida.*
[31] *Jugo* literally means juice. Professor Allison Peers translates it as sweetness.
[32] M.C. II, xii, 6.

The master then gives three tests to determine whether a soul has advanced from meditation to contemplation. These three tests were already known to contemplatives and set down by Tauler.

The first is that it cannot meditate nor exercise the imagination, nor enjoy as it was used to do; but now it finds dryness in that which beforehand used to satisfy emotion and bring profit. Yet it should not cease from any meditations which are profitable unless the soul fall into a state of peace and quiet.

"The second sign is that there is no longer any desire to occupy imagination or emotion in other particular things, outward or inward. I do not say that there is no movement (for even in deep recollection, there is swiftness and ease of mind), but that the mind has no taste deliberately to fix attention on other things.

"The third and most certain is that if the soul enjoys to rest alone with loving attention to God without particular consideration in inward peace and quiet and refreshment, without acts and exercise of the faculties, memory, intellect, and will, or at least any action which is discursive, moving from one thing to another; but only with attention and general affectionate awareness, without particular exercise of thought or understanding of what it is aware." [33]

If this last is lacking, the soul often falls short of the gift of contemplation, because the two preceding symptoms or indications may well proceed from a state of depression or exhaustion. So subtle and lofty is the peace distilled by contemplation into the soul that it may scarcely be recognized or felt. Then the saint gives one of his mystical interpretations: he takes the text: "I watched like the sparrow alone upon the house-top." "Alone" means alienated and abstracted from things: the house-top signifies the elevated state of the mind—and so, says the saint, the soul remains as though ignorant of all things, because it knows only God without knowing how it knows Him.

Nothing, says San Juan, is so serene and pure as this divine light which comes in a general and confused awareness of God.[34] Let us beware of visions and fancies, for over them the demon has power.[35]

[33] *Ibid.*, xiii, 2, 3, 4.
[34] *Ibid.*, xv, 3.
[35] *Ibid.*, xvi, 4.

II

Does God, then, allow the imagination to work? and if He does, why? He does so because His operations are tranquil, and because He moves all things according to their own nature, and so he draws men gradually upward.[36] First, therefore, He seeks to elevate the natural man, by moving him to profit by things which appeal outwardly, and here the saint puts first sermons, then "seeing holy things," then fasting, and then the use of the scourge, the discipline, which he calls "to macerate the sense of touch with penitence and holy rigour." [37] And when the senses are somewhat disposed, He is accustomed to educate them further, giving them certain supernatural rewards and pleasures, the more to confirm them in good, offering them certain supernatural communications, such as visions of saints and holy things, seen as it were by the natural eye, sweet odours and locutions, and extreme pleasures of sensation, by which He much strengthens the taste for virtue and alienates the taste for evil things. And thus, in turn, He educates together the inner faculties of sensations, that is, the imagination and fancy, accustoming them to the good with considerations, meditations, and edifying discourses, in all of which He instructs the spirit. . . . And so, step by step, God proceeds to raise the soul towards the most interior—not that it should be always necessary to keep so precisely this order of first one thing, and then the other, because sometimes God does one without the other, and may affect the outer life through the inner life, and all together: for God knows what will suit a soul, and how to reward it: but ordinarily things happen, as Fray Juan has said.[38]

What did St. Paul say to the Corinthians? "When I was a child, I spoke as a child, I understood as a child, I thought as a child. But when I became a man, I put away childish things." [39] As long, says San Juan, as we hold fast to the outward appearance of things, which are those of a child, we will never come to those realities of the spirit which are the perfect man.

[36] Cf. Dionysius, *De Divinis Nominibus*. See Rolt's translation, pp. 152, 153.
[37] M.C. II, xvii, 4.
[38] *Ibid.*, II, xvii, 4.
[39] I Cor. XIII, 11; cf. XVII, 1.

12

In this passage San Juan places himself wholly on Catholic ground, with a clear assertion of that hierarchy of men, and that growth in graces, which account so well for the elasticity of the Jesuits. Both they and Fray Juan wanted, like St. Paul, to reach out to every man in whatever way he could be reached. Again, San Juan applies a text from the Psalms: "He sendeth forth his ice like morsels, for who is able to endure his frost." [40] If God were to ask the full sacrifices of contemplation at once, none could abide it; and so the experiences of purification and elevation are given in morsels; but however gradual the course, the end is clear; and that is to live gradually less and less by images, sensations, fancies, emotions, or anything pertaining to the outward man. For even if revelations come from God, they may be misunderstood.[41]

Christ is all. In Him dwelleth all the fullness of the Godhead bodily: in Him are hidden all the treasures of wisdom and knowledge.[42] Know Christ, and Him crucified, and that will be enough.[43]

And so said Fray Juan: "In all we have to be guided by the law of Christ made Man, and by His Church and by His ministers, humanly and visibly, and in this way remedy our ignorances and spiritual languor that by means of such a life we shall find abundant medicine for all our ills. If any man errs from this path, it is not merely curiosity, but audacity, and there is no need for supernatural means of belief, but only the teaching of Christ made Man, as I say, and of His ministers, who are men." [44] And again he quotes St. Paul, whom he calls "my Apostle."

With these precautions clear in view, he now devotes the eight remaining chapters of his second book to the analysis and list of visions and revelations. With characteristic finesse, he applies his tests and places each matter in its place: he distinguishes between visions, revelations, locutions, and spiritual feelings. Here he becomes very subtle: he had noticed that in normal apprehensions there comes a time when the mind itself apprehends and makes its own the image

[40] Psalm CXLVII, 6 (Vulgate).
[41] M.C. II, xvii, 8.
[42] Col. II, 3.
[43] I Cor. II, 2.
[44] II Cor. II, 2.

of the sense. Well, it was so that God was apt to reveal His secrets to the spiritual man, who would seem to hear, or see, or perceive some fragrance or delight within the sense. Such visions come in a flash, and produce an effect of quiet illumination, joy like that of glory, sweetness, purity, and love. But the soul must not lean upon them. Words may seem to come as whole sentences, or as a single utterance, heard as it were from a third person; [45] or yet again as a reality so deep within the soul that they are indistinguishable from the effects which they immediately produce: [46] such are touches of union which are wrought passively within the soul which is humble and detached.

For in all things the principle is the same: faith is God's secret working on the mind; and the more exterior and startling are the signs, the less are they directly beneficial or even free from danger.

[45] II, xxxii, 1.
[46] II, xxxii, 2.

"For this reason so many fall from God who have attained to Him, because they cling to Him with their weakness, not with their strength." [1]

I

IN the third book of the *Ascent,* Fray Juan treats of memory and will, and of the precise lures and dangers which disturb the soul which either by memory dwells upon, or by will desires, any of those lower things by resting in which one fails to attain to God. What are the weaknesses, the softnesses, the deceits, the amusements by which men of religion generally, and Catholics, in particular, are likely to be caught, remaining among childish things when they ought to push on with the valiancy of men to men's rewards?

This question Fray Juan answers with the most searching insight—and well he might do. He had an acute brain refined by a philosophical training of marked subtlety. This training had explained to him how at a particular moment the mind assimilates to itself the impressions of the senses, so that in fancy and imagination there was an inner life of poetry closely connected with elevating words. He had had a very thorough theological training centred on the Bible, worked out with the fathers, in formal but precise eloquence that completed the intense effort of his own spiritual life; he had lived all his life among men of hard sense and abounding energy, who were embarking on huge exploits; his country's fame was rising to its meridian; and his own sense was refined not merely by poetical elevation, a love of beauty and the artistry of words, but by the friendship of a brilliant, charming, experienced, and saintly woman who, by the grace of her own *naïveté,* and by a spontaneous gift of expression which contrasted with his formal university training, was one of the great writers of her time: after all this, he had ample opportunity both to measure the amount of insincerity and mischief in convents, and he himself, in long and exhausting travails, had been stripped of any comfort that habitually comes the way of man.

[1] Meredith, *Richard Feverel.*

This process of purgation and enrichment—accompanied as it was by the keenest exercise of intellectual subtlety and the most delicate appreciation of beauty in Nature and in words—had not been lived alone. For seventeen years Fray Juan had been living in Community; for ten years he had been a director either of friars or nuns. He had furthermore been made the victim of his brethren's fury. He had received, therefore, a very thorough training in the ways of piety; he had enjoyed quite unusual opportunities of exploring the religious conscience.

He now set out to apply his knowledge in the intense light of his own mind and life. For he was both the most passionate and the strictest of them all; he maintained the highest standards; he had carried to the furthest extremes the stripping of self; he had refined his sensibilities with an extraordinary amount of fasting; he had the clear, direct, intense intuition which comes from a sincere and single-hearted life of holiness. And, finally, he had been schooled by trials undesired.

Let us not wonder, therefore, if his insight seems remorseless or his standards severe. He needed to be severe. Not only was the Church in Spain tainted with worldliness and factions, as indeed all Churches are; but also, with a quarter of her hot-blooded, proud, and sometimes lazy people in religious houses, the country, as he knew too well, was often more ostentatious and pietistic than thorough in her religion; and one extreme needed to be balanced by another in the scheme of "reparation."

2

With all this clear in our minds, let us then look more closely at *The Ascent of Mount Carmel*. Let us remember why Fray Juan insisted on self-renunciation, and let us also remember that the language of the gospel is the uncompromising language—the language of extremes which gives the counsels of perfection, drawing very sharp distinctions between God and Mammon. "If thy right hand offend thee, cut it off and cast it from thee." "If a man say, thou fool, he shall be in danger of hell-fire." "Be ye therefore *perfect, even as your father in heaven is perfect*."

These are among the hard sayings strewn thick in Christ's discourses, and especially in the Sermon on the Mount. It is the same language, even if rather more philosophical, which Fray Juan spoke when he said: "To come from the all to the all, thou must deny thyself of all in all," or: "Firstly try to work against your reputation and desire that others should do so: try and speak in contempt of yourself and desire that others should do so: try and think humbly in contempt of yourself and desire that others should do so." This is indeed extreme; for it is not good for others to speak contemptuously of anyone, even of myself; but that is not the point for San Juan. He means to dig his fork so deep into our clay that he can tear out pride and self-conceit by the roots.

3

Before he had finished the second book, he had dealt in searching detail with the matter of faith in relation to the mind: that in obscure contemplation the mind should work not by its own powers, but by a special, supernatural grace given by God. In the third book he proceeds to apply the same searching method of mortification and removal to the memory and the will. His object is entirely to denude the noble palace of the memory, "to drag it from the limits and hinges of nature and to raise it above itself, that is above every distinct impression and apprehension to the height of hope in God the Incomprehensible." [2]

Impressions come to it, as to the intellect, by sight, hearing, smell, taste, and touch, and all that can be formed from sense impressions. All must be stripped and made void. The imagination must be blurred, and the memory absorbed in a supreme good, in deep oblivion, noticing nothing. Only so, bared of all forms and impressions, it will rise to the supernatural and attain to union with God. Oblivion can fall upon it, drowning memory and imagination, and for a time the faculties, including sensation, are suspended.

At such times the worshipper is the victim of absent-mindedness. People forget their meals, and are unaware of what they have been doing: not that these are actually signs of *perfection* (for at a more

[2] M.C. III, iii, 5.

advanced stage, this trouble passes); but it does actually mark a step which is quite normal in the spiritual life.[3] In fact it really is most important to recognize that persons in the state of temporary forgetfulness and absent-mindedness are being led in their way by the Spirit of God. This apparent vagueness has to do not only with the things of the world: it can affect religion and prayer: it may be a matter of intercession, for God will enable such worshippers to intercede only in the way He wishes: they will not be able to control their prayers by their own choice.[4] The truth is that "God alone moves the faculties of these souls to do those works which are meet, according to the will and ordinance of God, and they cannot be moved to do others; and thus the works and prayers of these souls are always effectual."[5] Or it may be some practical duty: as to this he may seem absolutely vague, and yet at the time and in the way it ought to come, it will come to his soul, and the memory will be stirred. All kinds of counsels come in this way to the soul, without people knowing how they come, or how they know what they know. They develop an extraordinary intuition, and can only say, "The worker of all things who is Wisdom taught me all things."[6]

4

But San Juan teaches plainly that, whereas for the practical man there is nothing more valuable than an exact memory of what he has experienced by hearing, sight, taste, smell, or touch, yet for a man who is being led to direct communion with God, it becomes not merely allowable, but necessary, to forget all these things, and let them sink into oblivion. The fact is that the more the mind is given to God, the more the memory will act under His guidance, which is far more efficacious than our own ability or choice.

It is true, says San Juan, that though a soul will hardly be found that is moved by God in all things at all times, and has such continual union with God that without the mediation of any form its faculties are ever moved divinely, there are yet souls who in their operations are very habitually moved by God, and these are not they

---

[3] *Ibid.*, ii, 8.
[4] *Ibid.*, 10.
[5] *Ibid.*
[6] Wisdom, VII, 21.

that move themselves of their own strength: [7] for, as St. Paul says, the Sons of God—those, that is, who are transformed and united in God—are moved by the Spirit of God.[8] If God is working within them, how can their work be other work than His?

5

It is perfectly plain that San Juan is here applying to the contemplative life a psychological phenomenon which meets us in all the spheres of special talent or genius. For all of us the very condition of remembering is that we should forget: success in any sphere implies concentration, and concentration means freedom from distraction. We cannot crowd the mind with every kind of interest and details, and at the same time attain to a striking success in creative work. As Mr. Churchill said in his *Essay on Moses*: it is by seasons of withdrawal to the desert that psychic dynamite is formed for the explosive work of history.[9] And if this is true in all matters of natural excellence, obviously it must be still more true when the mind passes into the high state where God guides it with His eye, or makes it wise with what He tells it within. On the one hand are all the distractions of the world: desires, falsehoods, imperfections, opinions, loss of time, and all the things which breed inferiority in the soul. But if all these distractions are lost from sight, if all these natural interests and inclinations are erased from the mind, if, in a state of oblivion, of expectation and of hope, we turn to such texts as "Speak, Lord, for thy servant heareth," or "Be still and know that I am God," or "I will listen to what the Lord God will speak within me," [10] or "I will bring her into the wilderness and speak comfortably to her," [11] then we shall hear music clear above the din of earth.

"Let the soul then remain enclosed without anxieties or troubles, and He that entered in bodily form to His disciples when the doors were shut and gave them peace, though they neither knew nor thought that this was possible nor how it was possible, will enter

[7] M.C. III, ii, 16.
[8] Rom. VIII, 14.
[9] See Winston Churchill, *Thoughts and Adventures.*
[10] Psalm LXXXIV, 8.
[11] Hosea II, 14.

spiritually into the soul, without it knowing how He does so, when the doors of its faculties—memory, understanding, and will are enclosed against all apprehensions. And He will fill them with peace, coming down upon the soul, as the prophet says, like a river of peace; [12] he will take from the soul all misgivings and suspicions, disturbances and darkness which caused it to fear that it was lost or on the way to perdition. Let it not lose its anxiety to pray, and let it wait in detachment and emptiness, for its blessing will not tarry." [13]

6

The next twelve chapters apply to the memory much the same tests as San Juan had already applied to the intellect and the imagination. Not merely distractions and worldliness, but visions and locutions—not to speak of self-esteem and presumption—may all tend to keep a man back in the world of Nature, and prevent him from giving himself to that far more wonderful mode of life by which God raises the soul to the mystery of His own blessedness and holiness.

There is only one use of remembrance of things past: neither to grieve at grievances foregone nor to dwell upon past joys, but only to think of those which themselves came from uncreated knowledge. For then memory produces touches and impressions of union with God which is the aim "towards which the soul is being directed." By no form, image, or figure which can be impressed upon the soul does the memory recall these (for these touches and impressions of union with the Creator have no form), but only by effects which they have produced upon it of light, love, joy, and the renewal of the Spirit"; for when such things as these are remembered, they are wrought anew within the soul. Memory by hearing them makes them habitual; memory and hope combine as choice, to give the direction, and therefore the quality, to a mind; thus contemplatives should advance "from strength to strength and unto the God of Gods appeareth every one of them in Sion."

[12] Isa. XLVIII, 18. Then had thy peace been as a river and thy righteousness as the waves of the sea.
[13] M.C. III, iii, 6.

7

In Chapter XVI of the third book of *The Ascent of Mount Carmel*, San Juan goes on from the dark night of the memory to the dark night of the will. He remembers that Boethius had mentioned the four passions of joy, hope, grief, and fear; he wishes these to be centred in direct union with God alone, that we may love the Lord our God with all our heart and mind and soul and strength. "The whole business of attaining to union with God consists in purging the will from its affections and desires, so that thus it may no longer be a human will set on things below, but become a Divine will made into one same thing with the Will of God." [14] He then proceeds to treat of the good things, or blessings in which men rejoice: firstly, things of the world, physical attractions, things which give pleasure to the senses, and secondly, those higher favours which are in turn, moral, supernatural, or spiritual.

With regard to the first of these, he is on familiar ground: many are the warnings in the Bible against riches, prosperity, and success. San Juan carries these warnings as far as a wife and children. Natural attachments, even if healthy, may result in a certain blunting of the mind with regard to God, so that He is, as it were, hidden in a mist: they may end in worldliness and covetousness. By giving up the things of this world, one attains to liberality, freedom of soul, clearness of reason, freedom from worry, and peaceful confidence.

If people set their minds on physical attractions, they may despise others, become unduly passionate or luxurious, dull to heavenly things—they may, in a word, be proud, passionate, or vain. If, on the other hand, they give up all this, they become calmer, humbler, purer.

And now come the pleasures of the senses, in so far as they may be found in Church, or during prayer. For even these may be dangerous. San Juan applies a test: whensoever a person hears music or other things, and sees pleasant things, and is conscious of sweet perfumes or tastes things that are delicious and feels soft touches, if the thought and the affection of the will are at once centred upon God, and if that thought of God gives him more pleasure than the movement of sense which causes it, then it is a help. The test and the

[14] M.C. III, xvi, 3.

means of purification, therefore, are not merely self-denial, but praise and thanksgiving.

But if this is not happening, then sight may lead to vanity, immodesty, and carelessness; hearing to gossip, censoriousness, and waste of time; "from joy in sweet perfumes may come loathing of the poor," [15] and dislike of humble though necessary tasks; from taste can come gluttony, drunkenness; from touch may come all kinds of luxuries and impurities, leading us to moral cowardice, inconstancy, and fear. But if we deny ourselves in these things and mortify our senses that better things may live, the result is swift. We become stronger, more agile, clearer in mind. The spiritual takes charge. That which is born of the flesh is flesh, that which is born of the spirit is spirit, and for every fleeting joy that has been renounced comes a far more exceeding and eternal weight of glory.[16]

Now all these things are what many an ascetic has said before and after San Juan. He differs from them, if at all, only in being more precise and searching in his psychology. But few have warned people as he does of the subtler dangers of complacency in their own virtues: for the Christian, he says, must rejoice not in the performing of good works and the following of good customs, but in doing them for the love of God alone without respect to aught else so ever. Good works, fasts, penances, almsgiving depend for their value not on the amount or extent of them, but on the love of God which inspires him who does them.[17] Otherwise there will be spiritual pride, judgment on others, dependence on others' approbation, a complacency that clogs progress, while self-love causes charity to grow cold. Let us, therefore, free ourselves from spiritual envy, spiritual sloth, and be poor in spirit that we may extend the kingdom of heaven.[18]

8

We read in the New Testament of certain peculiar powers and gifts: healing, miracles, prophecies, interpretations, visions. "The practice of these has an intimate relation with the profit of man, and it is with a view to this profit and to this aid that God gives them,"

[15] M.C. III, xxv, 4.
[16] *Ibid.*, xxvi, 8.
[17] *Ibid.*, xxviii, 9.
[18] *Ibid.*, xxix, 5.

but nevertheless these things profit little unless they are used for the highest purpose, which is the serving of God in true charity. Fray Juan works out this point with even more illustrations than usual from the Bible. He insists that if people set their heart on miracles of this kind they too easily make compacts with the devil: vainglory may easily tempt them. But man's heart should be set on such lofty things that only God shall be exalted,[19] and the more God is served without signs and miracles, the more easily the soul rises above this world to understand things beyond what signs and miracles can demonstrate.

Finally, San Juan comes on the subtlest point of all, the point about the pleasures of worship and prayer. He speaks most carefully of the use of pictures and images,[20] and then of oratories, places dedicated to prayer, and festivals. His whole teaching is summed up in the sentence that "for a matter as intimate as converse with God, one should choose that place which least occupies and most transcends the human side of our natures. And then it must not be a place that is pleasant and delectable to our feelings (such as some habitually contrive to find) for, so instead of the recollection of the spirit in God, naught is achieved but recreation and pleasure and feelings of delight. Therefore that place is good which is solitary, and even wild, so that the spirit wholly and directly soars upward to God, not hindered nor detained by visible things: for even though these sometimes help to raise the spirit, that is better done by at once forgetting them and resting in God." [21]

The living temple is the interior recollection of the soul. Let us therefore make our bodies into these living temples of the Holy Spirit, that He may dwell with us. Always, always let us remember that *God is a Spirit,* and they that worship Him must *worship Him in spirit and in truth.*[22]

9

The mystic teacher is coming to the end at last of his subtle category of warnings and encouragements: there is a final word about

[19] *Ibid.,* xxxv-xxxvii.
[20] M.C. III, xxxv-xxxvii.
[21] M.C. III, xxxix, 2.
[22] St. John iv, 24.

insistence on ceremonies, about eloquence in sermons, about the value of associations. Always the same precision of balance: all times and places and aids and associations are rightly appointed and good up to a point; but not beyond it: for the soul must always fix the movement of her love in recollection on God alone: we must love Him, and Him alone, with all our heart and mind and soul and strength. The Kingdom of God is within us. Such is from beginning to end the teaching of the first, and indeed of every treatise, of San Juan de la Cruz. Such is the climbing of Mount Carmel.

His treatise has seemed to many, even of those in the monastic life, to be hard and depressing; it has seemed to ask more than one can give; it has seemed harsh and puritanical. If even monks or nuns read this treatise alone, they can indeed be misled. But when we place it in its proper place in the history of Spain, and in the life and development of an extraordinarily refined, sensitive, imaginative, passionate, and eager Spaniard, when we relate it to the poem it expounds, it becomes not only clear, but natural, logical, inevitable, and, finally, refreshing, and encouraging. It will not be simple at the first reading, he himself had said: the moisture will take a little time to sink to the roots; but once the occasion and the poem are appreciated, once the principles are grasped, the treatise will explain itself; the philosophical background will show the logical training: the theology of the Church will give a special and intense wealth of significance to a doctrine that comes direct from the Bible and from Christ; and not merely the monk, the friar, and the nun, but those that are in the world, and even those who have not accepted the discipline of faith and worship, will see the radiance and beauty of the views which come at every turn of the climb, different for every climber, and which lead up from the shores of Galilee to the heights of Sharon and of Carmel.

This ascetical treatise on the dark night of the soul and the hard climb up the mountain were written by a man who, though he took as his sign the Cross, spoke, even of holy things, so gaily that the friars he ruled loved to have his company when they walked out for their amusement: for, as one of them said, "he would make us all laugh." [23]

[23] *Works*, E. Allison Peers, III, 362.

Drowned in the dark . . .
I would behold beyond a mortal gaze,
Behold ev'n now, ev'n here
The beauty strange, the ecstasy extreme
Of what should this divine gloom best beseem.[1]

I

AFTER the rebellious chapter at Almodovar in 1579, as we have seen, the leaders of the Reform had fallen into trouble together. Antonio, Gracián, and Mariano Azzaro were thrown into prison, Teresa confined in her convent at Ávila.[2] Such, we remember, was the situation when Fray Juan went to El Calvario in 1579 and began to write his poems and treatises, while the Conde de Tendilla took up the cause of Madre Teresa, with the results that we have seen. The Nuncio had agreed that he would forgive all but Gracián.

Still the fight continued. The King, anxious to secure the full advantages he had gained for Teresa, instructed his ambassador in Rome to secure the approval of the Pope himself. Two friars of the Reform were to be chosen by Teresa and her friends to go to Rome to present the full case to the Quirinal: [3] meanwhile she set about for the means to arrange for this long, expensive, and difficult journey, which would, she knew, be impeded in every possible way by her well-meaning but thoroughly unscrupulous enemies.

A providential fortune now favoured her. Romance unlocked the doors of difficulty. An hidalgo in Ávila wished to obtain a dispensation for his marriage to a cousin. He agreed to take the two friars disguised in his retinue. Madre Ana at Beas now took up the affair. One of her novices had just arrived with a dowry of 400 ducats, which were at once handed over to the enterprise. The foundress at Ávila was fuller than ever of admiration for her favourite. "While I

[1] Laurence Binyon, *To the Summer Night.*
[2] Cunninghame Graham, II, 241.
[3] *Ibid.*, II, 246.

have the name," Teresa wrote, "she does the work." [4] Thus it was
that the two disguised friars began their dangerous journey to Valencia. "God bring them back safely," wrote Teresa. "I long for the
hour for him to leave Spain for fear any accident should occur to him,
which would be a perilous juncture": sometimes threatened by the
sails of Moorish pirates, sometimes shaken and seasick in storms,
sometimes becalmed, the two friars made their way into Renaissance
Rome to the Court of Gregory XIII, with their letters from Philip
the King.

The Pope referred them to Cardinal Montalto, who himself afterwards became Pope, as Sixtus V. His Eminence at once lent a con-
siderate ear. Diplomacy counselled agreement with the King, who
was the main support of the Papal cause not only in the vast provinces
of the New World, but in the diplomacy of France, England, and
the Netherlands. Religion advised the support of high standards for
the religious orders. The two friars who had arrived poor and disguised in Rome with the ducats provided by Madre Ana of Beas soon
found themselves supported by numerous Princes of the Church. A
General Chapter of the Carmelites was then sitting. The prayers of
Teresa were supported by the pressure of diplomacy; yielding to this
combination, they decided to admit the Reform, and a Brief accordingly was issued in June, 1580. [5]

When the news of this reached Spain and Santa Teresa, she set to
work in favour of her project, her protégés, and in particular of
Gracián. She arranged for a chapter of all the superiors of her Reform. They met on March 4, 1581, at Alcalá de Henares. [6] They
elected Gracián as their provincial, though only by a majority of one;
and it was now to be seen how far Teresa was right in her estimation
that his enthusiasm and eloquence, his distinguished name, his velvet
personality, had suited him to be the ruler of her company.

2

But while these things were hanging fire, while all seemed lost,
while Fray Juan was cut off from Madre Teresa, with all the mem-

[4] Stanbrook, Life, p. 86.
[5] Ibid., pp. 86, 87.
[6] Cunninghame Graham, II, 315, 316.

ories of outrages in his mind, and rumours of fresh intrigues and compulsion meeting him at every turn, he acceded to the adjurations of Madre Ana and her nuns to explain his poems.

Not until we have all this biographical background, not until we clearly envisage what Fray Juan knew of his Carmelite enemies and the Nuncio, not until we recall that Teresa's champion was the King, and the King acting against the Nuncio, can we understand the second treatise of Fray Juan. Let us, then, picture how he had been refreshed by the company of congenial Carmelites, delighted with what he saw of Nature. He loved the sierras, with their rain, their rare air, and their flowers; and he loved the wooded valleys with their birds and streams. "The mountains," he said, "have the quality of loftiness: they are enormous, extensive: they are beautiful, charming, flowery, and fragrant . . . the solitary valleys are quiet, pleasant, cool, shady, abounding in fresh water, and by the variety of their groves and the sweet song of the birds, they greatly recreate and delight the senses, in their solitude and silence giving refreshment and rest." [7]

But let us at the same time recall that these charms of the world, and the delightful enthusiasm and sympathy of Madre Ana and her friends at Beas, only served to heighten the contrast with what he had gone through, and what many of his friends were suffering still. While on the one side there was thanksgiving and relief, on the other there was still strain and indignation. He had learned to take the keenest and loftiest delight in Nature; for it was always leading him to contemplation. But if he thought of his brethren in the priesthood, life presented a picture far from idyllic. At the background of his quiet life in the valley of the Guadalimar was intrigue: this was still being worked out with a violence such as he had experienced himself, by men who, though priests, were Spaniards, unregenerate, contumacious, and lusting for fight.

3

Therefore, when he had completed *The Ascent of Mount Carmel*, he began the exposition of the stanzas on *The Dark Night* all over again. In the *Ascent* he had taken simply the idea of darkness, to write a treatise on self-renunciation; but this treatise, elaborate as it

[7] C.E. XIV, 6, 7.

was, proved to be incomplete: it had not explored and mapped the temptations of the religious, as he knew them. The saint felt he must go over the ground once more: he must warn the pious of yet more subtle snares of self-love in the sense of piety itself, and he must give a fuller account of all those sufferings which are not chosen by the soul, but come when, in His special care for it, the Supreme Lover purifies it through suffering to an intenser love of Himself.

Intenser love: intenser beauty: a night of amorous joy leading to dawn. These are the themes which occupy a poet who wanted never to stop short at æsthetic experience, never to remain solely with his own sensations, however refined and high, but always to lose them in direct converse with a Lover whose object was to shine through them in heavenly radiance and teach him that everything in creation was not only beautiful in itself, but beautiful as a revelation of the Mind that made it. The poem consisted of eight stanzas. The *first two,* he said, were to explain the effects of the spiritual purgation: firstly, that of the realm of feeling and imagination in human nature, and, secondly, the subtler world of Spirit. The *remaining six* were to explain the various and admirable effects of spiritual illumination and the union of love with God.

The poem itself is redolent of passion: an exquisite and delicate sense, first of the desire, then of the joy of the ardent lover, breathes through every verse with the same rapture as in the *Song of Songs,* and his own *Song of the Spirit.*[8] The dark night, he says, is but another name for the narrow way by which certain souls pass to the perfection of love, which is the high and blessed union with God; but the poem which tells this is one of the great love-lyrics of all literature. It is thought by some that it was composed in the cell at Toledo; and it is very likely indeed that it was there first conceived; but, since it is rich in the imagery of a night escape, it was probably completed after he had fled away. For it links together his two vocations: the first to join the Carmelite order at Medina, for which he had had to escape at night from the hospital where he was working: and, secondly, his escape from the prison of the Carmelite Observants at Toledo, that he might join with others in a life of fuller renunciation and contemplation. The third significance of the poem

[8] Although the literal rendering of this expression would be *Canción del Espíritu,* I think it a suitable equivalent in English for *Cántico Espiritual.*

is the escape first from the senses, then from the natural reason, which he had already treated (as we have just seen) in *The Ascent of Mount Carmel*. But behind all this there was something, as he was afterwards to insist, which could not be explained. For there is always the viewless power which attends the mystery of words, and all the host of shadowy things, where darkness makes abode. From line to line,

> The fairy fancies range,
> And lightly stirred,
> Ring little bells of change
> From word to word.

The bells of fancy, then, ring through every cadence of this poem, which in Spanish is infinitely melodious and evocative. It has been several times translated into English, but never better than by Professor Allison Peers, who keeps the original metre combined with a literal and scholarly translation. The following version is offered as the record of a personal reaction:

> In the dark dead of night,
> With longings all alight
> As loves, ah fortune blest!
> I made my secret flight,
> My house being now at rest.
>
> Disguised that dark amid,
> I by love's ladder did
> Descend, ah fortune blest!
> Always in darkness hid,
> My house being now at rest.
>
> So through blest night I came,
> None saw to guess my name:
> Nought could mine own eye see,
> No light was guiding me,
> Safe from my heart's hot flame.
>
> Where none there was to see,
> That flame was guiding me
> Clearer than noon's own sun.
> Expectant there was he
> To whom my mind had run.
>
> O night which was my guide,
> O night fairer than dawn,
> O night which to the side
> Of lover brought his bride,
> **And then didst make them one!**

My heart flowered out in bloom,
For him was all its room.
There sleeping I remained
And him I entertained.
Winds played through cedarn gloom.

Past towers blew an air bland
While long his locks I fanned,
When on my neck a wound
Was made by that mild hand,
And all my senses swooned.

I stayed: he let me rest
My cheek upon his breast,
All things had end; as there
Released I all my care,
Among those lilies fair,
In that oblivion blest.[9]

4

Such were the stanzas in which the contemplative breathed out
once more the secret of his inner life: once again, as in the *Song of
Songs,* the fervent imagery of nuptial attraction told more of the
soul's quest than any other words could tell. *Ubi caritas et amor, ibi
Christus.* Love can tell most of God, since God is love. And, since
the highest occupation of the soul is to grow like God, to mirror him,
Contemplation is itself love in its purest and most sacred union; this
poem, therefore, might have been at once made into a chant of contemplation. But he first connected it with all the snares of the monastic life.

5

Let us, then, first consider a fervent soul: it loves to pray at length;
it takes pleasure in rigours; it finds satisfaction in fasts and in divine
and holy exercises. Yet, even so, it is true that all our righteousness is
as filthy rags, which must be cleansed and made pure. For in them
all can lurk and grow, as Fray Juan de la Cruz had seen, a new form
of each of the seven deadly sins: firstly, spiritual pride and self-satis-
faction in the feeling that they are superior to others; and yet anxious
to seem better than they are, or very impatient with their own faults.[10]

[9] Cf. pp. 222-3.
[10] D.N. I, ii.

But there are others who, even as they do more, feel more their own imperfections, and the greatness of God, so that they would give their heart's blood to serve Him better. Secondly, there is spiritual avarice: either to be always having experiences or collecting articles of piety. But what is truly needed is that God Himself shall take us by the hand to purge us in the dark fire.[11]

Yet another trouble comes out of luxury which can give the body and the complex mechanism of sex their own pleasure in spiritual experiences. Some take a base delight in these; in others, soul and body are so subtly united that when the soul loves the body responds also.[12] The test is which does a soul prefer; for in the dark night these affections range themselves in their proper order. Anger can also find its way into the life of prayer, either because people are irritated after their prayers to come down to earth; or lose patience at another's faults, or even at their own. But the ideal is to be humble and meek in spirit.

Then there is spiritual gluttony, such as afflicted Angel of St. Gabriel at Pastrana with his undue austerities. Thus, monks can turn virtue into vice; others take an undue pleasure in the sensations of Holy Communion, whereas the least of the advantages of the Sacrament is that it delights the emotions.[13] Others are always avid of spiritual experiences; others flee penances and the way of the Cross. The cure of all these things is temptations, trials, and dryness.

Envy is yet another fault. People cannot bear to see others living intenser spiritual lives than their own. Others simply give way to boredom and refuse to make an effort. All these things are causes for those further trials which are the dark night leading to the day.

One of the first signs that they are being purified is a distaste both for the things of the world and the things of God. Everything loses its flavour, and yet they persevere in a desert and pathless land where no water is, until at last comes a solace as subtle, as delicate, as difficult to grasp as the air. And here again one meets the beginning of the true mystic life of contemplation. And from now on we see the advantages of this purer, deeper life with God: it is an intense charity. Gradually all those subtle spiritual returns of the seven deadly sins

[11] D.N. I, iii.
[12] D.N. I, iv.
[13] D.N. I, vi.

are purged away; and the house of the soul is at last at rest in true and selfless love. And now it had made religion sane. For was not Pope right when he said: "The worst of madmen is a saint run mad"? [14]

6

San Juan now comes back once more to that special sphere of his: the dark night of the spirit. This is the subject of his second book of the *Dark Night,* where, in the opinion of both Fray Crisógono and Professor Allison Peers, he attains to the summit of his prose writing. It was that subject which we have already seen to be treated fully both by Dionysius the Areopagite, and Denys the Carthusian. It was the revelation which came with the suffering and the dark: "my understanding went forth from itself, turning from the human and natural to the Divine; for when it is united with God by means of this purgation, its understanding no longer comes through its natural light and vigour, but through the Divine Wisdom wherewith it has become united. And my will went forth from itself becoming Divine: for being united with Divine Love, it no longer loves with its natural strength after a lowly manner, but with strength and purity from the Holy Spirit; and thus the will which is now near to God acts after a higher manner, and similarly the memory has become transformed into eternal apprehension of glory. And finally, by means of this night and purgation of the old man, all the energies and affections of the soul are wholly renewed into a Divine temper and a Divine delight." [15]

This is infused contemplation, which is also called mystical theology. San Juan is here following very closely on Dionysius, but he always introduces personal touches of his own: this Divine Wisdom, he says, is not only night and darkness for the soul, but is likewise affliction and torment. The first is because of the height of the Divine Wisdom, which transcends the talents of the soul, and in this way is darkness to it; the second, because of the soul's vileness and impurity, in which respect the purgation brings it pain and affliction and

[14] Pope, *Translations of Horace.*
[15] D.N. II, iv, 2.

is also dark. Here Fray Juan applies a verse from the Psalms: "Darkness and cloud are round about him." [16] Self-renunciation is painful, just as a bright light is painful to sore eyes; and, furthermore, it shows the soul its own impurity. "Why," asked Job, "hast Thou set me against Thee, that I am grievous and burdensome to myself?" [17] Man is in fact oppressed with the weight of God's greatness; and yet the heaviness of God is but His kindness and His mercy.

Nor is this the only pain: the habitual affections and attachments are torn away; but what the soul feels most in this condition is its clear perception, as it thinks, that God has abandoned it, and, in His abhorrence of it, has flung it into darkness. That is what had happened to himself at Toledo. Friends and creatures withdraw. The temporal, the natural, and the spiritual all fail to console, and the soul seems to go down into hell. All suffered then, said San Juan, body and soul. Here, indeed, the mystics receive the purgation of purgatory; for one hour of purgation here is more profitable than are many there.

David, Job, and Jeremiah supply the saint with many an expression of affliction as he describes how the spirit is humbled, softened, and purified; how it grows so keen and delicate and pure that it can become one with the Spirit of God, according to the degree of love which His mercy is pleased to grant it; for there are times of solace when the soul feels and experiences great sweetness of peace and loving friendship with God. But again these are disturbed, and distresses return, with symptoms of nervous exhaustion: there are distractions and forgetfulness, so that a man does not know what he has been doing or thinking.[18]

At this point San Juan returns to the metaphor of the window: as it gives more light when it is cleanest, and is therefore most invisible, so does contemplation transcend the natural powers of the soul, darkening it and depriving it of all outward affections and apprehensions, and emptying it of all its own faculties and desires, both spiritual and natural. And yet this poverty is the way to wealth, this exhaustion to power. Having nothing, we yet possess all things.

[16] Psalm XCVI, 2 (Vulgate); D.N. II, v, 3.
[17] Job xxiii, 6. D.N. II, v. 5.
[18] D.N. II, viii, 1.

7

In the tenth chapter, San Juan takes, as many a mystic had taken before him, the metaphor of fire. He had watched the fire driving out the sap from a bough of wood: he had seen the bough blacken and char in the smoke; and then, when the bough was dry, it had caught fire, and gave from itself all the glow and beauty of flame. Just so it is with the fire of mystic love: it too makes the soul seem ugly; it too drives out the humours and sap of our lower nature. Then we apply to ourselves new standards which show up many faults that human nature had disguised. And here, says San Juan, "we can learn incidentally how souls are afflicted in purgatory: for the fire would have no power over them were there no imperfections to burn. Whether on earth or beyond death, when the imperfections are consumed, the affliction of the soul ceases and the fruition remains." [19]

But here on earth this is a long process, many times repeated. For after the lower imperfections have been purified, the higher ones remain; the suffering of the soul becomes more intricate, subtle, and spiritual in proportion as it refines away the more intimate, subtle, and spiritual imperfections.

Not yet has the mystic doctor completed his dissertation on afflictions: the long, disquieting story of our imperfections has not yet been told; the tragic theme becomes subtler: but the writer never ceases to insist that if we but trust and love, there is a blessedness in every suffering. He says once more that this time of trial, the more severe it is, is but the favour and goodness of God, Who is to the souls to be strengthened by suffering infinitely more tender, infinitely more solicitous than they can dream. If He sends them suffering, He is doing more for them than they could do for themselves: "For with those hands, howsoever well they may serve thee, thou wouldest never labour so effectively, so perfectly and so securely (because of their clumsiness and uncleanness) as now, when God takes thy hand and guides thee in the darkness, as though thou wert blind, to an end, and by a way thou knowest not; nor couldst thou ever hope to travel with the aid of thine own eyes and feet." [20]

The saint quotes from a great passage of Job:

[19] D.N. II, x, 5.
[20] D.N. II, xvi, 7.

Stand still and consider the wondrous works of God.
Dost thou know how God layeth his charge upon them,
And causeth the lightings of his cloud to shine?
Dost thou know the balancings of the clouds,
The wondrous works of him which is perfect in knowledge?

How thy garments are warm,
When the earth is still by reason of the south wind?
Canst thou with him spread out the sky
Which is strong as a molten mirror?
Teach us what we shall say unto him
For we cannot order our speech by reason of darkness.[21]

He did not write down the whole passage. Only on three or four occasions did he take from the Bible more than one phrase at a time. He simply asks, "Dost thou know the balancing of the clouds, and the perfect sciences?" And he answers from the Psalms: "His paths are in the great waters, and his footsteps are not known." [22]

8

After this he changes his metaphor: following sundry predecessors on the subject, he compares the mystic path to a ladder. He illustrates this idea of a ladder from the Bible, and he speaks of those alternations of longing and joy, of storm and calm, by which the soul seems to ascend and to descend. "The reason for this is that as the state of perfection which consists in the perfect love of God and contempt for self cannot exist unless it have those two parts which are the knowledge of God and of oneself, the soul has of necessity to be practised first in the one and then in the other, now given to taste of the one that is exaltation and then to experience the other which is humiliation, until it has acquired perfect habits, and then this ascending and descending will cease, since the soul will have attained to God and become united to Him, which comes to pass at the summit of the ladder, for the ladder rests and leans upon Him." [23]

If, in the true mysticism of contemplation, the soul sinks into the deep oblivion where it finds God, the favour is ineffable. Neither the devil, nor yet angels themselves, can know "the intimate and secret

[21] D.N. II, xvii, 8. Cf. Job xxxvii.
[22] Psalm LXXVII, 19.
[23] D.N. II, xviii, 4.

communications which take place then between the soul and God." [24]
These communications, since the Lord Himself works them, are
wholly Divine, and sovereign, for they are all substantial touches of
Divine union between the soul and God; in one of these the soul
receives a greater blessing than in all the rest, since this is the loftiest
degree of prayer in existence.

For these are the touches that the Bride entreated of Him in the
Song of Songs: "Let him kiss me with the kisses of his mouth."
Then at last—with his lips upon the lips of his Beloved—could the
mystic say that his house was at rest.

9

He had finished the exposition of his second stanza; and now we
might expect to hear of all the windows of a transfigured life in his
exposition of the remaining six. But no! Again San Juan ends his
treatise abruptly. He has given us the full account of his soul's hardships and torments in its search for God. He has shown that tribulations return and return; he has shown that the life of piety is thick
with subtle snares. He demands that the sacrifice of self shall be complete, not only in the realm of feeling, but in the acceptance of trials
which no man can apply of his own will because they are sent from
on high, and burn us with a supernal fire.

10

The subject of the writer here is not the problem of suffering, or
why God permits evil. He never quotes any of those central texts
which relate to suffering. He does not remind us that St. Paul filled
up that which is lacking in the sufferings of Christ: [25] nor does he
repeat that "whom the Lord loveth He chasteneth, and scourgeth
every son whom He receiveth." [26] Still less does he give us any meditations on the Passion and Crucifixion of Christ. He never once
quotes from the Liturgy, with its reference to Adam's fall as a happy
fault and a truly necessary sin, in that they had led to man being

[24] D.N. II, xxiii, 11.
[25] Col. i, 24.
[26] Heb. xii, 5, 6; quoting Prov. iii, 11, 12.

VENERABILIS IOANNES A CRUCE,
CARMELITARUM DISCACEATOR.ᴹ PARENS.

QVID. Ioannes, vis pro cruce?   NULLA maior, pro labore
Crucem, Domine, te duce: Nulla maior, ex amore,
Crux, mea dilectio.   Optio, petitio.

Alardo de Popma fecit

SAN JUAN DE LA CRUZ IN AN EARLY PRINT BY ALARDO DE POPINA

raised to a yet happier state by his union with Christ his Redeemer.
He knew all these things: every Catholic theologian must know
them.[27] But he himself keeps to one subject: the subject of contemplation or mystical theology: by which the soul enters into direct and
loving communion with God, and lives hidden with Christ, by faith
and hope and love. His theme is the theme of Dionysius the Areopagite, the theme which was made so familiar and so charming by
Henry Vaughan in his poem, *The Night.*

> Dear night! this world's defeat,
> The stop to busy fools, care's check and curb,
> The day of spirits; my soul's calm retreat
>   Which none disturb!
> Christ's progress, and his prayer-time,
> The hours to which high heaven doth chime.
>
> God's silent, searching flight,
> When my Lord's head is filled with dew, and all
> His locks are wet with the clear drops of night;
>   His still, soft call,
> His knocking time, the soul's dumb watch,
> When spirits their fair kindred catch.
>
> Were all my loud, evil days
> Calm and unhaunted as is thy dark tent,
> Whose peace but by some angel's wing or voice
>   Is seldom rent,
> Then I in heaven all the long year
> Would keep and never wander here.
>
> But living where the sun
> Doth all things wake, and where all mix and tyre
> Themselves and others, I consent and run
>   To every myre;
> And by this world's ill-guiding light
> Erre more than I can do by night.
>
> There is in God, some say,
> A deep, but dazzling darkness: As men here
> Say it is late and dusky, because they
>   See not all clear.
> O for that night! where I in Him
> Might live invisible and dim.

Vaughan did not expound his poem: he never told us whether his
night meant pure contemplation and oblivion: but whether he was
content to take up the idea of Dionysius or whether he had heard of

[27] For a concise but excellent account of them, see Dom Bruno Webb: *Why Does God
Permit Evil?*

San Juan de la Cruz, he has become aware of the same secret, the same mystery: he feels the same need of withdrawal into quiet and stillness, and there, retired, he finds his eyes opening to the day of the spirit.

II

How clear and how refreshing seems the idea of the Dark Night when Vaughan describes it so! how rapturous and exquisite it seems in the poem of San Juan! And yet what suffering and misunderstanding were implied! For even the man of prayer must do his drudgery, and there are times when he will seem morbid, or exhausted, or weighed down with a hidden sin.[28]

San Juan has therefore two peculiarities in his treatment of the Dark Night: in the first place, as we saw, he makes it an essay on the imperfections of pious people, more especially of those living in a religious house. We need not recall of how much of these he had already had direct experience: direct in two ways: for, firstly, to a nature so Castilian, so determined, so rich, so sensuous, so passionate, the lurking temptations of which he writes could not have been unknown: had they been so, the life of Fray Juan would be infinitely less edifying; the struggle would have lacked zest: secondly, they impinged upon him with violence from those around him, not only bringing him personal afflictions, but also affecting him by his sympathy. For natures such as his live within themselves the experiences and travails with which their imagination has to deal in the hearts of others. What they hear, they feel. Their chords vibrate to every sound borne in to them. They share with St. Paul solicitude for those with whom they live: who is weak, he asked, and I am not weak: who is made a scandal, and I blush not? [29]

12

In every word of Fray Juan, the refinements of psychological analysis are quickened by being made personal: just as everything that is personal is refined by the study of philosophy.

[28] *Mount Carmel*, Prologue 4.
[29] II Cor. XII, 29.

But there is in these two treatises, in spite of their thorough searching of their own ground, one marked defect. They each end abruptly. At the beginning of *The Dark Night* Fray Juan said he would explain not merely the first two, but all the stanzas: nevertheless, he stops at the first two.

Why? The reasons surely are two. Firstly, he was wearied out with the struggles of the Reform, which were still uncertain in their issue; darkness and doubt still encompassed him. The second point is subtler: the doctrine of transcendence which he took from Dionysius was full of hidden splendours; but he could not make of transcendence alone a theme for his own joys. Dionysius had used his mysticism as a basis for sublime speculations on the Nature of God. These absorbed both the mystical and the poetical tastes of Fray Juan: they seemed to shine as revelations, but his own mind could not remain with ease on these heights of speculation. He was less oriental, more concrete, more exact—in a word, he was a Castilian. And, besides, he was a poet, with a poet's susceptibilities to passion and to beauty. There was to him something most dear and exquisite in the symbolism of the exterior world. Try as he might to put by the beautiful things he loved, and to worship the invisible alone, he was aware that he loved them still; they opened his secret raptures. That was the meaning—was it not?—of his *Song of the Spirit*.

And did not the Church draw him in the same direction? The Church insisted on reaching to human nature. Day after day, he said the Mass which brought him the presence of Christ, not as a transcendent mystery, but as immanent mystery, a presence in flesh and blood—a food he received himself and gave to others—Holy Communion.

For Fray Juan was not an oriental mystic: he was a Christian; not only a Christian, but a Catholic; not only a Catholic, but a Spaniard; not only a Spaniard, but a Carmelite, dedicated to the Madonna; he was not only a Carmelite, but a baroque writer, in the baroque period, the period of Titian, of Berruguete, of the Escorial, of El Greco, which was to lead to Montañés and Roldán; he was not only living his life among friars and nuns with all the loyalties and habits of a sacramental life of exterior observances, but also among poets and artists.

13

To tell the truth, both *The Ascent of Mount Carmel* and *The Dark Night,* masterly as they are, are incomplete. They take us to the walls of the garden: they hardly guide us in. "I do not now think of expounding all the breadth and plenteousness embodied in the fertile spirit of love," said San Juan himself about his *Song of the Spirit,* "for it would be ignorance to think that expressions of love which can be conveyed mystically, such as those of these stanzas, can be adequately explained by words of any kind." [30] Besides, he insisted that his written work was complementary to that already written by Santa Teresa.[31] If these things were true of *The Song of the Spirit,* they must be equally true of *The Dark Night.* The real secret, therefore, is in neither of these treatises.

Taken in themselves, they might even be a little dangerous: and it is, indeed, no wonder that they have depressed many good people who did not know the circumstances in which they are written, and who had not felt and guarded, as they read, the rapture of the poem, and its evocations of love and joy. The two first prose treatises are indeed works of great power and worth. But their full doctrine was not even attempted in prose till afterwards; and it had already been suggested, with all the mystery that music can convey, in the poems of which the treatises expound only one aspect.

Without first placing them in the personal history of Fray Juan, without always holding in mind the expression, *kindled with yearning love,* without concentrating firstly on the poems, and then awaiting his later treatises, we fail to understand his genius, and the reason why he has been named by the Church as a master, when the Church has not given that name to Dionysius, even at his most sublime, and seldom refers to Proclus with whom Dionysius shares whole chapters of his work.[32]

To the poetical mind of Fray Juan, God was never more transcendent than in His Immanence.

[30] Prologue I, 1.
[31] C.E. XII, 6; Allison Peers, II, 72.
[32] See F. Stiglmayer, *Proclus,* quoted by Dom C. Butler, *Western Mysticism.*

So shalt thou see and hear
The lovely shapes and sounds intelligible
Of that eternal language, which thy God
Utters, who from eternity doth teach
Himself in all, and all things in himself.
Great universal Teacher! he shall mould
Thy spirit, and by giving make it ask.[1]

I

IT was in the depth of his search for the symbolism of meadow, grove, or stream, in the significance of some image or design, in the viewless power of words, and above all in what these conveyed to a mysterious stillness of his own mind and spirit, that Juan de la Cruz found the path to the heavenly heights where he was filled to the utmost his nature could contain, and then enlarged that he might contain yet more.

In all his treatises one theme recurs. It is the excellence of the prayer of quiet. It is the need of the mind to rest in the Lord.

So ardent a mind as his, with its intense energy of analysis, its metaphysical subtlety, its sensitiveness to impression, its active imagination, and its responses to the urge and drive of passionate desire, was from time to time tired out: it often needed rest.

Such a rest is, of course, a necessity to the nervous system—for nervous systems have their own symptoms of exhaustion which react on the spiritual life; but also, as both Santa Teresa and San Juan insist again and again, in this very need of repose comes the sublimer favour. For it is in this time of quiet, where there is no discourse of reasoning, no use of memory, no play of imagination, no definite act even of the will, but a stilling of all in a vague general impression of loving confidence and confiding love, that the spirit begins to live with the more especial and peculiar grace which is not human but divine. An attitude of receptivity and passiveness is the seed-ground of mystical contemplation. In other words, the better way

[1] Coleridge, *Frost at Midnight.*

can never be learned except by those who have made effort enough,
or endured enough, to have their nerves tired out.

It is to explain this that San Juan wrote *The Ascent of Mount
Carmel*, and, though he does not mention it expressly in *The Dark
Night*, his whole treatment implies his desire to guide spiritual directors. But he returns to the subject once more in *The Song of the
Spirit;* and most distinctly of all, in his final treatise—*The Living
Flame of Love*—he breaks in on his rapturous account of the life of
blessing and joy in advanced contemplation—such as is known in
the sixth and seventh mansions of Santa Teresa—to inveigh at great
length, and with the utmost severity, against those priests who do
not know enough to welcome the prayer of quiet which is the very
essence of mysticism and the most direct of all the ways by which
man may enter into that mental communion with God, where the
soul is given completely into His hand for Him to mould according
to His own designs.

2

We saw that the two earlier treatises of San Juan are incomplete:
we must also admit that they are diffuse. They are actually marred
by repetition, and their style in general is cumbersome.[2] He writes
as a lecturer, or a teacher, who finds that to drive a point home, he
has to repeat it again and again; and when he has said it in one way,
then say it in another.[3] There is, says Fray Crisógono, a lack of
proportion and correspondence in the construction: tiresome repetition, occasional bathos, and sometimes in his efforts to attain the explanation of a doctrine, extreme verbosity.[4] His style is sometimes
for pages monotonously exclamatory. His phrasing can be careless,
and even incorrect.[5] The fact is that he was going over his ground
again and again, as a teacher does when he is trying to explain a
new and difficult subject. As a method of teaching, that is excellent;
but the standards are absolutely different when we assess the prose
of literature. Nevertheless, there are many sublime passages of great
richness and fervour; and there is an extraordinary strength in the

[2] *Works*, E. Allison Peers, I, 47.
[3] *Ibid.*
[4] Crisógono, II, 144, 145.
[5] *Ibid.*

skill with which the writer pursues his theme into its recesses. Like Burke, he could wind into his subject like a serpent. And at all times we can appreciate his high originality, and the poetical taste by which he anticipates Bunyan in always jewelling his work with gorgeous phrases from the Bible, especially from certain poetical books of the Old Testament: Jeremiah, Job, the Psalms, the Song of Songs, and Wisdom.[6] His one incessant subject of study was the Bible, and he knew an impressive amount of it by heart.[7]

3

But in the realm of literature his outstanding fame is not established by his prose: his masterpieces are always his lyrics. And to them we must always come back:

> "So sublime is his poetry," wrote the greatest of Spanish critics, Menéndez y Pelayo, "that it scarcely seems to belong to this world at all: it is hardly capable of being assessed by literary criteria. More ardent in its passion than any profane poetry, its form is as elegant and exquisite as any of the finest works of the Renaissance." [8]

Poetry, said Fray Juan himself in his Prologue to *The Song of the Spirit, has a greater power than reason.* The soul which has known the raptures of love, and the riches of its dream, knows more than any genius can express: poets know those groanings of the spirit within us which cannot be uttered. "And it is for this reason," says San Juan, "that, by means of figures, comparisons, and similitudes, they allow something of that which they feel to overflow and utter secret mysteries from the abundance of the spirit rather than explain those things rationally. These similitudes, if they be not read with the simplicity of the spirit of love and understanding embodied in them, appear to be nonsense rather than expressions of reason, as may be seen in the Divine *Songs of Solomon* and in other books of the Divine Scripture, where, since the Holy Spirit cannot express this abundance of his meaning in common and vulgar terms, he utters

---

[6] *Works,* E. Allison Peers, III, 459-464.
[7] *Ibid.,* I, xlii.
[8] *Ibid.,* I, xlviii.

mysteries in strange figures and similitudes. Whence it follows that no words of holy doctors, despite all they have said and yet may say, can ever expound these things fully, neither could they be expanded in words of any kind. *That which is expounded of them, therefore, is ordinarily the least part of that which they contain."* [9]

Let us, therefore, above all read and enjoy the poems. The indescribable communion which comes from song where music adds so much of its mystery to the pattern of words will teach us further "that love which comes from abounding mystical knowledge," under the influence of which these poems were composed.[10]

There is, then, much that a poetic admirer like M. Baruzi can add to all the expositions of the theologians. He can point to a region of rapture where the soul learns by admiring beauty; what the soul feels and knows, it can suggest rather than convey, for the mysteries it knows are infinite. "Let no one believe," said Fray Juan himself, "that this thing is not more than what can be expressed of it." He has opened a window on a garden stretching beyond all human sight in beauty after beauty: and "to learn the immediacy of the things of God, the only fit language is to hear and feel it for oneself, and to enjoy it and to be silent as to what it tells." [11]

Why is it that a song or a poem can convey what a prose treatise cannot convey of the deeper mysteries of the spirit? The answer is this: It is because when the soul is rapt in the contemplation of the eternal beauty, it admires both the splendour and the order of the universe. Beauty is in fact the delightful resplendence of a spiritual and intelligible perfection: *ordine di perfezione ammirata*—as Agosto Conti wrote in *Il Bello nel Vero*. And the spirit that enjoys this resplendence of the truth is stamped by and therefore mirrors it in the sense of order which the spirit enjoys, and which it conveys in composition, balance, harmony, or pattern. That is why Meredith set as a test for truth the question, "Is it accepted of song?" That is why St. Paul said that as we survey the mirror of perfection, we are changed from glory to glory as by the Spirit of the Lord.[12] That is what San Juan meant in *The Song of the Spirit,* when, talking of

---

[9] C.E., Prologue 1.
[10] *Ibid.*, 2.
[11] Baruzi, p. 366. The words are the *ipsissima verba* of the poet.
[12] II Cor. III, 18.

the eyes he longed to meet, he wrote: "I always crave and limn them in my dreams"; that is why Dante said of Beatrice: [13]

> *Negli occhi suoi ardeva un riso*
> *Tal ch'io pensai co' miei toccar lo fondo*
> *Della mia grazia et del mio Paradiso.*[14]

As a man in love floods his whole life with his romance, so the artist, the musician, and the poet, if seeking for true beauty, are impregnating with it the deepest processes of the mind: "In the fresh years," wrote Conti, "when the heart unfolds to unaccustomed feelings, and the eyes wander in desire from beauty to beauty, and a mysterious instinct runs from fancy to fancy, and from sigh to sigh, and the ears crave for song and sound, all these appearances of Nature, being gathered together in the mind and heart, suddenly reappear to us in dreams—inspired, alive, at once like our previous experience and new, in an image of beauty, in a love never seen or experienced, with its own inward light and undefined harmony, so that on awakening the soul longs for the vanished dream: and this inward power—which arose from inspiration and yet was spontaneous—is the same which inspires verses in the poets, and statues and pictures and buildings in the designer, and in the musicians immortal melodies." [15]

The words of Conti are reinforced by a Dominican scholar, who finds in his own experience a counterpart of the mystical intuitions of Plato.

"This summer evening, I gaze at a country scene. Some trees, a river, then the hill where the sheep are grazing. Not a sound: everywhere calm. And in this scene I am alone: it and I are alone together. I am familiar with all its details, I can describe them, or sketch their outlines. But, as a matter of fact, they do not interest me: I am not really looking at them. They compose the mirage which is before me; they are its elemental matter; but other is the image of beauty, and other what the eye of my soul admires. For what the inward eye admires is as it were an ideal image, within that discerned by the

[13] *Paradiso*, xv, 34-36.
[14] And such a smile was burning in her eyes
  That with my own I seemed to touch the depths
  Both of my grace and of my Paradise.
[15] *Il Bello nel Vero*, ch. v., para. 16.

nerves of sight. Here are the trees, the water, and a gentle green slope. I see them and I do not see them. I can say what they are, but beyond these objects—or better within them—I see another scene, distinct, eternal, of which there is only a sort of reflection. From the first awakening of interest, from the moment that, perceiving the image, I was aware of its beauty, this *double* ideal, which occupied my soul, has as it were absorbed the visible matter. And this inward gaze finally assimilates what I saw with the nerves of sight. My eyes are fixed on concrete things, but they travel further. They penetrate and pierce the object. And insomuch as still and silent I gaze, this double wakening as it were from a long sleep, arises and takes form to the inward eye, living with a new and mysterious life. The scene is invested with its soul; and this soul speaks to my soul. We are attuned to one another: we are in communion. It is in me, and I find myself again in it. And suddenly, at this contact, I am filled with the realization of a life of measureless expansion. The scene and I together share in this mysterious unity. We love one another. One same love unites me with these things and melts them into my being. We are bound together in kinship. And from this mutual love, from this reattained unity is born joy, which is the father of fullness, of harmony, of submission to a higher order which at the same time draws me out of myself and completes me. I am but a finite being; yet this sort of ecstasy which has rapt and delighted me in another finite being gives me for a few moments the intoxicating sense of the infinite. Peace, order, fullness—O fleeting joy and ecstasy in beauty!" [16]

It came, this high felicity, from an act of knowledge which gave the sense of a Presence, for contemplation did both. And what was the Presence but that of absolute Being, intuitively discerned? It was essential, delightful: it awakened love; and this admiring contemplation of something recognized as perfect and complete is the highest work of reasoning, for it becomes mystical and sublime. [17]

It is this experience to which San Juan was referring when he said at Beas of his verses: "Sometimes I searched for them: sometimes God gave them to me." [18]

[16] Festugière, *Contemplation selon Platon*, pp. 345-346.
[17] *Op. cit.*, p. 347.
[18] Bruno, p. 210.

4

Let us then enjoy a poem which he never expounded:

I know the fountain ever springs and flows
  Even now in the night's hush.

Eternal, it will ne'er its tale disclose.
Yet well its hidden depths my spirit knows,
  Even now in the night's hush.

Dim is our life and sad, one truly sayeth;
And yet joy's water spring I know by faith
  Even now in the night's hush.

Its origins I know not; who can know?
For from these origins all rivers flow
  Even now in the night's hush.

I know that nothing can have purer grace.
Both heaven and earth drink deep and haste their pace
  Even now in the night's hush.

Well know I that its deep no man can plumb—
To that profound abyss no spirits come,
  Even now in the night's hush.

Naught can obscure its sparkle diamond-bright,
Its gleaming brilliance from whence comes all light,
  Even now in the night's hush.

I know its streams life and refreshment tell
To skies, to peoples, to foul deeps of hell,
  Even now in the night's hush.

I know besides that still a new stream flows,
Brimming almightiness, whence those waters rose
  Even now in the night's hush.

And from these mingling floods, I know another flow
Proceeds. Did those precede it then? Ah no!
  Even now in the night's hush.

So these three streams flow their eternal course
Unrivalling and mutual in their force,
  Even now in the night's hush.

The eternal tide flows hid in living bread
That with its heavenly life we too be fed
  Even now in the night's hush.

And here it calls to all: and here we will
Our craving voids mysteriously fill
Even now in the night's hush.

This living stream for which I thirst and long
Provides my sup, my surety and my song
Even now in the night's hush.[19]

It is impossible to read such a poem without taking wings for the
flight of contemplation by which the faith and hope of the poet raised
themselves in his Catholic life, and as a worshipper fed on Christ in
his heart by faith with thanksgiving.

5

This in fact leads to a paradox. The object of San Juan de la Cruz
is to do away with meditation and lead the soul where it gives over
its action in a wise passiveness to the operation of a power other than
its own. *"In this state,"* says Fray Juan, *"the soul can perform no acts
but it is the Holy Spirit that moves it to perform them."* [20] His object is to lead men inward to the most sacred mystery of their being,
to the centre of the soul, for "the centre of the soul is God." [21] Now
the more the soul approaches these inward and spiritual graces of the
life God has given it, the more it moves from the discourse and
analysis of reason. All the processes of the mind are accompanied by
another sense, another quality of living.[22] Even though the mind is
busy, its impulsions and its secret are in a quiet communion when it
knows, in a way that is dim to consciousness, and yet that is fixed
with an authority of conviction which it regards as sovereign, that
it is sustained by this communion: for the communion is a sharing
with a power, with a wisdom, with a love that are all one, as the
Three in One are God.

Mystical writers insist that, above the highest work of the discursive reason, even when it is raised above itself by the grace of faith,
there is another faculty—united to the rest of man's being, though
above it—a depth or a peak, said Louis de Blois, which is more inti-

[19] For a more literal rendering see the beautiful translation by Professor Allison Peers,
Works, II, 454, 455. For original see p. 235.
[20] *Living Flame*, I, 4.
[21] *Ibid.*, I, 12.
[22] Cf. H. Bremond, *Prière et Poésie*, XII.

mate and more sublime than our three highest faculties, for it is there these three faculties originate. "There reigns an absolute tranquility in the deepest silence, for no image can penetrate there. There dwells in hiding the Divine presence.—A Paradise, the Kingdom of God, which is God Himself within us.—A bare and shapeless abyss, beyond time and space, its *raison d'être* being a certain perpetual adhesion to God and yet it is essentially within us, it is us, the very essence of our soul." [23] In this mystical temple of the mind, says St. Francis de Sales, "there are three partitions which are three different degrees of reason. In the first, we discourse according to the experience of sense, in the second according to humane sciences, in the third according to faith; but beyond all this we discover a certain height, or highest point of reason, and the spiritual faculty, which is not guided by the light of discourse or reason, but by a simple view of the understanding and a simple touch of the will, by which the soul yields and submits herself to truth and the will of God." [24]

To this "selfless self of self most strange, most still," fast furled beyond gauge or guess, the soul owes the intense and rapt communion of mystical theology.

The more a life has experience of this communion, the clearer becomes its view that, though the communion can sustain and inspire thought, yet it is not thought. In it all thought, even the thought about God, seems to be exchanged for a more direct, a more intuitive knowledge: faith vanishes into darkness, a darkness lit by fires. And so, too, with memory and hope, for all that can be recalled and all that can be desired seem to be found, and are found, in a life which fills the whole capacity of desire, as it does of knowledge: hope, therefore, is fulfilled in this sense of immediacy, of timeless being. As San Juan puts it: "When the soul has attained to Him according to the whole capacity of its being, and according to the force of its operation, it will have reached the last and deep centre of the soul which will be when with all its powers it loves and understands and enjoys God." [25] Understanding completes the work of faith: enjoyment satisfies the flights and eagerness of hope: both of these are merged in another activity in "the love which unites the soul to

---

[23] Quoted by H. Bremond, *Prayer and Poetry* (Eng. trans.), pp. 110-111.
[24] *Traité de l'Amour de Dieu*, Book I, ch. xii, para. 2. Cf. Dionysius, quoted on p. 65.
[25] *Living Flame*, I, 12.

God," [26] because love above all renders us like Him. It is the entry into Christ, who is the Way and the Life.

6

But we are still enquiring how this new act to move inwards, to strip oneself of created things, and to forego all intercourse with them can be not merely combined with the passion and beauty of the poet, but better expressed in the sensuous images of poetry than in the discourses of the theologian. With magisterial precision San Juan answers us in a great passage of *Song of the Spirit*. He shows there that when the mystic race is finished, and a man attains to the wisdom which sees all things in God, he learns how God is in all things; and then all that was lost is found. Most people build up their knowledge of God by what He has created:

> and by those hid ascents climb up to Thee
> Who art in all things, though invisibly.

But the mystic, if by cultivating his gift of abstraction he communes with the transcendence merged in the deepest centre of the soul, can learn about creation more directly from God Himself; for in Him and with Him and through Him are all things.

While the outward world hints and stammers what He is, the soul, therefore, rapt into still communion, which transcends the imperfect offices of prayer and praise, understands them all in Him, and sees, therefore, how He is in them. Both by searching God through creation and looking to creation from the heart of God can we come to wisdom; but Fray Juan insists that the way of interior prayer is the better and clearer. "For when by this essential love, the soul is commingled with the Ineffable and so awakens to glory, although it is true that the soul is now able to see that these things are distinct from God, inasmuch as they have a created being, and it sees them in Him, with their force, root and strength, it knows equally that God, in His own Being, is all these things, in an infinite and pre-eminent way, to such a point that it understands them better in His Being than in themselves. And this is the great delight of this awakening: to know the creatures through God and not God through

[26] *Ibid.*

the creatures: to know the effects through their cause and not the cause through the effects: for the latter knowledge is secondary, and this other is essential." [27]

7

"But God, as the soul is enabled to see, is always moving, ruling, and giving to all creatures being and virtue and graces and gifts, containing them all in Himself, by His power, by His presence and by their partaking in His reality. So that in one single glance the soul sees that which God is in Himself, and that which He is in the creatures. Even so, when a palace is thrown open, a man may see at one and the same time the eminence of the person who is within the palace and also what he is doing. And it is this, as I understand it, that happens in this awakening and glance of the soul. Though the soul shares the reality of God, as does every creature, *He draws back from before it some of the veils and curtains which are in front of it, so that it may see of what nature He is, and then there is revealed to it and it is able to see (though somewhat darkly, since not all the veils are drawn back) His countenance full of graces and beauties.*" [28]

At last the process is explained: God moves all things gently and according to their nature; and at times He gives flashes of His beauty through a sense of inward communion; and the more this power of communion is developed, the more will be seen. So that there are always two ways to the secret of the universe, the way which adores His transcendence and the way which cherishes His immanence. But these two ways interchange and intermingle as the universe exhibits a double movement, downward from God and upward towards Him, for all things are returning to prefection through Him from whom they took their origin. [29]

The poet, therefore, who gives in music and beauty a hint of his delight in the perfection he has found, will always best convey the power of communion. Literature is not merely a decorative accompaniment to worship: it can be a spontaneous revelation of the mystery by which created things are a living, visible garment of God; and

[27] C.E. IV, 5; Allison Peers, III, 209.
[28] C.E. IV, 7; Allison Peers, III, 210.
[29] *Living Flame*, IV, 7. Cf. Collect for Easter Even in the Roman Missal.

everything, if looked at rightly, is but a symbol, and therefore a disclosure, of things unseen, and of the underlying reality which is the mind of God.

8

Nowhere is this doctrine so clear as in San Juan de la Cruz; his thorough philosophical training was combined with an analytical psychology, which traced the process of knowledge to that region where images are perceived and felt: he had his peculiar power over this region of the memory and feeling of images, so that he could make certain words peculiarly evocative.

All these things were one with the passion of his temperament, and his experience of love as a violent magnetism, first of desire,

> If I see not thee,
> What use have eyes?

and then of rapture

> O night which to the side
> Of lover brought his bride,
> And then didst make them one.

He was not afraid of passion: he had learnt from the *Song of Songs* to welcome it: he was still more familiar with it in the works of Boscán and Garcilaso, and though he did not accept the contention of Luis de León that *The Song of Songs* was a human drama, yet its imagery was constantly affecting him to reinforce all the instincts of his own prodigal temperament.

The crude Freudian would say that this passion for the unseen lover was but an ebullition or at best a sublimation of the carnal in his nature: San Juan had anticipated that contention; for he actually says that men who live by the impulses of physical sex will assess all motives accordingly.[30] But the Freudian explanation is soon refuted by the technical treatises: they make it perfectly clear how the flesh of the mystic was subdued to the spirit: his impulses of love were both ordered and exalted. As San Juan himself says, "all the harmony and ability which the body gives to man's human nature

[30] *Living Flame,* IV, 8.

served him for greater recreation and as a help towards a knowledge
and love of God in peace and concord with his higher part." [31] There,
in the inward man, the ways of human love are outdone. In this
inward communion in the hidden part of the soul, God, as the Very
Being of Love, assails the faculties with His glory and greatness so
loftily that the human side of the mind no longer understands, and
the spirit "soars aloft through high and noble knowledge and through
excesses of love most strange and singular." [32] In this high and noble
knowledge, theology enabled San Juan to be particularly clear and
precise.

God's scheme is a hierarchy, for all things in the world are related
to God in Christ, Who in His Incarnation exalts them all with Himself: the creatures, says San Juan, are as it were traces of the passing
of God, for in them He has left pointers to His greatness, power,
wisdom, and other perfections. But the creatures are the *lesser* works
of God, Who made them as it were *in passing*.[33] *The greater works*,
wherein He revealed Himself most clearly and to which He paid
most heed, are those of the Incarnation of the Word and the other
mysteries of the Christian faith. Now, according to the faith, God
and Man in the Incarnation are one Christ, not by conversion of the
Being of God into flesh, but by taking the nature of man into the
Divine.[34] As Fray Juan read day by day in the Missal, God, Who
had marvellously formed the nature of man, by ways yet more
marvellous had redeemed it that man should be a partaker of the
dominion and the glory of God.[35] But, since man is within the realm
of nature, and mirrors the realm of nature in his mind, and thus
assimilates it, therefore, when Christ accepted human nature into His
own, He raised all creation to take its part in his Divineness. In the
words of San Juan, in uniting Himself with man, He united Himself
with the nature of them all. This is expounded with precision in *The
Song of the Spirit:* " 'The Son of God is the brightness of his glory
and the express image of his substance.' It must be known, then, that
God looked at all things in this image of His Son alone, which was
to give them their natural being, to communicate to them many nat-

---

[31] C.E. XXXII, 5; Allison Peers, II, 154.
[32] C.E. XXXII, 1; Allison Peers, II, 156.
[33] C.E. V, 3; Allison Peers, II, 49.
[34] Athanasian Creed.
[35] Roman Missal, Offertory prayer.

ural gifts and graces and to make them finished and perfect, as He says in *Genesis* in these words: 'God saw all the things that He had made, and they were very good.' To behold them and find them very good was to make them very good in the Word His Son. And not only did He communicate them their being and their natural beauties when He beheld them, but also in this image of His Son alone He left them clothed with beauty, *communicating to them supernatural being.*" [36] This was when He became man, for when He thus exalted man into the beauty of God, and in uniting Himself with man He united Himself with the nature of all creatures, He consequently exalted them all into His Being and Glory. "And therefore this same Son of God said: *'I, if I be lifted up from the earth, will draw all things unto me.'* And thus in this lifting up through the Incarnation of His Son and in the glory of His resurrection according to the flesh, not only did the Father beautify the creation in part, but He can say He left them all clothed with dignity and beauty." [37]

9

So much was Catholic philosophy: it was the logical conclusion to belief in the Incarnation and Ascension of the mysterious Second Person of the Infinite Trinity. But to this corollary mysticism immediately added something more. It added a revelation of God in nature by the communion of loving admiration of the excellence of creation. As San Juan said: "After all the philosophical doctrine, I will go on and speak rather with the heart and faculties of a mystic: in the vivid contemplation and knowledge of the creatures, the soul sees with great clearness that there is in them such an abundance of graces and powers and beauty, with which God has endowed them, that, as it seems to the soul, they are all clothed with marvellous natural beauty, derived from and communicated by that infinite supernatural beauty of the image of God, whose beholding of Him clothes the world and the heavens with beauty and joy, just as does also the opening of His hand: *Thou openest thy hand and fillest all things living with blessing.* And therefore the soul, being wounded in love

[36] Allison Peers, *Works,* II, 50; C.E. V, 3.
[37] *Ibid.*

by this trace of the beauty of her Beloved which she has known in His creatures, yearns to behold the invisible beauty." [38]

This passage explains with perfect precision both the mysticism of nature and the mysticism of love. It harmonizes Juan de la Cruz with Donne, with Vaughan, with Traherne, with Wordsworth, with Coleridge. But none of them ever approached such masterly precision.

That in the words which have both the rhythm of music and the pattern of art mysticism may be turned to poetry, so much we have known. It needed a poet's combination of mysticism with theology to make the Christian reasons for it clear and distinct.

For when the poet looks back at the created world, how beautiful it has become: on the way thither it had been mere ugliness in comparison with that end on which his gaze was fixed, the infinite beauty of God.[39] This was what the saint wrote in *The Ascent of Mount Carmel*. But in *The Song of the Spirit*, which is the outpouring of his heart when it has arrived at union, he says that "all created things are lovely . . . they are crumbs that fall from God's table." [40] We cannot find a better statement of his doctrine than that of the young Carmelite of Ávila who has recently given us the most searching of all studies of St. John of the Cross: "Applying to beauty that double process of perception so peculiar to mystics from the Middle Ages on," writes Fray Crisógono, "he teaches us to discern the infinite beauty through its dim reflection in that which is created, and to discover the charm of natural beauty by the light of the infinite beauty, so that we remain with our eyes fixed upon that primal glory." [41]

In the saint's own words, the soul of the mystic is "pierced with love for the countenance which it has recognized in beautiful creations, longing to see that beauty which has made them." If once the veil of nature seemed ugly, now it is pierced by the brightness of the scene which the soul had seen behind it and now sees through it. The mystic now becomes a poet: he sees nature with an eye of rapturous vision which identifies its impression on the sense with what St. Augustine had called the intellectual light which gives to all things

---

[38] C.E. V, 5; Allison Peers, II, 50, 51, quoting Psalm CXLIV, 17 (Vulgate).

[39] M.C. I, ii, 4.

[40] C.E. V, 2.

[41] Translated from Crisógono, *San Juan de la Cruz*, II, 49.

their intelligible splendour. The poet tells of the rapture which, in a fitting gleam of vision, had rejoiced and rested him, but which finally becomes the inalienable possession of the mystic. It is in this state, "with the soul filled with pure sentiments awakened by the beauty it has contemplated, with the heart and the imagination steeped in the light which has vibrated through them from that beauty, that the intelligence rises to concepts which are sublime: it thinks without effort, and its ideas flow serene and mild as from a hidden well. The moment of artistic creation has arrived. If the mystic writes or speaks —and fain he almost must—he will express concepts of exceeding beauty, striving to robe them in that beauteous light in which his own soul is steeped. His work will be to create, for it will be to reproduce the beauty of his spirit." [42]

This is what San Juan de la Cruz does in his poems, even in his prose, but above all in the *Song of the Spirit*. As in the *Dark Night*, he had emphasized the spirit of detachment which is the inner and less beautiful part of the spiritual system (for the foundation is naturally less beautiful than the edifice raised upon it), so in the *Song of the Spirit* we trace the mystic way anew from the point at which the symbol is irradiated by the beauty which it veiled.[43]

> Mi Amado, las montañas,
> Los valles solitarios nemorosos,
> Las ínsulas extrañas,
> Los ríos sonorosos,
> El silbo de los aires amorosos.
>
> La noche sosegada
> En par de los levantes de la aurora,
> La música callada,
> La soledad sonora,
> La cena, que recrea y enamora.[44]

[42] Crisógono, *San Juan de la Cruz*, II, 43.
[43] *Ibid.*, II, 46, 47.
[44] The mountains high and fair,
  The lonely vale and grove,
  The sounding streams, the islets scattered there,
  The murmuring amorous breezes of the air,
  These are to me my love.

  The night still and serene,
  Dawn with its wings of hue and sheen,
  The desert's sounding chord
  Like air that trembles still where music's been—
  With these I feast on love. They are God's board.

An alternative translation by the writer.

Each creature to the view of the mystical poet has its peculiar gifts: each sings his own tune of praise. The soul which, in the tranquil wisdom of holiness, is disposed to admire all things, not only those which are above but also those which are below, to the degree that each has within it what it has received of God, hears from each its own musical witness of what He is.

When the eyes of the saint rested upon a stream or river (and he rejoiced especially on summer nights to see the water mirror stars) he would lift up his heart in fervour, and fresh fancies would decorate his praise.

Although San Juan de la Cruz writes of nature in the tone of the Platonists, he definitely accepts Aristotle's theory that the soul learns what it knows by the traffic of the senses with outward things. This Thomistic doctrine was elaborated by John Bacon, who, as we saw, was also a Carmelite and whose theory St. John of the Cross certainly studied. He departs in no way from the Aristotelian or the Thomistic theories of knowledge: they insist that there are three stages of reality: the exemplar idea in the mind of God; the concrete thing which expresses this idea in outward form; and the concept of it in the perceiving mind. And the relation between these three was made clear when St. Thomas developed the theory of Aristotle; his philosophy survived in Salamanca when most of Europe gave way to Renaissance Platonism on the one side, and, on the other, into acceptance of the outward thing as final.

But the great mystic of the Spanish Renaissance was subtle enough to take advantage of the medieval theory. In his theory of knowledge he showed that first the exterior senses perceive the material object: an image is formed in the inner physical faculties; and then, while the faculties are working upon this image, there is an inner reaction on the passive spiritual faculties of the intelligence.[45] Here is the link between mind and body—for the imagination can recall a sensible

[45] *El processo del humano conocimiento, según San Juan de la Cruz, és el siguiente: percepción del objeto material por los sentidos exteriores: formación del fantasma en los potencias corporales o orgánicas interiores: actuación del entendimiento agente sobre el fantasma sensitivo, y formal intelección por el entendimiento pasivo. Luego, queda la imagen de la cosa entendida, imagen espiritual en la memoria intelectiva, y sensible en la fantasia.* Crisógono, *San Juan de la Cruz,* I, 90, 91. The argument is based on the *Subida,* ch. iii, p. 42; ch. xi, pp. 145-147. *Cantico: canc.* 38, v, 4, p. 365; *canc.* 14, v, 5, p. 240. *Subida,* ch. xii, p. 304; ch. vi, p. 389; Edition of Silverio. The whole subject is subtly discussed in Book I, ch. ii, of *San Juan de la Cruz,* by Crisógono.

perception, while in the intellect there remains an essential knowledge. Imagination, in other words, is the medium of knowledge as it is of creation.

This fact—so important to the understanding, and therefore to the criticism of art—is made still more significant by San Juan's clear statement of the relation between the informing idea and the shape of things in the exterior world. In the psychology of man there is so subtle an interrelation between body and mind in imagination that it is clear there is a terrain on which they meet, a secret and delicate sense, an energy or an ether which is neither purely physical nor purely intellectual, but something between the two; [46] so, in the exterior world, between the intelligible reality which Aristotelians call the form and between the sensible and subsidiary reality which we call the form in modern language, there is a common energy where act meets potentiality. By this double mediation the mind of man habitually communes with the reality of which creation is the symbol.

But if, by a process of detachment from sensible satisfaction, man learns to commune direct between his own heart and the heart of reality, he sees beyond the sign to what it signifies: all is made more spiritual, and therefore more intense in beauty. Intuition enables a soul to contemplate true reality in each single creation, and can add to eye or ear or touch its own delicacy of appreciation. All are familiar with what temperament adds to creative work, but not all know what spiritual insight gives by deeper knowledge of a latent perfectness. Temperament merges into insight as creative work ascends to the fuller revelation of beauty.

There is, therefore, between the mystic and the creator, which includes the poet, a close kinship. Each has the gift of being absorbed in an admiring contemplation; each thirsts and longs to know that which he admires; each does this with such effort that spells of acute exhaustion, sometimes prolonged, seem to dull and deaden his faculties. But each has the power to see so intellectually that the impressions of his sense are as one with intuitive vision. In this intuitive vision, the knower mingles with the known. His heart and will are so absorbed in his act of contemplation that the knowledge and the

[46] A learned Dominican so explains the word *Psyche*. See A.-J. Festugière, O.P., *L'Idéal Religieux des Grecs*, Excursus B.

symbol which expresses it concentrate heart and mind together in an act of admiration which is joy and love. For this act becomes a means of union between two distinct lives, two distinct realities.[47]

What develops the human lover into the lover of beauty is a peculiar attitude of heart, mind, will, and body to react in the pursuit of an ideal object. The distinction between the lover as mystic and the lover as artist is that the one aims at the soul's immediate communion with the beauty he loves, and the other concentrates on appreciation of the symbol, or in creation through a patterned representation of the scene or event or truth which was symbolic. But, since it is the nature of all good symbols to share something with what they signify, so the symbol, when it is contemplated with the lover's whole attention, draws him to communion with the reality it signifies.

> What thing long contemplated, alters not
> Its seeming substance, as the deepening mind
> By contemplation passes out of thought
> Immenser worlds to find? [48]

In like manner the mystic, even though on his path he denies attention to symbols, so that he may be wholly given to the love which meets him in the depths of the soul and transforms him into the being he loves, yet finds that the spiritual and uncreated love with which in those depths he is united, far from cutting him off from joy in created things, reveals them to him as he proceeds further in the intenser beauty which shines behind and through them.

For alike in the innermost heaven and in the human heart, and in the presences of living things innumerable, there flies and nests a bird-like spirit, a spirit of electrical and magnetic sympathies felt in the blood and felt along the heart, a spirit subtle and generous as love; because this spirit *is* love; and love's voice is song; and the delight of love's eyes is in beauty. Love, drawing from this spirit the secret of both form and intuition and joining them in the imagination, sees them joined also in the life and changes of a nature which, meaning a process of generation, means also a process of love, and contains the secret of the universe:

[47] For a fuller treatment of this subject, see Crisógono, *San Juan de la Cruz,* II, ch. i.
[48] Laurence Binyon.

And for all this, nature is never spent;
There lives the dearest freshness deep down things;
And though the last lights off the black West went
Oh, morning, at the brown brink eastward, springs—
Because the Holy Ghost over the bent
World broods with warm breast and with ah! bright wings.

O Strength and Stay upholding all creation,
    Who ever dost Thyself unmoved abide,
Yet day by day the light in due gradation
    Dost still through all its changing courses guide.

Grant to life's day a calm unclouded ending,
    An eve untouched by shadows of decay,
The brightness of a holy death-bed blending
    With dawning glories of the eternal day.

Grant this, O Father, gracious and forgiving,
    Through Jesus Christ, Thy Coeternal Word,
Who with the Holy Ghost by all things living
    Now and to endless ages art adored.[1]

Each moment call from earth away
My soul that lowly waits Thy call.
Speak to my inmost soul and say
I am thy love, thy God, thy all.
To do Thy will, to hear Thy voice,
To taste Thy love, be all my choice.[2]

I

THE life of Fray Juan de la Cruz at Baeza had been full, but not exhausting. He had his friars to train and govern, he had to mix with the life of the University. In 1580 an epidemic swept over Europe: its symptoms were a painful cough and fever. It was to kill his mother at Ávila. Attacking all Spain, it reached Baeza, and made the Carmelite College into a hospital, such as that in Medina in which Fray Juan had laboured as a boy. And here he renewed the old solicitudes, while the kindly townspeople provided mattresses for the friars, who till then had slept on bare boards.

[1] Translation of the ancient hymn, *Deus Rerum Tenax Vigor*.
[2] From a hymn of G. Tersteegen, translated by John Wesley.

Stories of the solicitude and gaiety of the Prior gathered. Once at Christmas he was seen dancing as he dandled an image of the Holy Child. He heard the confessions of many simple people. He was often in ecstasy, and when he could he said his Mass in honour of the Blessed Trinity; for he said there is none holier in heaven. It led him to the summit of contemplation.

It was from such a life as this that he was called back to the cold spring of Castile to attend at Alcalá the first chapter of the Reform, the chapter which resulted from Roca obtaining in Rome the Papal Brief. The chapter opened on March 3, 1581. The expenses for it were paid out of the Royal Treasury. It was attended by the Conde de Tendilla. Fray Juan was appointed Definitor for Andalusia, under a Superior, Fray Diego. And then there came the voting for who was to be the Provincial of the order. The rivalry was between old Fray Antonio de Heredia and the brilliant young Gracián. With a majority of one, Gracián was confirmed in the position which Madre Teresa had designed for him.

Great rejoicing marked this definite establishment of the Reform. There were debates, there was a solemn Mass, there was a sermon by Gracián. So passed the Sunday. "On the Monday following," relates Mrs. Cunninghame Graham, "it was unanimously decreed by the chapter to offer up perpetual prayer for the Catholic King; some of the weekly scourgings in community were to be devoted to the same purpose." [3] On March 13 the Constitutions were finally drawn up according to Teresa's direction. Her joy overflowed. It all seemed like a wonderful dream. "However much we had wished it, we could never succeed in doing it so well as God has done it." [4]

2

Yet a few days later, her motherly heart was thinking of the friar who had suffered and whom she loved so much. Teresa was growing old. What greater treat than now to see him once more after those four years of separation? "I forgot," she wrote on March 23 to Gracián, "to ask you for my Easter cake. May God grant that you will hear my request. I must tell you that I had once to console Fray

[3] Cunninghame Graham, II, 316.
[4] Loc. cit.

Juan de la Cruz at the grief he felt when he found himself in Andalusia: he cannot abide the people there. I told him that if it would please God to give us a separate province I would plead to have him brought back to Castile. Now, he begs me to keep my word: he is afraid of being elected Prior of Baeza, and warns me that he will beg you not to confirm the election. It would be only reasonable to give him this consolation—provided it is in your power—for he has suffered enough." [5]

But the Reverend Mother did not get her Easter cake. Fray Juan not only languished for Teresa and his native air: he was not only anxious to avoid being elected Prior of Baeza. His poetic mind preferred to be freed from all the responsibilities and cares for banal things which always come with administration. But he was not allowed to be near Teresa. He had been sent eastwards to Caravaca to inaugurate a new community there. And when he came back to Baeza he felt very lonely. On July 6, 1581, he wrote from there to a Prioress in Castile, Madre Catalina de Jesús. It began with his accustomed greeting:

"Jesus be in your soul, my daughter Catalina. Although I know not where you are, I desire to write you these lines, trusting that your Mother will send them on to you if you are not with her; and, if you are not with her, be comforted with me, for I am in exile farther away still, and am alone down here; for since I was swallowed by the whale and cast up in this strange fashion, I have not been found worthy to see you again, nor the Saints that are up yonder. God has done all things well, for, after all, desolation is a file, and the endurance of darkness is preparation for great light.

"God grant that we walk not in darkness. Oh how many things I should like to say to you. But I write in complete darkness, realizing that you may not receive this letter: so I break off without ending it. Commend me to God." [6]

His longing once more to see Ávila and Santa Teresa was, however, not denied. It had been suggested that a house of nuns should

[5] Bruno, p. 230.
[6] Allison Peers, *Works*, III, 264-265.

be founded at Granada, and after it was proposed to Madre Ana de Jesús at Beas, it was decided that Fray Juan should go to Ávila and beg Teresa herself to come to Granada. So once more, after five years of separation, once more, and for the last time, the two friends met. Teresa felt she must go to Burgos. She could not come south again: there she could safely leave things to her favourite Ana. "Wherever she is," said Teresa, "I am not required, for I know that she will act with more intelligence than I." [7] But she had once more felt lonely at Ávila, and the visit of the friar she loved was the greatest consolation. "As it is natural to wish to have one's love returned, it cannot be wrong," she wrote a few days later, "because Our Lord also wants His love returned." [8]

Yet she had been her old self in those last days: on one occasion Teresa, making her confession to Fray Juan, had told him that the affection she felt for him had affected her formal attitude of respect to him. Juan, with an air of assumed gravity, said as soon as she had finished speaking: "You should correct that, my daughter." Teresa had been delighted to tell this story to her nuns. [9] This charming interchange of respect and intimacy was now renewed. At one time they were as they talked together like seraphim, afire for the Majesty of God; at others, when he spoke of our Mother, she made the playful answer, "Father, why do you not call me 'My daughter'?" [10]

3

It was the last year of Teresa's life. Her work was done. She did go that autumn to Burgos: she saw the gateway, the towers, the spires which give such a gorgeous outline to the city of the Cid Campeador as one looks at it across the river Arlanzón. She may have visited its churches: she must surely have surveyed the glooms and glories of the great Gothic cathedral, and visited the neighbouring convents of Miraflores and Las Huelgas—and then back through Placencia to Ávila.

At Ávila she had disquieting news from Andalusia. Her favourite,

[7] Bruno, p. 234.
[8] Ibid., p. 232.
[9] Ibid., p. 485.
[10] Ibid., p. 232.

Madre Ana, had gone from Beas to Granada to found a new house there. Teresa had already noticed that this gifted mystic, whom she so generously praised, had an itch for command, which made her act without consulting either the founders or the council. She had taken it ill that Gracián had addressed her as president, not as prioress. Of her own free will, she had gone off to Granada, with her favourite nuns as her own companions there, and sent back to Beas those who had come to meet her. Teresa, when she heard this, was very angry indeed, and she decided to send a letter that would bring Ana to her senses. "In the same way as you sent those poor women back so many leagues, when they had barely arrived (for I don't know how you had the heart to do it) you might also have sent back those who came from Beas, and even others along with those; for your having been so wrong has been a terrible discourtesy, especially when you felt you were giving trouble. . . . *Nothing is to be gained by founding new monasteries unless those who live in them lead holy lives.*

"Any kind of attachment, even though it be to their prioress, is utterly against the spirit of the Barefoot Carmelites, and checks all improvement in the spiritual life. . . . It is the beginning of factions and rivalry and of many other calamities, if it is not checked at the commencement; for this once at least for mercy's sake be guided by me; and afterwards, when you are more settled and they more detached, may have them back again if you think fit. Truly I know not who they were, for with great secrecy you kept it from me and our father,[11] nor did I think your reverence would take so many thence, but I imagine that they are the most strongly drawn to your reverence.

"I beseech you, reverend Mother, to consider that you are bringing up souls for brides of the Crucified, and that you crucify them in rooting out your will and putting an end to these childishnesses. Consider that you are carrying the order into a new kingdom and that your reverence and the rest are obliged to act with the courage of men and not with the weakness of women. What matters it, my Mother, whether the Provincial calls you president or prioress or Ana de Jesús?

"Of a truth, I have been greatly put to the blush that after so

11 Gracián.

long my reformed nuns should pay attention to these mean and paltry things." [12]

Yet Ana had lapsed so little from grace that, instead of at once destroying this letter, she preserved it for record and for history.

4

More pressing anxieties disturbed Teresa from another quarter. Gracián had neither the astuteness, the wariness, nor the strong inflexibility required for a Spaniard in a position of power. His authority was being undermined by a Genoese whom he had received a few years before into the order at Seville. This man had the name of Nicolao Doria. Disloyally, Doria listened to complaints, disloyally he promulgated criticisms. For Doria had all the ruthlessness and unscrupulousness which certain people have in mind when they talk of "a strong man."

Teresa noted a few months before her death that he was insisting that everything should be carried out according to his own way of looking at things: [13] she was again pained and shocked; she knew that Gracián was too conciliatory to opposing factions; "do not think of making yourself an Andalusian," she wrote once, "for you are not of the temperament to deal with them," but Doria's lack of scruple shocked her. "I do not understand some kinds of sanctity," she wrote in warning to Gracián. "I say this for him who does not write to you; and the other who wishes everything to be done as he thinks fit, has tempted me. Oh, Jesus: how little there is perfect in this life!"

There was yet one more journey for Teresa over the roads of Castile. At Alba de Tormes was the Duchess of Alba, who was such a powerful and helpful friend, and was now expecting another baby: and here too was old Fray Antonio, and a convent which needed the eye of the Foundress. But she had hardly arrived in Alba in the autumn of 1582 when she was taken ill. "God help me, my daughter," she said, "how tired I feel: it is more than twenty years since I went to bed so early." [14]

---

[12] Cunninghame Graham, II, 369-370.
[13] Bruno, pp. 285, 286.
[14] Cunninghame Graham, II, 378.

When on the journey thither she had heard that evening from a messenger that the Duchess of Alba had already been delivered of the baby she was expecting, Teresa had made a characteristic comment, "Thank God, there will no longer be any need for this saint." When the Duchess, recovering, came to visit her, Teresa was disturbed to find that they had spilt on her bed-clothes some oil with a nasty smell. She tried to have the offence covered up; but no, the Duchess would have the bed-clothes drawn up to their proper place, and as she did so found the smell delicious.[15]

A little later they brought Holy Communion to Madre Teresa. Those watching her, as they did so, saw her face change and light up with a majestic and resplendent lustre; her age no longer withered her: her features grew as serene and smooth as in her girlhood. Then her consciousness began to fade. "After all, Lord," she said again and again, "I am a daughter of the Church." She asked forgiveness for her sins, hoping to be saved through the Blood of Jesus Christ. And then she recited the *Miserere:* "Make clean my heart within me and take not Thy Holy Spirit from me: the sacrifices of God are a troubled spirit: a contrite and a broken heart, O God, thou wilt not despise."

Cor contritum et humiliatum: those were the other words she kept repeating: but towards evening on October 4 her face suddenly took on a more brilliant splendour and beauty; then, in a last aspiration of love, her soul took flight.[16]

5

At that same moment, Ana de Jesús in Granada found beside her a nun whose face was so glorious that she could not discern whose it was. "Surely I know this nun," she said to herself as the presence, coming nearer, grew so dazzling that she could see no more. Many of Teresa's monks and friars had a like vision that night. "We here in heaven," said the vision to one of these, "and you there on earth must be one in love and purity—we above beholding the Being of God, and you on earth adoring the Most Holy Sacrament." [17]

Such is the woman whom the Nuncio denounced, the Church

[15] *Ibid.*
[16] *Ibid.,* 381.
[17] *Ibid.,* 382.

canonized, and Spain took with Santiago as her patron saint. Nor did
they disdain to offer her the honours of profane life. It was natural
enough that the University of Salamanca should give a doctorate to
a writer so enchantingly Spanish in her mixture of ease and distinction. But we must be prepared for the fact that she is also a colonel
of artillery. And not far from her first convent in Ávila, the butchers
have named her patron of their slaughter-house.[18]

[18] *El matadero de Santa Teresa.*

A VIEW OF THE ALHAMBRA AT GRANADA
From a drawing by J. F. Lewis, R.A.

Thy saints in holy lustre round Thee move,
Like stars about Thy throne set in the height
Of God's ordaining counsel, as Thy might
Gives measured grace to each, Thy power to prove.

Let Thy bright beams disperse the night of sin.
Our natures all shall feel eternal day
In fellowship with Thee, transforming day
To souls erewhile unclean, now pure within.[1]

I

IT was early in that same year of 1582 that Fray Juan de la Cruz had been elected Prior of Los Mártires in Granada and followed Madre Ana thither. He found his new home in one of the most famous and the most beautiful scenes in Spain. Los Mártires was on a height above the city, close to the romantic lines of the Alhambra. It enjoyed a delightful view over the Vega with its shining rivers, the Darro and the Genil, its orchards, its vineyards, its villages, its roads, and its lines of poplars. In the orchards were the fig, the pistachio, the pomegranate; in the gardens oleander and myrtle. Above the Vega the ground rose wild and high to the south-west, till it culminated in a great line of snows in the Sierra Nevada. Farther up the hill was a delightful Moorish retreat, the Generalife, a little palace with water sparkling in the Moorish style down a long central conduit bordered on either side by cypresses. Farther away was a great royal domain, the Soto de Roma.

The Alhambra itself was an enchantment: its reddish walls threw on the scene an outline as romantic as their colour was pleasing. Its impressive gateway, its spacious courts, its delightful chambers with their Moorish tiles, its sparkling fountains, its windows with their indented arches opening on views over the gorge below and over to the caves in the hill opposite, the Albaicín where the gypsies lived, and below to the ancient town with its great baroque Cathedral—

[1] Written anonymously to a composition of Gibbons.

here was everything that could inspire and please a poet.[2] The Alhambra itself was one of those works of genius which speak insistently to the imagination every time one sees them.

Here for six years Fray Juan was to find his home, while he went off on long journeys over the hills and plains of Andalusia to the sea, to Málaga, to Córdoba, to Caravaca, and Buljalance to inaugurate yet more foundations: he travelled as far west as Lisbon, and when he came back it was to build a cloister. At times also he returned to Beas. It was during one of these visits that he wrote the last five stanzas of *The Song of the Spirit*.

> With joy, beloved, we
> Will scale the hill to where the mountain steepens,
> And all thy Beauty see
> Where living waters be
> Pressing in further where the denseness deepens.
>
> Now sudden let us go
> Where roughest caverns of the rock seduce us,
> And since they hide us so,
> There can we drink enow
> The pomegranate's most luscious juices.
>
> There thou'lt to me display
> That which my soul was always naming.
> And then, my life, my fay,
> I'll take for one more day
> The favour that my love long since was claiming.
>
> The zephyr's breath and balm,
> The darkling nightingale's enchanted singing,
> The woodland's fondest charm,
> The starry night and calm
> With flames which burn my flesh, no torment bringing.
>
> None spied us there, I deem,
> Aminadab no longer lurked around.
> My siege stilled to a dream,
> Till, spying the sparkling stream,
> The lancers from their saddles leapt to ground.[3]

Madre Ana asked him to write and tell her what all this meant. He told her, as we have seen, that in his poem much more was suggested than words could explain.

[2] For a further account, see *Granada*, by E. Allison Peers.
[3] Pp. 228-9, stanzas 36-40.

All words, though culled with choicest art,
Failing to give the bitter of the sweet,
Wither against the palate, and the heart
    Faints,—faded by its heat.

Nevertheless, for what words were worth, he now proceeded to link to the evocations of his poem a prose dissertation on the mystic way: "Although I write here of certain points of scholastic theology concerning the interior commerce of the soul with its God, it may not have been in vain to have talked somewhat after the manner of pure spirit, for though Your Reverence may lack the practice of scholastic theology wherein are comprehended Divine Verities, you lack not that of mystical theology, which is the science of love and wherein these verities are not only known but experienced." [4]

2

In *Mount Carmel* and *The Dark Night* Fray Juan had written systematic, one might use the word scientific, treatises. They are less literary expressions than psychological charts prepared in view of the spiritual life in its relation to the faculty of mysticism or contemplation. The two remaining treatises are much more literary; they are more spontaneous; they move in spheres of imagery and beauty; and they speak much less of asceticism and purgation than they do of love in its yearning, its joy, and its beauty. All four treatises are dealing with the same broad theme: the spiritual quest; but here is a far completer mysticism.

The object of the Christian scheme, he explains, is so to perfect and fulfil our incorporation into the Christ that we shall share God's life and glory, being transformed from glory into glory till we take our place in heaven. Then at last the soul that is united and transformed in God breathes God in God with the same Divine breathing with which God, while in her, breathes her into Himself.[5] The Christ has given us the power to become the Sons of God. San Juan took from a great passage of his namesake, the Evangelist, an elucidation of the inmost purpose of the Christ: "As thou, Father, art in Me,

[4] C.E. Prologue.
[5] C.E. XXXVIII, 3.

and I am in Thee, even so may they be one and the Same Thing in
Us; and I have given them the glory which Thou hast given Me,
that they may be one and the Same Thing as We are one and the
Same Thing. I in Thee and Thou in Me, that they may be perfect
in one; and that the world may know that Thou hast sent Me, and
hast loved them, as Thou hast loved Me; namely, by communicating
the same love as to the Son, though not naturally as to the Son, but
as we have said by unity and transformation of Love. Neither is it
to be understood here that the Son means to say to the Father that
the saints are to be one thing in essence, and in nature as are the
Father and the Son, but rather that they may be so by union of love
as are the Father and the Son in unity of love. Wherefore some
possess these same blessings of participation by the powers of nature;
and for this reason they are truly God's by participation, equal to
God and his companions. Therefore St. Peter said: 'Grace and peace
be complete and perfect in you in the knowledge of God and of Jesus
Christ our Lord according to the wholeness of that divine power given
to us for life and worship through our knowing Him that has called
us with and through His own glory and honour. For, through those,
exceedingly great and precious promises have been given to us that
through them we might be in communion with the Divine nature':
and that," added San Juan, "is for the soul to have participation in
God, working out in Him, in company with Him, the action of the
Most Holy Trinity." [6]

This is a costly treasure; and San Juan in this song does not omit
to remind us of the price, of which he had already told us so much
in his earlier treatises, but now he explains that this is less a matter
of choice than of a much more sublime and complex process.

A soul, not to follow too much the desires and devices of the heart,
must be prepared by self-denial, by humility, by prayer, by all that
patience recognizes as the Cross of Christ; but she will also find that,
by a subtle law, she has against her all those common inclinations in
ordinary people which are called the world: first, the favour of the
world will leave her, and she will lose friends, credit, reputation, and
even property; secondly, a wild beast no less terrifying, the renunciation for ever of the satisfactions and delights of the world and of all
that the world offers will confront her. Thirdly—and this is greater

still—the tongues of men will rise up against her, and will mock her, and will proffer many sayings and gibes against her, and will set her at naught. These things are wont to prejudice certain souls in such a way that it becomes supremely difficult for them, not only to persevere against the wild beasts, but even to be able to set out on the road at all.

But a few more generous souls are wont to meet other wild beasts which are more interior and spiritual, in difficulties and temptations, tribulations and trials of many kinds through which they must need pass. Such God sends to those whom He will raise to high perfection. "Many are the afflictions of the righteous, but the Lord will deliver them out of all." [7]

The dominant interest is always the definite experience of contemplation; but now the emphasis is changed. The theme of this treatise is the desire and rapture of the life of love, and the richness and delight both in religion and in nature which come to the man of prayer. Before the writer had been in a desert and pathless land: now in holiness he sees God's own glory and beauty by the development of God's gift within him, and he sees it, therefore, in his own soul as well as in the exterior world.

Dionysius had long since described the eternal beauty as the cause of the harmony and splendour in all things, flashing upon them like light the beautifying communications of its originating ray. It was one with the power of love which drew both like to like, and all to the primal love. "The eternal beauty," says Dionysius, "contains in a transcendent manner the originating beauty of everything that is beautiful; and by the beautiful all things are united together; and the beautiful is the beginning of all things, as being the creative cause which moves the world, and holds all things together in existence by their love for its own beauty. And it is the goal of all things, and their beloved, as being their final reason for existence (for the desire of the Beautiful is the cause and source of life) as it is also the pattern, or exemplar, to which their peculiar type conforms." [8]

Fray Juan took up this passage as before he had taken up Dionysius on the theme of Love, and he exalts it with rare subtlety into

[7] C.E. III, 6, 7; Allison Peers, II, 44, quoting Psalm XXXIII, 19 (Vulgate).
[8] De Divinis Nominibus, IV, 7.

literature. "Let me be transformed by thy beauty that being alike in beauty, we may see ourselves both in thy beauty, so that one beholding the other, each may see his own beauty in the other, the beauty of both being thine only and mine being absorbed in thine. And then I shall see Thee in thy beauty, and thus I shall see me in thy beauty; and I shall see myself in Thee in thy beauty and Thou wilt see Thyself in me in thy beauty. My beauty shall be mine, mine shall be Thine, and I shall be Thou in it. This is the adoption of the Sons of God." [9]

For *The Song of the Spirit* is always a mystical philosophy in which the sublimest raptures are very closely linked with revelation and Catholic thought.

3

From the beginning, the treatise, like the poem, is the confession of one who has fallen passionately in love with God, who longs for Him to enlighten and strengthen the understanding; to calm and refresh those deepest instincts, cravings, and movements of the heart and mind which Thomistic philosophy calls *voluntas,* and which are, of course, much more than that mere decision and determination which we are apt to mean by the word will; to satisfy also a combination of the two in that continuance of looking before and after which begins as memory and ends as hope. To these first cries of longing and desire nature gives her own revelation; but that is not enough. It awakens only an intenser eagerness and longing for inward communion, and a burning fervour of desire. "The favours and visits of God to the soul are wont to be great in proportion to the affections of the fervour and the yearnings of love which have preceded them," and from this deep inward fervour of the soul itself in the exercise of mystical prayer comes the delight of the marriage or union which shows God both as the splendour indwelling creation, and as the power transcending it, for of Him it is a sketch and a symbol.

San Juan traces this through many favourite things in nature: he sees farther into the ways of God through the Indies, discovered by the navigators: "The strange islands are girt around by the sea and

[9] C.E. XXXV, 3.

are far away over the sea, withdrawn and aloof from the communications of men. Thus there are conceived and generated in them things very different from those here, of very strange kinds and with virtues never seen by men, so that they cause great surprise and wonder in those that see them. And thus, by reason of the great and admirable novelties and the strange impressions far beyond the common knowledge of God in the soul, He is here called strange islands. There are two reasons for calling a man strange: either because he lives in retirement from men, or because he is excellent and singular among other men in his deeds and works. For both these reasons the soul here speaks of God as strange: for not only has He the strangeness of undiscovered islands, but His works, His ways, and His counsels are strange and new and marvellous to men . . . only to Himself is He not strange, neither to Himself is He new." [10]

There is the richest wealth and splendour of experience here related in the account of the joys, the favours, the distractions, the temptations of the life of the spirit. For there is every variety of experience, every kind of appeal to the imagination, and they are subtly interwoven both with one another and with the Bible. "In the horror of the visions of the night when sleep is wont to occupy men, fear came upon me and trembling and all my bones shook." [11] Such are the words of Eliphaz the Temanite. San Juan takes them up in the melodious line:

> Miedos de las noches veladores.[12]
> (The terrors which keep vigil in the night.)

For sometimes fear and affright, he tells us, come to men from God, and sometimes the devil assails them with horror. For the travails and the anxieties of the spiritual life cut deep into the quick of feeling.

4

But at last beyond the spiritual betrothal comes a deeper union still, as the soul presses deeper into contemplation. In *The Ascent of*

[10] C.E. XIII, 8; Allison Peers, II, 78.

[11] Job iv, 13, 14.

[12] Some have suggested "miedos voladores," believing this to be an echo of the line "A sagitta volante in die." Psalm XC, 5 (Vulgate).

Mount Carmel, San Juan had argued that to attain to the all one must renounce all. The doctrine remains, but it is now expressed with a gentleness and romance that make it seem wholly gracious. Remorseless logic is exchanged for a picture of happy lovers.

"A strange characteristic of those that are in love is this, that they are far more desirous of enjoying each other's society when they are alone together and withdrawn from every creature than if doing so in the company of anyone. For although they be together, yet if there be any strange company present with them, even though they would not converse and speak together if they were away from them any more than they do in their presence, and though these others speak not, neither converse at all, their very presence is sufficient for the lovers not to have pleasure and enjoyment in each other. The reason for this is that, since love is the union of two souls, these two desire to continue alone." [13]

Such a picture of the sacredness in the communion of human lovers is very close to Donne's *Extasy.*

> If any so by love refined
> That he sowle's language understood,
> And by good love were growen all minde,
> Within convenient distance stood.
> He, though he knew not which sowle spake
> Because both meant, both spake the same,
> Might thence a new concoction take
> And part farre purer than he came.

For this mystery of union is what Meredith called "the first supernatural spring of the ripe senses into passion, when they carry the soul with them." San Juan says nothing of this, however, though the description certainly tells that he understood the most exquisite communion of friends or lovers. For the purpose here, the simile is enough, since as he immediately proceeds, "Now that the soul has been set upon this summit and perfection and freedom of spirit in

---

[13] C.E. XXXVI, 1. There is again an interesting parallel in Ossuna.

"A marvellous silence and most meet to be praised and admired is that of love. And thanks to it, our understanding having found by experience an idea which satisfies it, sinks into intimate silence; for many a time, we have had opportunity to see clearly by experience, when lovers are conscious of one another's presence, they are silent together and the love which unites them compensates for the absence of words."—Ossuna, *Tercer Abecedario,* trat III, p. 546.

If, as it appears, San Juan is indebted to Ossuna, yet once again he shows his power of personal interpretation.

God and the repugnances and contrarieties of its human nature [14] are burnt out, it has naught else to understand, no other exercise to employ it but to surrender itself with the bridegroom to the delights and joys of intimate love." [15]

5

Just as the bride finds that the joys of love lead to the travail of child-birth and a mother's tiring sacrifices, so the soul which has in mysticism attained this ultimate rapture asks for tribulations and sacrifices, as the continuation of its bliss. It seeks the very heaven of pain. "O that it might be perfectly understood how the soul cannot attain to the density and wisdom of the riches of God which are of many kinds unless it enters into the density of suffering in many ways, and the soul seeks therein its consolation and desire. And how the soul which indeed desires divine wisdom desires first to suffer to enter into it the density of the Cross. And therefore St. Paul exhorted the Ephesians that they faint not in tribulations, but that they should be rooted and grounded in love that they might understand with all the saints what is the breadth and length and depth and height and know the love of Christ which passeth knowledge, to be filled with all the fullness of God." [16]

Such was the treatise by which, as in a series of meditations and confessions, always interspersed with the fruits of philosophy and the sacred sciences, Fray Juan wrote to Madre Ana de Jesús. And it is indeed worthy of the poem. It has elevation, finish, exquisiteness. It is like the silken flowered embroidery on contemporary vestments. Colour, energy, endurance, fervour, exaltation, and bliss are interwoven in the poet's explanation of the spiritual life; for it is the record of his own.

It is precisely for the reason that this treatise in style, in quality,

[14] The word San Juan uses is *sensual*, but he had explained that:
"By sensual good we mean all those which in this life are perceived by the senses of sight, hearing, smell, taste or touch, by the inner working of the imaginative faculty which belongs entirely to the physical senses, interior or exterior."—San Juan, *Ascent of Mount Carmel*, III, ch. xiv, 1.
It is plain, therefore, that San Juan uses the word sensuality as equivalent to our human nature. It is everything which reaches the human spirit through the psychology of man.
[15] C.E. XXXVI, 1.
[16] C.E. XXXVII, 13.

as well as in exposition, is so close to the poem it expounds that it is of particular efficacy to those who, consciously or unconsciously, are living the spiritual life, and receiving, even if they have not realized it, the graces of contemplation in the enjoyment of true beauty. The reason is that it is so much less occupied with the asceticism of purgation, and so much more with the experiences where

> Thro' rapid glances of the inner life
> The soul is sentient of its own salvation.[17]

For mysticism, like beauty, and like holiness, spreads by irradiation; and there is no call to the spiritual life so powerful as the words which picture what it is. Therefore the mystics have dilated on its joy: joy is a word which in their writings is found again and again. And without it no one could understand their acceptance of renunciation and of suffering. "It is carrying austerity too far," said Santa Teresa, "to say that we ought to deny ourselves all human satisfaction if we do not at the same time speak of the sweetness and delight which will follow this renouncement, and of the pleasure it will bring us, even in this life." [18]

But quite apart from the fact that it is love and attraction which make the spiritual burden light,[19] we cannot see the beauty of holiness without to some extent admiring it: and what one admires is one's possession. As one reads, one drinks from the fountain of living waters:

> "Contemplation is dark and for that reason is called by its other name, mystical theology, which signifies secret and hidden wisdom of God wherein, without noise of words and without the service or aid of any bodily or spiritual sense, as in the silence and quiet of the night, hidden by darkness from all that

---

[17] See R. Sencourt, *Life of George Meredith*, p. 33.

[18] *Way of Perfection*, ch. xii.

[19] For fuller treatment, see Saudreau, *The Ideal of the Fervent Soul*, pp. xi-xxvii, and Ossuna:

"You must know that humility and magnanimity are two sisters, two companions so intimate that one is not found without the other. They are like two wings by which the woman, which is the soul, flies towards God and towards the solitude of contemplation. And as poverty of spirit does not stop short at the scorn of earthly things, but rises to the riches of heavenly things, so humility does not stop at the scorn of honours but rises to the sublimity of spiritual things."—*Tercer Abecedario*, trat XIX, p. 335 b.

attraction of "the central orb of righteous love," and the sense of
gracious rapture, of adoring calm which were the centre and essence
of the spiritual life. They were all summed together in what he wrote
of the living flame of love, which, both as a treatise and a poem, is
more personal than anything he had written yet. Admiring it, each
of us is an Abednego—hurled into the furnace of his heart.

2

O love with living flames that climb
Profound and dear the sear sublime,
    Thine ardour has begun.
Since thou'rt no longer hard to please,
Devour with thine imperial ease
    The web our meeting spun.

O scald and sear of purest love,
O wound enjoyed all ease above,
    O delicate, soft touch
Of hand which every ransom pays
And savours of eternal days
    And slaying, quickens much!

Resplendent lamps of blazing fire,
The blindest caverns of desire
    Where human senses go,
Caves terrible, profound, obscure,
Ye fill with piercing gleamings pure
    Outstreaming heat and glow.

How suave and gracious is the sense
Thou wakenest in my heart intense
    Abiding lone and still!
With what high love and delicate air
Thou breathest grace and glory there,
    My tranced being to fill! [4]

Such is the poem; and the opening of the prose exposition burns
with a kindred glow: "The soul feels itself to be at last wholly enkindled in Divine union, its palate to be wholly bathed in glory and
love, and from the inmost parts of its substance to be flowing rivers
of glory, abounding in delight, for it perceives that from its belly are
flowing the rivers of living water which the Son of God said would
flow from such souls. It seems to this soul that since it is transformed
in God with such vehemence and in so lofty a way possessed of Him,
and is adorned with such marvellous riches and gifts and virtues, it is

[4] P. 229.

very near to bliss, from which it is divided only by a slender web. And, seeing that that delicate flame of love which burns within it is, as it were, glorifying it with a glory both gentle and powerful, whensoever it assails it, to such a degree that, whensoever it is absorbed and assailed it believes that it is about to enter upon eternal life, and that this web of mortal life will be broken and that there remains but a very short space of time, yet during this space it cannot be glorified in its essence. The soul addresses this flame, which is the Holy Spirit, with great yearning, begging him now to break this its mortal life in that sweet meeting and encounter, so that of a truth he may communicate to it perfectly that which it believes him to be about to give to it, and to work in it whensoever he meets it—complete and perfect glory." [5]

San Juan now recapitulates the need of purgation and the gradual operation of fire upon the soul. He explains in a brilliant passage how, as souls advance towards perfection, they become aware of deficiencies of which at first they knew nothing. He had, it is true, written fully of this before, yet he elaborates the point once more, explaining how each soul suffers affliction as the force of the perfecting love struggles with human passions and imperfections.

3

This life, says San Juan, "is called a web for three reasons: first, because the spirit is enwoven with the flesh; secondly, because there is something which separates the soul from God; and thirdly, because this something is, as a web, transparent and the Divine glory shines through it." Such are the thoughts which San Juan read into the comparison of men to a spider, in the psalm *Domine refugium nostrum,* and the petition for the flame to devour the web expresses the intensity or passion of the contemplative.[6]

Then the treatise relates the touch or the impression of intimacy by which the blessed Trinity comes to live within the soul; for this burning light of the Holy Spirit does not destroy: it deifies.[7]

And so the struggle between flesh and spirit continues, the flesh

---

[5] *Living Flame,* I, 1.
[6] *Ibid.,* I, 26.
[7] *Ibid.,* II, 3, 5.

being as it were the curb that reins in the thoroughbred; the habits of life oppress the spiritual sense when the mind muses upon many things. At one time the writer explains how few are the souls of heroic temper to embrace endurances and tribulations;[8] at another he celebrates in fitting poetical prose the exquisite and delicate ways of providence, "O delicate touch, thou Word, Son of God, Who through the delicacy of thy Divine Being dost subtly penetrate the substance of my soul, and touching it wholly and delicately dost absorb it wholly into Thyself in Divine ways of sweetness which have never been heard of in the land of Canaan nor seen in Teman. . . . The more delicate is a thing, the broader and more capacious can it become; and it becomes the more diffusive and communicative, according as it is the more delicate. Thou delicate touch, so delicate that when naught is felt to the touch, thou dost touch the soul the more, and by penetrating deeply within it at thy touch, thou dost make it the more divine."[9]

4

Again and again San Juan insists on the needs of sacrifice, of effort, of suffering, of generosity, and above all of not going backward in the life of grace. First, of course, there are the bad directors who, always afraid of quietism or, as it was then called, illuminism, understand nothing of the prayer of quiet, but pound and hammer at souls like a blacksmith with a piece of iron. Some directors are so "pestilential" that they even put motives of human prudence before souls led by God to sacrifice.[10]

Indeed, one of the principal points of the teaching of San Juan is that, even if they are free from the limitations of incompetence which he had already described, directors should not attempt too much, nor should any lean too much upon them. No two souls are alike: "God leads each soul along different roads, and there shall hardly be found a single spirit who can walk even half the way that is suitable for another."[11] Directors must not assume any more direction than they can help; for it is God who Himself guides the spir-

[8] *Ibid.*, 23, 24.
[9] *Ibid.*, II, 16.
[10] *Ibid.*, III, 39-53.
[11] *Ibid.*, III, 51.

itual man with manifold gifts of grace. *"The Holy Spirit is the principal agent and mover of souls, and never loses his care for them"*: it is enough for directors to advise solitude and freedom and tranquility—freedom especially from any personal inclination of sense or soul. The director may aid the soul in all these ways. "But when the soul is detached from all knowledge of its own and from every desire and all affections of its more human side, and dwells in the pure negation of poverty of spirit, wholly emptied of the mist of sweetness, wholly weaned from the breast and milk (which is what the soul must be careful to do, as far as in it lies), it is impossible that God will not perform His own part. It is more impossible than that the sun should shine in a serene and unclouded sky; for as the sun when it rises in the morning and shines into your house will enter if you open the shutter, even so will God, who keeps Israel and slumbers not, still less sleeps, enter the soul that is empty and fill it with blessings. God, like the sun, is above our souls and ready to enter them." [12]

The building up of the soul is the work not of a director but of the Father of Lights from whom cometh every good and perfect gift. For if the Lord build not the house, he labours but in vain that builds it; and in every soul in the manner that seems good to Him God will build a supernatural building. [13]

But, apart from trusting too much to human guides, the soul can be deceived by the devil, who lures it back with sensations or emotions which are all too poor for those who should be advancing from these things of the human heart to a way of life all divine. [14]

Lastly, there is the soul itself which becomes restless, like a baby that will not be carried, but kicks to get to the ground, or the subject of a portrait who will not sit still while the painter paints him. Always the supreme thing is to surrender oneself wholly to the work of God. "For it must be known that *if a soul is seeking God, the beloved is seeking it much more,* and if it sends after Him its loving desires which are as fragrant to Him as a pillar of smoke that issues from the aromatic spices of myrrh and incense, He likewise sends after it the fragrance of His ointments with which He draws the

---

[12] *Ibid.,* III, 40.
[13] *Ibid.,* III, 41.
[14] *Ibid.,* III, 55, 56.

soul and causes it to run after Him. These ointments are His divine inspirations and touches, which, whenever they are His, are ordered and ruled with respect to the perfection of the law of God and by faith in which perfection the soul must ever draw nearer and nearer to God." [15]

The life of love is an unending progress, and no union is final, because the more the soul is enlarged, yet the more can it receive. Even when it is in the centre, it is not in the deepest centre. "The more degrees of love a soul has the more profoundly does it enter into God and the more is it centred in Him: and thus we can say that, as are the degrees of love of God, so are the centres each deeper than the other, which the soul has in God: these are the many mansions which He said were in His Father's house." [16]

So the *Living Flame* becomes a long argument for the mystery, the freedom, and the splendour of God's direct action upon the soul. *Those who are led by the Spirit of God, they are the sons of God.*[17] Fray Juan, in fact, believed with Carlyle that, at least in so far as we are mystics, we are a fire-breathing spirit host, who, even as we hasten across the earth may already be raised into the life of heaven: for

> We are such stuff as dreams are made on,
> And our little life is rounded by a sleep.

But advanced contemplatives are no longer living of themselves: they are living for God in God: they are giving to the Giver the very brightness that He gives to them; [18] a strange glory: a glory

[15] *Living Flame*, III, 27. This passage is but a variation on what he had already written in *The Song of the Spirit*:

"Even as the touch of the air is felt with the sense of touch, and the whisper of the same air is heard by the ear, even so likewise the touch of the virtues of the beloved is perceived and enjoyed in the sense of touch of this soul which is its substance; and the knowledge of these virtues is perceived in the ear of the soul which is its understanding. And it must be known that the amorous breeze is said to have come when it strikes delectably, satisfying the appetite of him that so greatly desires the refreshment, for then the sense of touch is soothed and refreshed, and with this soothing of the sense of touch, the ear experiences great delight in the sound and whisper of the air, much more than does the sense of touch in the touch of the air; for the sense of hearing is more spiritual."—C.E. XIII, 13; Allison Peers, II, 82.

[16] *Ibid.*, I, 13.

[17] *Ibid.*, Rom. VIII, 14.

[18] *Ibid.*, III, 67.

above all common thoughts and all memories known to men. For the glory with which God visits the soul is like the glory wherewith the understanding receives divine wisdom, and is made one with the understanding of God, for one cannot give save in the way wherein is given to him.[19] The soul by means of this transformation has become the shadow of God, so that it does in God and through God that which He does through Himself in the soul. What the Word, His Son, said to the Father become the words of that transformed and adopted soul: "All My things are Thine, and Thine are Mine, and I am glorified in them." The soul loves God through God. It praises Him as a duty, as the end for which it was created it finds itself filled with delight and blessing in offering this praise; and it thanks God and praises Him above all for who He is, and for His glory.[20] It is filled with joy and wonder at all that it possesses in Him.

5

The fourth part of *Love's Living Flame* describes the calm and peace, with the blessing and glory of the soul which has attained to unity with Him it loves:

> How sweet and gracious is the sense
> Thou wakenest in my heart intense,
> Abiding lone, and still.[21]

In this awakening of the soul, "the Word comes to it with such grandeur and dominion and glory and such intimate charm that it seems to the soul that all the balms and perfumed spices and flowers in the world are mingled and shaken and whirled together to procure it, and all the kingdoms and dominions of the world are moved, and the powers and virtues of heaven. And not only so, but all the virtues and inward realities and perfections and beauties of all created things shine forth and make the same movements, together and in unison." [22] For by the Word are all things made: and in Him is

---

[19] *Living Flame,* III, 68. Cf. C.E. XI, 7. They will live the life of God and not their own life, and yet it will be their own life, for the life of God will be their own life, and then they will say in truth: "We live, yet not we, for God liveth in us."

[20] *Ibid.,* III, 69.

[21] III, 27.

[22] *Ibid.,* IV, 4.

their life.[23] In Him they live and move and have their very being.[24] This sense of the presence of God in the power by which He upholds all things, bearing the Government upon His shoulder, is the consummation of the life and the contemplation of San Juan de la Cruz. The soul, he says, "is entrenched and remains terribly and firmly arrayed among them like ranks of armies, and made gracious and charming in the charm and graces of the created world." [25]

But here is no rhapsody: just as he had already interrupted his theme of glory to arraign the blacksmith directors of souls, so here he is well aware of the stark realities which divide human nature from the things of God: "For such is the law of nature of this kind of life which we live that we believe others to be as ourselves; and we judge others as we do ourselves, so that our judgment begins with ourselves and not outside ourselves. In this way the thief believes that others steal likewise; and he that lives sensuously that others live like him; and he that is malicious that others are malicious, his judgment proceeding from his own malice; and the good man thinks well of others, his judgments proceeding from the goodness of his own thoughts: so he that is careless and somnolent thinks that others are so. Hence when we are careless and somnolent before God, we think that He is careless and somnolent with us, as we read in the Psalms, where David says to God: Awake, why sleepest thou, O Lord?, attributing to God what is in man. It is God whom he calls to arise and awaken, though it is they who have fallen and sleep: for He that keepeth Israel never sleeps." [26]

6

At the end of *The Living Flame*, the writer sums up in one short passage the whole subject of the relation of God to the soul of man. God dwells secretly in all souls, hidden in their very being: for otherwise they would be unable to exist.

But between his manners of indwelling how great is the difference! "For in some He dwells alone, and in others not alone; in some he dwells contented, in others displeased; in some He dwells

---

[23] S. John i, 2, 3.
[24] Acts XVII, 28.
[25] *Living Flame*, IV, 10.
[26] *Ibid.*, IV, 8. Cf. Psalms XLIV, 23; CXXI, 4.

as in His house, ordering it and noting everything, while in others He dwells as a stranger in the house of another, where He is not allowed to do anything or to give any commands." [27] But where He dwells supreme, His inspiration is exquisite, delicate, beyond what is lawful for man to utter: for the Holy Spirit has filled the soul with blessing and glory, inspiring it with love of Himself in the heights and depths of God, above all that ear has heard or it has entered into the heart of man to conceive.

"And for that reason," says the writer at the last with quiet logic, "I leave speaking of it here." [28]

Thus there came a moment when even poetry had reached its term. But bright had been its journey. For to it all the qualities and perfection of God, His almightiness, His fortitude, His justice, His mercy, His truth, His uprightness, His dominion—all that flashed on the prophet on Sinai—showed that God is to the soul as innumerable lamps which give it light and love.

"The soul is completely absorbed in these delicate flames, and wounded subtly by love in each of them, and in all of them together more wounded and deeply alive in the love of the life of God, so that it can see quite clearly that that love belongs to life eternal, which is the union of all blessings. So that the soul in that state in some wise perceives and knows well the truth of those words of the Spouse in the Songs, where He says that the lamps of love were lamps of fire and flame. Beauteous art thou in thy footsteps and thy shoes, O prince's daughter. Who can recount the magnificence and rarity of thy delight and majesty in thy wondrous splendour?" [29]

[27] *Living Flame*, IV, 14.
[28] *Ibid.*, IV, 17.
[29] *Ibid.*, III, 4, 5. *Works*, E. Allison Peers, III, p. 163.

> *As the wild swan*
> *Voyaging over dark and rising seas*
> *Into the stormy air adventures on*
> *With wide unfaltering wings, the way he bore,*
> *When blue the water laughed beneath the breeze,*
> *And morning round the radiant beaches shone.*
> *So thou, through all this pain*
> *Endure, my heart, whither thy course was bound,*
> *Keep, keep thy passionate flight,*
> *Nor find thy voyage vain.*
> *Yea, till thou break, my heart, all meaner quest disdain.*[1]

I

IT was immediately after Santa Teresa had composed the Seventh Mansion of *The Interior Castle* that she faced the fiercest storms of tribulation. An experience as intense as this came to Fray Juan de la Cruz after he had written the passages on the final blessing and glory in *The Living Flame of Love*.

For it had not been enough to reform the order. It had not been enough to have Santa Teresa. It had not been enough to write *The Way of Perfection, The Interior Castle,* or even *The Ascent of Mount Carmel* and *The Dark Night of the Soul.* Just as Teresa had come into conflict with Tostado and the Nuncio, Fray Juan de la Cruz, when he had survived her, came into conflict with a new superior. In 1581 the charming Gracián had been superseded, and superseded in his own order, with the support of the Court, not by another Spaniard, but by that despotic and pharisaical Italian who had aroused the suspicion of the Founders. How do the records account for such strange things as these?

We recall that when in Alcalá in 1581, Gracián had been appointed the first Provincial, his majority was the bare majority of one. It was plain, therefore, that as an administrator he did not even then command the full confidence of his brethren in the Reform.

[1] Laurence Binyon, *Sursum Cor.*

Why was it that in the opinion of so many he failed to fulfil the high hopes that Santa Teresa had formed of him? Why did they distrust a man whom she so much admired? What, if any, were the defects of his spirituality, his brilliance, his eloquence, his charm?

The trouble with Gracián was that he was both a diplomatist, and a diplomatist not sufficiently determined. Diplomacy is something more than subtlety. It requires, at times, brutal frankness: it is not enough to manœuvre: one must sometimes overawe and overpower. That Gracián could not do. The man who can accomplish constructive work among men is he who can disregard their opinions, and claim the monopoly of the sound idea. He must see what can be done, and insist that it must be done. Gracián could do neither. He lacked the fighting spirit of the seraphic Mother. The sparkling radiance and magnetism of his Polish grandfather he had to perfection: he had also the Pole's courage: but he always avoided that shock and clash of personalities from which the strong man emerges with exhilaration and therefore *bonhomie*. There were other difficulties with Gracián. His eyes roamed the outer world for opportunities, and revelling in his gift of preaching, he planned to make the new order into a missionary order. But though he planned much, he effected little. And both in the order and in the Court, need was felt for a strong administrator. Doria, as we have seen, took advantage of Gracián's defect, and being both an autocrat and a tyrant,[2] he planned and he intrigued, and before long the quarrel broke out in fight.

2

In the hermitage of Pastrana, the portraits of Gracián and of Doria hang side by side. Gracián's expression is gentle, open; his features rounded. But Doria! Here is no trace of sympathy: here confident determination: the hooked nose, the bright eyes, the crude though smiling lips, the bold chin and the receding forehead express both the despotism of efficiency and the efficiency of despotism. Here was an administrator whose passion and talent were for finance. "Gracián was an idealist," writes Fr. Zimmermann, "his ideals being of the loftiest. Doria was intensely practical, cold, and calculating. Both were born leaders of men and could no more help having, each, a following than

[2] Bruno, p. 362.

a magnet can help attracting iron. Like Caesar, either might have been first in a village, but neither could have been second in Rome. Gracián with his idealism made numerous fatal mistakes, as he had done during his quarrels with the Calzados when he nearly wrecked Santa Teresa's work, imagining all the time he was doing wonders; it was exactly the same when he was Provincial of the Descalzos. Doria made no mistakes: Gracián was loved but not trusted by his subjects, for with his inconsistencies they never knew where they were. Doria was trusted but not loved: on the contrary, he was feared. . . . Gracián was inordinately fond of preaching, and spent whole seasons on this apostolic work when it was his manifest duty to attend to business; he wrote an incredible number of books, but nothing commensurate with his talents, nothing that survived him. Doria wrote nothing, but he was ever at his post: no detail escaped him, no individualistic initiative was allowed to side-track his clear line of action. While Gracián was Provincial great projects and high aims were resolved upon, but were pursued with something less than the required energy; during Doria's nine years of office all enterprise was stifled." [3]

Such were the contrasting types who brought faction into the order while Fray Juan was Prior at Granada. At first Gracián had sent Doria on a mission to Genoa to offer homage to the new Carmelite General Caffardo. Doria came back from Caffardo with a letter appointing him as the General's delegate in Spain, a letter which he produced after pressing his views on a chapter at Almodovar in 1583. But the Spanish friars had their own views, and they forced Doria to surrender the powers by which one Italian had set up another Italian as their master. For the Carmelites of Spain never forgot that they were Spaniards, and they were well aware that Doria was both a rigorist and a despot, as well as an Italian.

Meanwhile Gracián cherished his project of making the Reform into a great missionary order of preachers; and on this subject, too, there was argument. Some thought the Carmelites should live simply as contemplatives. "There are some," complained Gracián, "who think that the whole of Carmelite perfection consists in never leaving one's cell, in never missing an item of choir observance, even if the whole world was on fire." Fray Juan de la Cruz took the middle way

[3] Zimmermann in Bruno, pp. 378-379.

of an illumined wisdom: if the order were to extend, this must be
done as in the days of the apostles, "when our Fathers of old followed
the preaching of the gospel through all the provinces of the East and
then at once withdrew to the deserts, where they led a solitary and
monastic life, in order to win by divine contemplation God's grace on
behalf of those who were preaching to infidels." [4] He never forgot that
Dionysius had written, *"Of all divine things the most divine is to
co-operate with God in the salvation of souls."* His principle was that
the more the soul loves God, the more does it desire that He should
be loved and honoured by all men: for it seems to contemplatives a
very little thing to go to heaven alone.[5]

3

But he was well aware both that Gracián had not the gifts of an
administrator, and that others were too ambitious. He said so in a
chapter at Almodovar in 1584. The friars were by no means free
either of ambition, or of cunning; and he thought it well to reinforce
the uncompromising warnings of *The Dark Night.*

In 1585 in a chapter at Lisbon, he heard faction rise furious against
Gracián. Who was to succeed him? "The curse of Spain," says Professor Allison Peers, "is the pendulum." In a mood of impatience and
zeal, the Spaniards went, as they so often do, from one extreme to
the other. They rejected Gracián for their head; they elected Doria.

Fray Juan de la Cruz had already a shrewd suspicion that Doria in
envy and revenge would expel Gracián from the order.[6] Fray Juan
had not forgotten all that he had himself written of the faults of
religious men; and, above all, their pride. Doria, in fact, in struggling
against Spaniards, had, in recalcitrance and excess, become the most
difficult of them all. But he could not make the compromise they
made in favour of freedom. They could no longer vote for their superiors: their doings were subjected to minute scrutiny from outside.
Doria, in short, was an inquisitor. His rule was Tyranny.

"For Genoese and Venetians," wrote the Carmelite historian, "who
rule bears, tigers, lions, and wolves, the rod of iron may be tolerated,

[4] Bruno, p. 289.
[5] *Ibid.,* p. 290.
[6] Cunninghame Graham, II, 413.

and the arm upraised over their blood-stained necks, in order that they may be reduced to reason, and prevented from disturbing the Republic. But in religion, and especially in a reformed religious order, in which all are like simple, obedient, and submissive sheep, they resented the prying authority, they groaned: in colleges, in the humblest buildings, nothing was heard but cries, complaints, and murmurs." [7]

If he tyrannised over the order as a whole, he reserved his acrimony for Gracián. In his first chapter he announced his intention: "Let us cut off the rotten limb, and the body will recover its strength." [8] He tried to secure absolute power over the order. That he could not do; but he still pursued his enmity towards Gracián. He had not the means to expel him, but he could get him out of the way, if he appointed him to a post in wild, mountainous, perilous Mexico, which across the wide Atlantic was reached by the caravels of Philip II very slowly.

But even Mexico was not enough. Doria's financial skill had won him the favour of the King. He had the support of both Mariano and Roca. These secured from the Court a decree giving them absolute power to expel from the order any rebellious subject. It only remained to apply to Gracián the methods of the Inquisition. He was accused of publishing a pamphlet without obtaining permission, and even of freedom of intercourse with the nuns; on the strength of these charges, he was expelled from all meetings of the order.

At this point Gracián should have fought; but he was a man of conciliation. He longed, like Fray Juan, only for the peace and perfection of the spiritual life: he resigned from the post in Mexico to which he had been appointed. Doria took advantage of his mildness to stamp on him and crush him. The insinuations against Gracián remained unanswered, and he was driven from the order in disgrace.

This done, Doria invoked a chapter in Madrid on June 18, 1588. The fierce heat of the sun was not hotter than the passion living in the hearts of Teresa's Carmelites. But the fires, if fierce, were shrouded, and Doria proceeded to elaborate his plans. He divided the congregation into six provinces; the heads of each were to be nominated by himself, and this committee of six was alone to govern the

[7] Bruno, p. 311.
[8] Cunninghame Graham, II, 413.

order from their house in Madrid. Thus Doria attempted to apply to the Carmelites the military discipline of the Jesuits.

San Ignacio de Loyola admitted, however, no female Jesuits. In spite of being a son of Santa Teresa, Doria had forgotten the strong character of the women of Spain. For the Foundress was no solitary prodigy among her Castilian sisters. She was the type rather than the exception. Her prioresses knew perfectly well what were his designs and what their rights. They were supported not only by Juan de la Cruz. The other great poet of the time came forward to campaign for them. Luis de León, now freed from the Inquisition, was recognized far beyond Salamanca as one of the leaders of intellectual Spain; he was, as we saw long since, a fervent admirer of Santa Teresa. He now collaborated with Fray Juan to preserve Teresa's work.

Surely the two men who were so much alike in aim, in taste, in vision must have met. But if so there was no record of it. Each appeared to be working separately.

Guided by his sense of justice and his intimate knowledge of the Foundress, Fray Juan finally spoke out his mind. Doria watched him debating how best to silence him, then placed him in another post: he made him Prior of the new foundation at Segovia.

4

Of all the cities of Spain, Segovia offers the most striking sights. It is placed in a delightful corner of Castile. A few miles away are the woods and streams which lead up the richest valleys of the Guadarrama to the passes of Reventón and Navacerrada and the Peak of Peñalara. Except for the Royal Palace of the Escorial and La Granja, no city or monument nestles so close to the heart of the Sierra. The height, as at Ávila, is well over three thousand feet; and here are built a Roman (or Pre-Roman) aqueduct of red granite, a Gothic Cathedral, which had been completed in 1572, and, on a rock overlooking a gorge, a turreted castle, the Alcázar. Medieval builders, who loved picturesqueness, never set a castle more romantically than this as it towers above the confluence of two small rivers, the Eresma and the Clamorés. Its narrow walls shoot upward, flanked with delicate towers, round and slender as cylinders, and each peaked with its bartisan turret: here, straight from the Middle Ages of knight and baron, of

friar, of forays and of chivalry, is the purest romance of scene and
fancy. Here, martial and high, is the distilled spirit of Castile. The
aqueduct adds the majesty of organized empire, the Cathedral has
lightness, gorgeousness, and space; and from the heights one looks
on wild nature and wild sky, the plain and the sierra, always to bring
the eye back to the sharpest lances of the Alcázar.

Such was the city to which the generosity of Señora de Peñalosa
brought Fray Juan de la Cruz to await the vengeance of Doria: here
he passed the years from 1589 to 1591 building his convent, as he had
done at Los Mártires, with his own hands, and climbing whenever
he could to the lofty grotto which offered him, with the wide pros-
pect of the wide scene, of the sky, of the Sierra, and of the towered
city, the full advantage of Segovia's glory.

A letter to Doña Juana de Pedraza at Granada, written from Segovia on January 28, 1589, presents a picture of his mind.

"Jesus be in your soul. I have received all your letters and
have sympathized with your griefs and troubles and times of
loneliness, which, even when you have said nothing about
them, have always cried out to me to such an extent that even
with your pen you could not have said more. All these are rap-
pings and knockings upon the soul calling it to greater love.
God will provide what is best. God takes care of the affairs of
those who love him truly without their being anxious concerning them.

"In matters pertaining to the soul it is best for you in order
to be safe to have attachment to nothing and desire for nothing,
and to have true and complete attachment and desire to him who
is your proper guide, for to do otherwise would be not to desire
a guide. And when one guide suffices and you have one who
suits you, all others are either superfluous, or harmful. Let your
soul cling to nothing, for, if you fail not to pray, God will take
care of your affairs, for they belong to no other master than
God, nor can they do so. This I find to be true of myself, for
the more things are mine, the more I have of heart and soul in
them and the more anxious I am about them, for he that loves
becomes one with the object of his love, as does God with him
that loves him, since, one cannot forget him without forgetting

one's own soul; and for the object of one's love one indeed forgets one's own soul: for one lives more in the object of one's love than in oneself.

"O great God of Love, and Lord, how much of thine own riches dost Thou not set in him that loves naught and that takes pleasure in naught but Thyself, since Thou givest Thyself to him and makest him one thing to Thyself through love! And herein Thou givest him to love and have pleasure in that which the soul most desires in Thee and that which brings him the greatest profit. For we must not be without our Cross, even as our Beloved had His Cross until He died the death of love. He orders our passions in the love of that which we most need so that we may make the greater sacrifices and be of the greater worth. But it is all short, for it continues only till the knife is raised, and Israel remains alive, with the promise that his children shall be multiplied." [9]

"As a man of the Lord," says a contemporary manuscript, "his life was so celestial that it seemed he was no longer living in the flesh." [10] Two things he studied always with unwearying and impassioned scrutiny: the Bible and the stars. At this time, if we may believe a contemporary testimony, he wrote on high contemplation these lines:

> I entered in I knew not where,
> And there remained I, knowing naught,
> For I had far transcended thought.

The unspeakable, the transcendent, beyond all faculties and knowledge, a dowry from on high, a thought that thought no longer, a thing so secret, a knowledge so perfect of worship and of peace, an inclination, an experience so strong and absorbing that his sense was his no more, a cloud that, though dark, illumined the night of his wilderness.[11] Such were the sublime associations with which Fray Juan added from his orison to the pointed splendours of Segovia.[12]

[9] Allison Peers, III, 275-6.
[10] Baruzi, p. 217.
[11] Allison Peers, II, 448-9. Cf. p. 230.
[12] Crisógono, pp. 388, 390.

5

While he passed his hours in hymning his communion with the transcendent mystery, his friend Ana de Jesús was still fighting the good fight against prelacy. She was assured that the action of Doria contravened the intentions of Teresa; she therefore took a bold step: she decided on an appeal to Rome.

Whether the Holy See was favourable to the cause of Teresa, whether her friendship with the King was remembered, or whether Doria had aroused suspicion, the records do not tell us. What is certain is that the Pope acceded to the petition of Ana in 1590, as a predecessor had agreed to those of Roca in 1580. A brief granting her request reached Spain on August 20, 1590.

Doria raged: then with resolute craft he made his plan. The Pope was ill, and it was managed to postpone action till he was actually dead. Doria had time to do his work. By treacherous translations, he succeeded in giving a false idea of the testament of Teresa. But this proved ineffective. In the meantime, he cut off all communications with the nuns, and refused to make arrangements for administering the convents. The nuns had asked to have Fray Juan as their visitor. He better than any other knew the mind of Teresa. It was also suspected that his advice was the motive power behind their successful appeal to Rome; and after fresh intrigues in various directions, a chapter of the order was convened at Madrid by Doria on May 30, 1591.

It had some interesting business to discuss: what to do with the nuns, what to do with Gracián, and how to apply some three hundred new regulations worked out by Doria. The expedient of exile to Mexico, first devised for Gracián, was now applied to Juan de la Cruz.

"He saw," says Mrs. Cunninghame Graham, "the abyss into which Doria, blinded by his gigantic personal ambition, was bent on plunging not only himself but the order. He disapproved the constant and contradictory changes introduced into its constitution, subversive of all discipline and the origin of confusion. He pleaded—and we may judge (in spite of the carefully-worded and biassed words of the chronicler) that he pleaded ably and well—in favour of

Gracián. Forecasting the future, he warned them against taking any cruel and hasty resolution which they must afterwards repent. He pleaded for the nuns, and deprecated the Vicar General's harshness in chastising all for the fault of one or two—if fault there was. His noble and dispassionate words produced no effect on the passionate and prejudiced audience around him; for since the Priors had been deprived of a seat in the chapters, Doria had no difficulty in filling it with his own creatures who owed all to him. Suspicious of Fray Juan's complicity in the action taken by Ana de Jesús, knowing that if the Bull granted by Sixtus V was confirmed the office of Commissary General of the nuns would naturally fall on one of the heads of the order (and who more likely than San Juan de la Cruz?) Doria hastened to annul his appointment to the Provincialate of the Indies, bestowed on him by that very chapter—an election which had already afforded a theme for murmuring tongues, so obviously was it an attempt to secure his absence from Spain."[13]

Juan, therefore, was disgraced, was deprived of his offices, and made again a simple friar.

Did it grieve him? For an answer, let us look forward to July 6, when he wrote two letters to his nuns. One was to Ana de Jesús at Segovia:

> "Jesus be in your soul," he began. "Since now that I am free, and no longer have charge of souls, I can, by Divine favour, if I so desire, enjoy peace, solitude, and the delectable fruits of forgetfulness of the self and of all things; and so for others, it is good for them also to be without me as they will then be free from the faults which they would have committed through my unworthiness.
>
> "What I beg of you, my daughters, is that you beg the Lord to continue his favour to me, for I still fear that they make me go to Segovia and not leave me wholly free, although I will do what I can to escape from this also; but if this cannot be, Madre Ana de Jesús will not have escaped from my hands, as she supposes, and thus she will not die with the regret that, as she thinks, the opportunity to be holy is over."

[13] Cunninghame Graham, p. 426. This is confirmed by Bruno, pp. 329, 330, and Baruzi, p. 215.

So much for the fidelity of Ana. Such was the way in which these Spanish saints kept their sense of humour. And still writing for quaintness' sake in the third person, he sent her the assurance that whatever happened she should not be forgotten, for, said he, "I still desire her everlasting good."

> "Now till God gives us them in heaven let her occupy herself in practising the virtues of moderation and patience and desire to behave in suffering in some measure as did this our great God when He was humbled and crucified, for this life profits nothing unless we imitate Him. May His Majesty keep you and increase you in His love, amen, even as His holy and beloved bride." [14]

Such was his last farewell to the woman who had so often consoled, encouraged, and inspired him at Beas, the woman to whom we owe the first two of his masterly treatises on mysticism. On the same day he gave another Segovian nun a yet deeper revelation of his secret: after admitting that he was still anxious for Gracián, he wrote:

> "As to my affairs, my daughter, let them not trouble you, for none of them troubles me. What I greatly regret is that trouble is attributed to him who has none; for these things are not done by men but by God who knows what is best for us and ordains things for our good. Think only that God ordains all. *And where there is no love, put love and you will draw forth love.*" [15]

6

He knew that he should receive no honours. When a man at Segovia had suggested those he had answered with the dry shrewdness of the Saints: "I shall be thrown into a corner like an old rag." [16]
Such was the spirit in which, in the summer of 1591, San Juan de la Cruz went off as an exile to the lonely rock of La Peñuela in

---

[14] E. Allison Peers, II, 295-6.
[15] *Loc. cit.*
[16] Bruno, 473.

the Sierra Nevada for his last weeks on earth. He found it a shrine
of silence, recollection, and austerity.

But if Fray Juan de la Cruz had passed beyond the power of discord to disturb his inward peace, discord still was strident, and still
it threatened all on which Teresa and Juan had set their hearts. The
first step towards ruining their work was to damage their reputation.
Fray Diego de Evangelista and Fray Francisco Crisóstomo, therefore,
attempted during these months to work up all possible calumnies
against Fray Juan. "With perverse malignity they threatened and
menaced the terrified nuns into vague admissions and utterances which
were falsified or embellished by the secretary who took them down:
and the Commissary loudly proclaimed that it was his purpose to
cast out from the order him who had been Teresa's first and greatest
recruit. The universal burst of resentment and anger which hailed
these base calumnies against a man whose life had been so absolutely
spotless and free from reproach convinced Doria that there were
limits beyond which even he could not go with impunity." [17]

Meanwhile Fray Juan lived as he had always lived. In the earliest
morning he rose to praise God in wild scenes: he spent much time
alone: he knew that Doria had sent a friar to gather accusations against
him,[18] that every effort was being made to discredit him in order to
expel him from the order, as Gracián was to be expelled and driven
out of Spain. But he did not realize how far injustice could be
pushed. "They cannot take the habit from me," he wrote, "even for
incorrigibility and disobedience, and I am quite prepared to amend
my ways in all wherein I have strayed, and to be obedient, whatsoever penance they give me." [19] That was perhaps his last letter, for
it was written from Úbeda, where they had taken him when he was
very ill. He had written on September 21 to Doña Ana de Peñalosa
to say that on account of this fever he was leaving La Peñuela for
Úbeda.

The poor man had had a miserable journey, riding down on the
mule, with a high temperature, ulcers, the itch of erysipelas, and an
appetite for nothing except asparagus, which was miraculously pro-
cured. When he arrived at Úbeda he was given the poorest and small-

[17] Cunninghame Graham, p. 427. This story is confirmed by Bruno, p. 330.
[18] Bruno, p. 334.
[19] E. Allison Peers, *Works*, III, 298.

THE ALCAZAR AT SEGOVIA, WITH THE CATHEDRAL IN THE BACKGROUND

est cell in the convent. It had nothing in it but a pallet and a crucifix. The Prior who had once been reprimanded by Fray Juan found now his opportunity for revenge: he did everything he possibly could to annoy him, until old Antonio de Heredia, who had been with him at Duruelo, came over to intervene on his behalf. His sufferings remained extreme: his abscesses were like those of Job: and when the rough surgeons of the time cut through the putrid flesh to the bone, the patient was in torment. One kindly friend brought in some musicians to distract him, but he would not allow any alleviation of the sufferings, for he offered them as a sacrifice; those who had watched him saw that "he seemed to have great content at his wounds," so, when the pain had been greatest, he was heard to repeat the words, *Haec requies mea in saeculum saeculi.* They were from the psalm *Memento Domine David:* "This is my rest for ever and ever: here will I dwell, for I have desired it." [20] And so the weeks passed till, on December 7, they made it known to him that he was dying. His answer was, "I was glad when they said unto me we will go into the house of the Lord."

At the last, the Prior repented of his revenge, and was seen at the foot of the dying friar's bed in tears.

As the dying saint became aware that he was to die at midnight on Friday, December 13, he grew yet more silent and peaceful. But his face became radiant when on the Thursday evening he received Extreme Unction. As the sun sank, "I shall be to-night in heaven," he cried exultant. The night deepened. Antonio de Heredia returned and reminded him how they had laboured together to support Madre Teresa. "Father," answered Fray Juan, echoing her, "this is not the time to be thinking of that: it is by the merits of the blood of our Lord Jesus Christ that I hope to be saved." He, too, had recited that *Miserere,* which speaks of a contrite and a broken heart.

But at last the poet's taste turned back to *The Song of Songs:* he heard again and he repeated the rapturous words of passion which were the very essence of his mysticism: [21] his at the very last was "a heart in love with God," [22] and breathing the secrets of love and beauty, and to the echo of his favourite poem, he heard the bell strike

[20] *Works,* E. Allison Peers, III, 370. Cf. Ps. CXXXI, 14 (Vulgate).

[21] This passage is condensed from Bruno, pp. 356-364.

[22] C.E. IX, 5; Allison Peers, II, 61.

midnight. As he said the words "Into thy hands, O Lord, I commend my spirit," the friar who was supporting him saw above the bed a great sphere of light, like that of sun and moon and stars together, sparkling, soft and intense: a sweet perfume filled the room. Those around perceived that he whom they watched no longer breathed: a triple crown seemed to circle his head: his face shone with a brilliant pallor: his expression was one of peace and joy.

So died on December 15, 1591, the coadjutor of Santa Teresa, the Carmelite friar, Fray Juan de la Cruz.

7

If he had died as a captive, he had died also in an atmosphere of intrigue; even after his heart had ceased to beat, they were still trying to manufacture calumnies.[23] But there is a strong power in death: it lends its august unquestionability to many a humble soul; and survivors exchange their sense of irritation at differences and peculiarities for a discovery of all there was to praise. Doria could do no more against Fray Juan; but there still remained the friend of his, whose story was charged with the drama of the reform.

The personality of the friar chosen as chief by Santa Teresa—all the more striking because his temper was conciliatory and mild—was now the target for the fiery darts of Aminadab. In 1592 Doria so elaborated the contrivances he had used against San Juan that he succeeded in expelling Gracián from the order in disgrace. Ana de Jesús was a prisoner in Salamanca; Maria de San José, another of Teresa's chosen, was banished to La Cuerva to die there. As a simple priest, Gracián made his way to Alicante to take ship for Rome. At Alicante the son of the hostelry served him and became his devoted friend. The two spent Holy Week in assisting at the stately ceremonies at Valencia, and finally sailed from Viñaroz. When Gracián arrived in Italy, he found that Doria had, through King Philip's influence, closed all gates against him; he fled for refuge to Sicily to the hospital of Santiago.

On October 11, 1593, after he had embarked at Gaeta for Rome, he was captured by a Turkish Galliot. For some days in the Bay of Naples, he watched pirate galleys swooping on passing barques. A

[23] Bruno, p. 477.

few days later the Turks landed on an island off the coast of Barbary, and finally he was imprisoned in the baths at Biserta. From there he was conveyed to Tunis; and for two years, after being stripped to the skin and branded with red-hot irons, he was in the baths there, his feet in gyves.[24] But in time he impressed his captors. The Sultanas sent him presents of their own food, the baker a daily loaf. Many came to converse with him: many believed him beneficent.[25] He won them over, if not to his religion, at least to himself. Among the camels and their drivers beside the white walls between the intense blue sea and the intense blue sky, he became part of the world of Africa. Amid the turbaned piety of Islam, he performed many acts of Christian charity; and in ministering to the wretched he found a happiness that made his prison among the Moslems seem a haven of peace from the Catholics of Spain, of whom not one would pay enough to ransom him. Yet even here his happy respite was disturbed. His charm again betrayed him: he converted a Moslem. For this, of course, he was treated with extreme rigour: "what we suffered from fleas," he wrote, "and from filth, stench, rats and fear of phantasms that went about those caves was of itself a certain kind of martyrdom: for the worst dungeon of a Christian prison is a delightful garden in comparison to what one goes through here." [26]

At last, by the agency of a Jewish money-lender, his fetters were thrown off, and he was safely lodged with the French consul. The Moslems, relenting, greeted him with warmth. But his Jew, anxious to get a ransom for him, conveyed him in 1595 to Biserta. Finally, he crossed to Genoa, and as a beggar made his way to Rome. There at last his suit was heard; and Pope Clement VIII ordered that he should be reinstated in his order.[27] But though Doria's body was already in the grave, his spirit was still active in his party, and Santa Teresa's chosen was still refused by the Carmelites of Santa Teresa's reform. Then a curious thing happened. The unreformed, since they saw in him a criticism of their reformed brethren's zeal, received him with honour, and in every sense made the most of him. For five years he remained with them in Rome. Then again, after sailing the African coast, in 1601 he returned to Spain to revisit his

[24] Allison Peers, *Studies of the Spanish Mystics*, II, 157.
[25] Cunninghame Graham, II.
[26] *Ibid.*
[27] Allison Peers, *op. cit.*, 158.

family. Finally, as a Carmelite he drifted to Flanders, where, in admirable treatises, he combated the dangers of quietism, already developing there. He also, under the title of *Peregrinación de Anastasio,* wrote the story of his adventures. As a master of the spiritual life, and a friend and coadjutor to Santa Teresa, therefore, he was faithful to the last.[28] One of his works was so much praised as to lead to an English translation.

At Brussels he died on September 21, 1641, at the age of sixty-nine.

Such was the end of the man whom Santa Teresa had found enchanting, to whom San Juan de la Cruz had proved so faithful a friend. He had, it is true, a defect, which in a religious leader is great: he lacked the malice or caution which is so often necessary among the sons of Adam. But for the rest his faults were few.

His story is not inapposite: for his end provides an interesting picture of what might well have happened to his friend Juan de la Cruz, if the poet's body had not proved too fragile for his intense trials. For, when all was said, Fray Juan de la Cruz had been not altogether unfortunate to die when he did die, on that winter night of 1591, obscure, suffering, and calumniated, in the remote valley where the Guadalimar cleaves its way through the Sierra Morena to flow on to the waiting Atlantic.

As for him to live had been Christ, so to die was gain—gain in more ways than one.

[28] Allison Peers, *op. cit.,* p. 159.

Love has no convicts or slaves but brings all things under its obedience with a force so delightful, that, as nothing is as strong as love, nothing also is as sweet as its strength. The virtues are in the soul to moderate its movements: and charity, as first of all the virtues, governs and tempers them all not only because the first in any species of things serves as a rule and measure to the rest, but also because God, having created man in his image and likeness, wills that as in himself, so in man, all things should be ordered by love and for love.[1]

I

FOR there are some men who live with such intensity, or whose place in history is so significant, that their fuller power on earth is exerted after their death. They find, with Mary Queen of Scots, that in their end is their beginning. This is particularly true of a saint who is a writer. The life of San Juan de la Cruz continues among men as a beacon to mysticism, and as a poet.

> Further and further still,
> Through the world's vaporous, vitiate air,
> His words wing on, as live words will.[2]

His personality and his record as a living man certainly enhance his fame and clarify his meaning; but his writings have a life of their own. His doctrine survived among Carmelite writers in Spain, and it is particularly worthy of note that Ana de Jesús went to a Convent at Dijon, where she came into touch with Ste. Chantal and St. François de Sales. The doctrines of Santa Teresa and San Juan are beautifully paraphrased in *Le Traité de l'Amour de Dieu* by St. François de Sales, which appeared just before the complete works of San Juan, and this treatise is perhaps the best comment on them available to English readers. In Spanish there are also admirable treatises by

[1] St. François de Sales, *The Love of God*, Book I, ch. 6.
[2] Thomas Hardy, *Poems*.

Madre Cecilia del Nacimiento, available in the edition by Fray Gerardo of the Works of San Juan de la Cruz.

It was, however, always Teresa who captivated the hearts of that age, as we see in the case of Crashaw. With regard to San Juan, we can trace extraordinary resemblances in Vaughan. There was the Night: there was the call of mysticism to humility:

> O supreme bliss
> The circle, centre and abyss
> Of blessings, never let me miss
> Nor leave that path which leads to thee
> Who art above all things to me.
> I hear, I see all this long day
> The noise and pomp of the broad way.
> I note their coarse and proud approaches,
> Their silks, perfumes, and glittering coaches.
> But in the narrow way to thee
> I observe only poverty,
> And despised things; and all along
> The ragged, mean and humble throng
> Are still on foot; and, as they go,
> They sigh and say, Their Lord went so! [3]

—to retirement:

> Leave, leave, thy gadding thoughts.
> Who pores
> And spies
> Still out of doors
> Decries
> Within them nought. [4]

—and the immediate reward:

> O joys! Infinite sweetness! With what flowers
> And shoots of glory, my soul breaks, and buds;
> In what rings
> And hymning circulation the quick world
> Awakes and sings! [5]

and above all in the celebration of the Night; a celebration which is found again in the Second Act of Wagner's *Tristan und Isolde*.

But San Juan has affinities with all our poets who record a mystical communion.

From the psychological point of view, there is no better introduction to him than Wordsworth with his love of the stars, of midnight,

[3] *Silex Scintillans.*
[4] *Ibid.*
[5] *Ibid.*

of blank ocean and mere hill as a means to still communion when the soul loses itself in the oblivion of worship. This is described also by Coleridge in the lines:

> God only to behold and know and feel
> Till by exclusive consciousness of God,
> All self annihilated, it shall make
> God its identity, God all in all,
> We and our Father one.[6]

It is true that San Juan is always the Catholic theologian, that he is treating of a theme special to his Church and his belief, that he describes the end more luxuriantly, and the process with more precision. He relates more exactly the immanent to the transcendent; but he always leaves the poetry to raise us on its viewless wings when the dull brain perplexes and retards. Literature, therefore, provides one introduction to his genius.

2

If Vaughan echoes in quiet tones the mystical Christianity of San Juan, Wordsworth amplifies the meaning of the word contemplation, and the very idea of creation in regard to it. The third thing, San Juan said, "which the soul desires to see by means of love is the wood and its graciousness. By wood God here means all the creatures which exist within His life; because as all the trees and plants have their root and life in the wood, so creatures celestial and terrestrial have in God their root and their life. And this, says the soul, because there God will manifest Himself in so far as He is life and being to all creatures; she knows in Him their beginning, span of life, and their very selves, because without Him the soul attains nothing nor counts to know them by way of the spirit. The soul much desires to see the graciousness of the forest, which is the grace and wisdom and graciousness which is given by God not only to each creature in itself but to the sage and ordered relation of one to another, and of those above to those below. And to recognize this mystically is a thing of great delight, for it is to have knowledge of God Himself." [7]

This passage on the universe San Juan relates immediately to the

[6] *Religious Musings*, lines 41-45, Globe edn., p. 54.
[7] C.E. XXXVIII, 8. Cf. *Works*, E. Allison Peers, II, 180.

idea of night: "This night by which the soul desires to see these things in mystical experience, because that contemplation is dark, and so it is called by the other name of mystical theology which means a hidden and secret wisdom of God, in which, without noise of words and without the service or help of any sensation of body or spirit, in the silence and quiet of night, dark to the senses and nature, God informs the soul in ways most mysterious and secret without its knowing how: which some masters of the spiritual life call to understand by not understanding. For this is not done by the active intellect, as the philosophers call it, which works in forms and fantasies and apprehensions of things, but it is done, as far as can be passively within the intellect which has no definite impressions, but in its passiveness receives a knowledge of the being of things which is given without any active work or office of its own." [8]

How can this be? If we want a precise psychological account of the virtue of this receptiveness or passiveness, we may well turn forward to Wordsworth. His mysticism is not distinctly Christian: it bears no immediate relation to revelation: but it does explain with extraordinary effectiveness and beauty the psychological state of mystical receptivity, and its effect on its faculties. It is his desire to wait:

> With heart as calm as lakes that sleep
> In frosty moonlight glistening,
> Or mountain rivers, where they creep
> Along a channel smooth and deep
> To their own far-off murmurs listening.[9]

He could be like the River Duddon as it meets the Irish Sea:

> Prepared, in peace of heart, in calm of mind
> And soul, to mingle with eternity.[10]

He insists to Coleridge that

> there are Powers
> Which of themselves our minds impress;
> That we can feed these minds of ours
> In a wise passiveness.

[8] C.E. XXXIX, 9. Cf. *Works*, III, 180. Cf. p. 163, also 138, 139.

[9] *Works*, III, p. 363. The references are to Mr. Nowell Smith's edition in three volumes (Methuen, 1908).

[10] III, 165.

He asks:

> Think you, mid all this mighty sum
> Of things for ever speaking,
> That nothing of itself will come
> But we must still be seeking? [11]

In other words, he teaches that, if we wait in the passiveness of mystical contemplation, things, and the order and harmony of their relation, will reveal to the soul that which they have from God. Therefore he abjures personal talk:

> Better than such discourse doth silence long,
> Long barren silence square with my desire.
> To sit without emotion, hope or aim,
> In the loved presence of my cottage fire,
> And listen to the flapping of the flame
> Or kettle whispering its faint undersong. [12]

For out of this quiet waiting comes the great flight of the spirit:

> Wings have we—and as far as we can go
> We may find pleasure; wilderness and wood,
> Blank ocean and mere sky support that mood
> Which with the lofty sanctifies the low. [13]

He praises the skylark singing in "a privacy of glorious light," as a type of the wise "who soar but never roam." [14] He delights in "the vacant and the pensive mood" as awakening "the inward eye which is the bliss of solitude." [15]

He uses the word imagination, not as the faculty of dealing with images but as

> another name for absolute power,
> And clearest insight, amplitude of mind
> And Reason in her most exalted mood.

and these cannot act but in the exercise of intellectual, of spiritual love:

> Love that breathes not without awe,
> Love that adores, but on the knees of prayer
> By heaven inspired.

[11] Wordsworth, III, 327.

[12] III, p. 342.

[13] III, p. 343. Cf. Ossuna, *Tercer Abecedario,* trat. R, ch. 2, cxxvii, "inspired by good thoughts, the soul rises and flies on the wings of desire to rise more quickly to God."

[14] II, 353.

[15] II, 313.

He insists that we hear echoes of the voice of eternity:

> Have not we too, yes we have
> Answers and we know not whence,
> Echoes from beyond the grave,
> Recognized intelligence? [16]

And who does not know his preciser description of the oncoming of mystical experience? Beauteous forms living on in the mind to awaken

> Sensations sweet
> Felt in the blood and felt along the heart,
> Mingle with feelings of remembered pleasure,

till at times comes a gift

> Of aspect more sublime. That blessed mood
> In which the burthen of the mystery
> In which the heavy and the weary weight
> Of all this unintelligible world
> Is lightened;—that serene and blessed mood
> In which the affections gently lead us on—
> Until the breath of this corporeal frame,
> And even the motion of our human blood
> Almost suspended, we are laid asleep
> In body, and become a living soul;
> While with an eye made quiet by the power
> Of harmony, and the deep power of joy,
> We see into the life of things. [17]

But Wordsworth could describe the experience of quiet yet more precisely than that. He does so in the *Excursion,* where a boy before a great scene of sea and solid earth could read in the silent faces of the clouds unutterable love. Then

> Sound needed none
> Nor any voice of joy; his spirit drank
> The spectacle. Sensation, soul and form
> All melted into him; they swallowed up
> His animal being; in them did he live
> And by them did he live; they were his life.
> In such access of mind, in such high hour
> Of visitation from the living God
> Thought was not; in enjoyment it expired;

[16] Wordsworth, I, 348.
[17] "Tintern Abbey."

> No thanks he breathed; he proffered no request.
> Rapt into still communion which transcends
> The imperfect offices of prayer and praise,
> His mind was a thanksgiving to the power
> That made him; it was blessedness and love! [18]

San Juan, as we saw, had explained how nature has been drawn up into heavenly places in the Ascension of Christ; he thus explains and justifies the natural mysticism of Wordsworth. Wordsworth, in return, is brilliant in psychological description: for no exacter description of contemplation was given by any Saint of the Church than by this English poet. And, like San Juan, he found that he attained this communion through wild nature, and that the blessedness and glory were always one with love.

Once, however, he had connected it also with a human romance when

> All paradise
> Could by the opening of a door
> Let itself in upon him.

This romantic experience of paradise and joy, however, did not lead to personal perfection. Far from it: carried away, partly by his trust in nature and partly by the delirium of his passion, he had allowed his joy to lead to an act which made him the father of an illegitimate child. After that he was more suspicious of the exaltations lent him by his impetuous blood; and never again did he connect a personal attraction or an amorous experience with his account of his spiritual life.

With San Juan things took a wholly different course. From his earliest years he had kept his body in rigorous subjection. He had embraced the heroism of self-denial. His life was consciously supernatural, his illumination, therefore, not nature but divine grace, and his appreciation of nature was allowed only in so far as he looked through nature to the supernatural, as made known to him by the inspiration of the Bible and the life of his Order. He had turned his desires away from the world, turned them to the jealous God within him; once this great emprise was accomplished, there was therefore no taint in the poetry of love. He connected it not with ebullition of the lower nature, but with the delicate exaltation of the ideal. In the

[18] "The Wanderer," I, 215-229.

life of grace, completed in the unity of the Church, natural experiences could lead to holiness more certainly than mystical experiences could do in a life like Wordsworth's, dedicated to nature. The poetry of Love seemed to Fray Juan as perfect an expression of his own eagerness for his heavenly lover, as had been, to saint after saint, *The Song of Songs*. Echoes from the literature of profane love had mingled with his appreciation of this poem, and in the mystical embrace, as he received the "touch" which melted his being into union, he found the completion of both his own heart and his supernatural longings, and fulfilled the significance of every image connected with them. Everything relating to love and passion was super-invested in beauty, and his delight in the images of love takes him through suffering to playfulness. And then, always in the company of the Bible, his soul grows radiant in his delight in nature, and nature's life, but always as revealing God within them.

3

Therefore, even when he insists that contemplation is dark night to the mind and its ways, and though he appears to write as though getting farther and farther from images and sensations, the Bible always kept him in the company of splendid words and images.

And so as a writer he is perforce at one with Santa Teresa, whose visions and similitudes are so remarkable. For she connected them with a new intensity of experience, far deeper than the ordinary processes of the mind: they told of the union of her soul with God. This union was not an image: it was an intuitive apprehension, but it pervaded her being, and she brought back from it something to which words could at least point the way, words which, sometimes in admirable prose, sometimes in naïve verse, were redolent of love and of beauty.

It was almost precisely similar with San Juan. The experience he sought was hardly an experience: it was even "so heroic and so rare as union with the Divine Love." But this union drenched his being, and left him with lofty apprehensions which, like crags with which the wind makes music, could be suggested in the poetry of personal love and bliss.

Had he not learnt in perfect adoration the full meaning of love's secret, and attained to the acme of its joy? That was the source of his poetry. "All a poet's emotional experience," wrote Laurence Binyon, "what he feels, what he thinks, what he hates, what he desires—passes into his verse and moulds its rhythm with infinite subtleties and minute reverberations, so that its beauty is irrevocably implicated in the richness and depth of the poet's spirit and wins thereby a living glow and changeful texture impossible to the most accomplished metrician who is a virtuoso and nothing more." [19]

4

So much for San Juan in relation to the poetry of nature and of love: he takes a central place in its history.

He is equally apposite to the religious philosophy of life and effort.

His self-denial was not inhuman; some of our own Victorian writers have thrown across the chasm between him and profane literature one of those bridges which literature, like all genius and art, is always throwing. One of these is itself a story of Spain: it is *Olalla* by Robert Louis Stevenson.

An officer wounded in the wars in Spain was recommended by his doctor to make a quiet convalescence among wooded mountains in an old country house or *residencia* at some distance from a remote village. The son of the house, Felipe, a wild, simple youth with the shyness of an animal and joys and fears that were all instincts, drove him there. He found many remains of decayed grandeur. It was a stipulation of the hostess, who was of princely family, that he should have nothing to do with her, her son, or her daughter. But the boy took to him, and gradually the hostess herself relented. What of the daughter?

Many significant incidents are related. There was, for instance, in the officer's room the portrait of a lady not without resemblance to Felipe. Both eyes and features, though of striking beauty, had a cruel and sensual expression. The idea of this enchantress haunted the officer, for he feared that, in all her beauty and sinister attraction, she might face him in the person of some descendant. Felipe served the officer, and at times would accompany him on a little ramble. On one of these walks the boy, having caught a squirrel, began to torture it.

[19] Binyon, *Essay on Dante*.

This infuriated the officer, who, however, soon forgave him, and increased his hold upon the boy. Felipe, he noticed, though generally inclined to sloth, and at times to cruelty, still showed the signs of some good influence.

It could hardly be his mother. The officer had seen her in a brilliant dress of some rich stuff, seated on a skin and leaning against a pillar. Her perfect features and noble pose gave her distinction: but the expression of her brilliant eyes was blank. There day after day he would see her, content in the comfort of the sun, and always in her beautiful face the same expressionlessness.

After a little time a sirocco blew up, uncomfortable and disturbing; and that night the officer's quiet was broken by pitiable yet hateful cries. Next day, the weather being again clear and quiet, he explored the house a little further; after wandering through galleries of portraits by famous masters, where he was struck by something common to all these handsome generations, he came into a room furnished for occupation, but severely, and wandering to the writing-table he saw, written in Spanish, the words:

> Pleasure approached with pain and shame,
> Grief with a wreath of lilies came.
> Pleasure showed the lovely sun,
> Jesu, dear, how sweet it shone.
> Grief with her wan hand pointed on,
>   Jesu, dear, to thee.

This was his introduction to Olalla. And it was Olalla, said Felipe, who kept him from going down. Next day, as the officer mounted the marble staircase to a gallery, his eyes met those of the lovely girl herself. Divine bounty had lavished on her colour, energy, slenderness, and spirit. Dressed with a cunning grace which showed her delight in life and beauty, she shone on the pale background of the world with the brilliancy of flowers. The officer, stricken with admiration, felt that her soul was more than worthy of its lodging.

Such was the girl with whom day after day the handsome young officer would exchange a look, and for whose approach he would crave, as a runner on a hot day thirsts for water. But the only time she ever spoke to him, it was to ask him to go away.

Then a horrible thing happened: he had cut his wrist on a window-pane, and going down to the courtyard, he called to his hostess. The

WHAT ENGLISH LITERATURE EXPLAINS 223

sight of blood wakened in her a frantic bestiality. She attacked him, bit him, sucked his blood, sprang at him with those ferocious cries he had heard on the windy night. Felipe and Olalla saved him; and as he lay ill afterwards, Olalla kept watch beside his bed. What then could follow but the avowals of love?

The answer of Olalla was to tell the officer the story of her family. Princely, masterful, and great, they were yet cruel and sensual in their pride, and a curse came upon them. Though their bodies retained strength and grace, their spirits fell asleep; their minds decayed: each generation went a little lower than the one before. The people around them feared to approach them: for their race was a menace to all around. Let it now, said Olalla, cease.

Though she longed to keep her lover, she would send him away; though she loved him, she so hated herself that her love was hateful to her. Though it killed her, let him go.

Next day he drove away to live in the village. But he could not tear himself from the neighbourhood where rapture had tarried with him incarnate. Sometimes in conversation with the priest, sometimes questioning the peasants, he sought to see a little further into the story of the accursed family, and of the saintly, heroic, exquisite being he loved. On her that curse had been for once arrested. She was on an eminence from which she could gauge her family's decline. But as the peasants warned him, the curse was there: the priest told him, too, that the girl knew best. And still he tarried.

Sitting one day upon a height from which he could see the *residencia* far away, he saw her coming up the hill. Though veiled, she was undisguisable. "I thought you had gone," she said; then, leaning upon a wayside crucifix, she pleaded with her lover once more: "Look up for a moment with my eyes and behold the face of the Man of Sorrows. We are all such as He was, the inheritors of sin; we must all bear and expiate a past which is not ours; there is in all of us, even in me, a sparkle of the divine. With Him we must endure for a little while, until morning return, bringing peace. Suffer me to pass on my way alone: it is thus I shall be least lonely, counting for my friend Him who is the friend of all the distressed; it is thus that I shall be most happy, having taken farewell of earthly happiness, and willingly accepted sorrow for my portion."

Such were the last words the lovely girl spoke to her lover, and though he was not a Catholic, he understood the significance of the symbol on which she leaned. "I looked at the face of the crucifix," he writes, "and though I was no friend to images and despised that imitative and grimacing art of which it was a rude example, some sense of what the thing implied was carried home to my intelligence. The face looked down on me with a painful and deadly contraction; but the rays of a glory encircled it and reminded me that the sacrifice was voluntary. It stood there crowning the rock, as it still stands on so many highway sides, vainly preaching to passers-by, an emblem of sad and noble truths: that pleasure is not an end, but an accident, that pain is the choice of the magnanimous, and that it is best to suffer all things and do well." Then he went down the mountain path, and the girl remained leaning upon the crucifix.

This story takes us far towards the heart of San Juan de la Cruz.

5

Eleanor Hamilton King, who brought out *The Disciples* in 1869, also takes us far in a sermon in verse which she puts into the mouth of Fra Ugo Bassi of the Italian Risorgimento. His text was "I am the True Vine: ye are the branches." The True Vine said the branches had grown till its leaves shone green in half the world: from its grapes rivers of juice were flowing: each twined with each, they, its branches, were all living from the Vine's central heart. And what is the life of the Vine? It does not grow at will like the weeds: it has no coloured fantasies of blossom for butterflies to kiss: the fruit of the Vine begins almost before the flower has bloomed. The Vine grows bound. It has its luxuriance of leaf and tendril, but the husbandman cuts deep and sure into its growth; yet, not the less, ripening into fruit, it yields itself with unabated life. Even its fruit is taken. Such is the life of the Vine and its branches

> each entwined
> With each, all living from the Central Heart.
> And you and I, my brethren, live and grow,
> Branches of that immortal human stem.
>
> .   .   .   .
>
> The vine from every living fruit bleeds wine.
> Is it the poorer for that spirit shed?
> The drunkard and the wanton drink thereof,
> Are they the richer for that gift's excess?

> Measure thy life by loss instead of gain;
> Not by the wine drunk, but the wine poured forth.
> For love's strength standeth in love's sacrifice
> And whoso suffers most hath most to give.
> I speak to those who suffer—they will know,
> Better than I the whole deep truth of it.

The preacher takes some instances. The dying soldier who waits in the life beyond for his bride and his child: the artist who finds that his ideal escapes his expression: the man haunted by remorse: the labourer with his sweat and travail: the invalid with long weakness and weary brain, with bitter darkness growing darker still—each shows the sacrifice, even in work, in love, and in joy. Is it not true that this world's unique opportunity is to accept suffering? What better confers the dignity of heroes?

> Our lives here are mostly in the power
> Of other lives, and each of us is bound
> To be his brother's keeper.

And not only, therefore, must we, like San Juan de la Cruz, take the Cross as our burden, but take it, says this poetess, "in the dark" —"not by sight, but faith."

> It were not hard to suffer by His hand
> If thou couldst see His face—but in the dark
> That is the one last trial.

So she, too, knew something of what was known by San Juan de la Cruz.

6

In the same Victorian England a very similar thought came to a distinguished Fellow of Trinity, at Cambridge. F. W. H. Myers was absorbed in psychical research; he wrote searching essays on the classics, and a delightful monograph on Wordsworth; but in his *St. Paul,* he too preached Christ crucified: Christ forsaken.

> Yea, it was well, and thou hast said in season
>   "As is the master shall the servant be."
> Let me not subtly slide into the treason,
>   Seeking an honour which they gave not Thee.

Never at even, pillowed on a pleasure,
    Sleep with the wings of aspiration furled,
Hide the last mite of the forbidden treasure,
    Keep for my joys a world within the world.

Nay but much rather let me late returning,
    Bruised by my brethren, wounded from within,
Stoop with sad countenance, and blushes burning,
    Bitter with weariness, and sick with sin.

Safe to the hidden house of Thine abiding
    Carry the weak knees and the heart that faints,
Shield from the scorn, and cover from the chiding,
    Give the world joy, but patience to the saints.

A promise and a pain: sorrow and sanctity: God renewing His love in His own pain: saints appearing like a heaven of stars, there are so many purified by pain—this is the secret of holiness: shame was its kingdom, reproach its glory, and its power, as the Castilian Carmelite found, was—the Cross!

7

In the same Victorian period of progress and comfort, a book for the sorrowful was written also by a scientist. James Hinton in *The Mystery of Pain* summed up the whole story of effort and discipline, in putting at the summit the faith which is blinded by the darkness of the night. "It is good," he wrote, "to be blest in health and strength and family and friends and prospects and success; in capacity and power and scope for usefulness; in love returned and growing with its return, giving and receiving more with every year, in deeds of wide beneficence which enrich the life of nations. It is good to be blest so: but not so good as to be sacrificed, poor and wretched, halt and maimed and bruised; heart-broken, spiritless, lost utterly—so sacrificed for man's redemption. That is to be like Christ. . . . Blackness of darkness and despair, and sorrow blotting out God's hand, and feebleness sinking without a stay—these are not failures. In these characters was written first the character of our deliverance: these are the characters in which it is renewed."

So much from our Victorians: all of them join with Teresa's friend to find in the love of Christ the lamp of fire which fills with blessing and glory the deepest caverns of the human heart. All of them understood something of what San Juan de la Cruz meant by what he wrote of darkness; each placed himself beside the Cross, though he developed his ideas—as they did not—in relation to complete Catholic theology, worked out in a Catholic life of sacraments and order.

8

But how far we are from understanding San Juan de la Cruz if we do not see that "clear before him through the darkness" there gleamed and burned a pillar of fire! He never ceased to be a Castilian of his age, a man of romance, a lover of beauty, a poet. It is as a poet that he lives on most vividly as a power in Spain, and in the world of letters. And it is poetry which best tells the secret of his mystical theology. Why?

Have we not already found the reason? It is that the admiration of beauty induces the transcendental feeling, as one of Oxford's noblest Platonists called it, which is one form of mystical contemplation. "Some common scene is simply pictured for the mind's eye; some place painted by memories and emotions is pictured for the heart; a face declaring some mood is framed in circumstances which match it and its mood, some fantasia of sound or colour fills eye or ear; some sudden stroke of personification amazes us; there is perhaps nothing more than the turn of a phrase, or the use of a word, or the falling of a cadence—and straightway all is done that the most elaborate and sustained employment of mythological apparatus could do; we are away in the dream world and when we presently return we are haunted by the feeling that we have seen the mysteries." [20] Mysticism is never served so well as by the high seriousness of poetry. Ronsard wrote:

> Dieu est en nous et par nous fait miracle,
> Si que les vers d'un poete escrivant,
> Ce sont des dieux les sécrets et oracles
> Que par sa bouche ils poussent en avant.[21]

Poetry is not merely a patterned excellence of imagery and sound. "The art of style," wrote Herbert Trench, "is to add to beauty and

[20] J. A. Stewart, *Myths of Plato*, p. 23.
[21] Ronsard, *Abrégé de l'Art Poétique.*

precision of expression the impression that reality lies behind the words, and the spirit of beauty in turn behind that reality." [22] And conversely, the fullest experiences of the religious mystic are more than a sense of silent communion: they illumine the world of phenomena, and indeed the whole scheme of life, with richest significance. For poet and mystic alike are enabled to see into the life of things: the outward beauty keeps mingling with life and life's own secret joy, and when the light of sense goes out, it is with "a flash that has revealed the invisible world." It is a high moment of exhilaration when

> The heart and soul and sense in concert move,[23]

that leads to high achievement in the revelation of life and beauty.

"The poet is, as Plato said, a winged being. It is not the action of visible and individual things which engenders his creation: he escapes their grasp and soars above them, receiving his inspiration from on high. But if the idea is born, as it were, by an immaculate conception, still, on the other hand, it is inconceivable that in its effect after development and expression the idea should disdain what the material world already offers. No thought can come to its full and real existence unless it becomes incarnate in a form, an image, a symbol." [24]

9

Nowhere is this symbol so subtle as in the evocations of a word. Words flash to the deepest cavern of human nature, illumining them with lamps of fire, and the fire is the eternal mystery. So it was that San Juan de la Cruz wrote about the glories and blessings of contemplation, and spoke of the unspeakable. So it is that he is steeped in the words of the Bible, so he knew that Christ has the words of eternal life. And since they are the words of eternal life, their wealth

[22] Written in pencil in a copy of Mr. Middleton Murry's *Problem of Style* in the library of the British Institute at Florence.

[23] Byron, *Don Juan*, II, Canto 168.

[24] Preface by Emile Boutroux to *Le Sens de l'Art*, by Paul Gaultier.

of significance is boundless. "For in His hand are both we and our words, all understanding and all acquaintance with divers crafts." [25] A spiritual sense of words is founded upon the literal one, and is more powerful.[26] Words which carry this life from the vast deeps to the mind's eye, and "pipe to the spirit ditties of no tone," were the means by which Juan de la Cruz found communion with the eternal; and through his words he offers this communion to us.

He is therefore the great vindicator of the Bible—the Bible not alone read, but learnt by heart and contemplated till it flashes with a new significance more intensely personal, more mysterious, more holy, as a book in a unique sense inspired.

In what sense is the Bible uniquely inspired? The human writers of the Bible were not necessarily conscious of their inspiration: they were used by the Holy Spirit to convey His revelation to men of faith as a musical instrument is used by a musician to convey his purpose to those responsive to music. It is the Holy Spirit who provides for those guided by Him the wealth of meaning in inspired words. He gives the Bible the cogency of a living voice of the Spirit speaking to spirits, even though the human writer remains himself with his style, his personality, his knowledge, his intention. In this household of the Faith, it is this living voice which speaks the words of eternal life.

10

San Juan de la Cruz was so absorbed in the Bible, and his own particular mysticism, linked with nature, that he leaves no word of his attachment to the traditional worship of the Roman Catholic Church. He accepted her judgment on his doctrine, yes; but how little does he say on the sacraments! Only once does he refer to baptism: "the day of baptism wherein the soul received total cleanness and purity, which the soul says here in these lines that He would give her at once in the same union of love." [27]

But *his works contain no mention of the Mass*. He did write in his verse

[25] Wisdom, vii, 16, 17.
[26] Aquinas, *Summa Theologica,* I, 1.
[27] C.E. XXXVII, 5.

> The eternal tide flows hid in living bread
> That with its heavenly life we too be fed,

but we must remember that when he expounded the line:

> Feast freshening us for love's delight,
> *La cena que recrea y enamora,*

he made no reference to Holy Communion. "It is to be known," he
writes that in "Divine Scripture *this word supper (or feast) is understood of the Divine Vision:* for, as supper is the end of the day's work
and the beginning of the night's rest, so this knowledge we have
called tranquil gives to the soul a realization of the sure termination
of things evil and the possession of things that are good." [28]

He refers only once to the Blessed Virgin, and then as an example
of wisdom—in *The Ascent of Mount Carmel*—and he certainly
vindicates the use of images; but one can hardly say that he en-
courages it. His extreme dislike of the Andalusians was due probably
not merely to their images, but to their love of the ceremonies and
diversions offered them by their Church.

In contrast to this, we have an absorption in the worship of the
Trinity, a celebration of the Incarnation—the praise of mystical
spirituality, and in one poem he shows a tender feeling for the
Passion; [29] with all these he takes a constant delight both in the
barrenness and the bountifulness of nature: in sierras, in strange
islands, in groves, streams, breezes, springs, meadows, flowers, perfumes, birds, dawn, rocks, caverns, fire, rays of light, and above all
the quietness and darkness of the night. He praises God for creation:

> The world, the clustering spheres He made,
> The glorious light, the soothing shade,
> Dale, champaign, grove and hill,

but above all he prefers the suggestion of solitude and mystery:

> The multitudinous abyss
> Where secrecy remains in bliss
> And wisdom hides her skill.[30]

[28] C.E. XIII and XIV, 28. Cf. *Works,* E. Allison Peers, II, 90.
[29] See the poem, "Un pastorcico solo está penado."
[30] Smart, *Song to David.*

II

In the spiritual life, also, he had his particular originality. Others have written of faith; others have written of love; but none has insisted as he does on the virtue of hope. By hope he means: first, the elevation and purification of memory; secondly, the cultivation of oblivion; and thirdly, the setting of affection upon things above. For "having hope in God gives the soul such wisdom and courage and aspiration to the things of eternal life that by comparison with what it hopes for then all things in the world seem to be, as indeed they are, dry and faded and nothing worth." [31] It is by hope that we say, "My eyes are ever unto the Lord." [32]

Here, then, are the two peculiarities of San Juan de la Cruz: first, to take from memory the noted experiences: whatsoever things are just, whatsoever things are pure, whatsoever things are lovely, whatsoever things are of good report: if there be any virtue, if there be any praise, think on these things.[33] And then risen with Christ to seek the things above that we may find our heaven now, in tasting and seeing this graciousness of the Lord; secondly, to study and to be so impregnated with the Bible that our minds, enlightened by faith, will ever be pressing on with ardour to the prize set before us; the prize which is the fullness which filleth all in all. And if mystical poets take us in their own way to their own realm, we must learn from other literature, more common and familiar, what he meant by *The Dark Night*. For all the words of the Bible are but reverberations of the one Word of God, by whom He made the worlds, that we might learn "the universal and public manuscript of nature," what by illumined literature He offers to the spiritual life in the Bible.

[31] *Dark Night*, Book II, xxi, 6.
[32] Psalm XXIV, 16.
[33] Phil. IV, 8.

It seems as if I could sit silent all day long with the thought of God overflowing my soul as the pebbles bathed in the Willow Brook. For thoughts are so great, aren't they, sir? They seem to lie upon us like a deep flood; and it's my besetment to forget where I am and everything about me, and lose myself in thoughts that I could give no account of, for I could neither make a beginning nor ending of them in words.[1]

Ab occultis meis munda me, Domine, et a peccatis alienis parce servo tuo.

Cleanse me from my secret faults, O Lord, and from the sins of others spare thy servant.

Psalm XVIII, 12, 13 Vulgate.

I

SINCE the love of creatures reproduces in, and delegates to, the world of nature that love which unites the Father with the Son by Whom He made the world, and since this created love is carried back with Him into the Divine Being; and since this is the object of creation; therefore *The Song of the Spirit*, in which the mysticism of Wordsworth is vindicated, is a light and almost playful song in the words of a young man's fullest joy in love and its attendant luxuries.

> The purest lines of blue and red
> Mingled to dye the curtain spread
> Over our flower-embroidered bed.
>   Shielded by claws [2] of lions.
> It was all made of peace and love,
> A thousand golden shields above
>   Spoke of Spain's noblest scions.
>
> For where thy footprints left their trace
> Youth's fairest now delight to race
>   A path replete with charm.
> There by the kindling of a spark

[1] George Eliot, *Adam Bede,* third page of Chapter VIII.
[2] Lit. *cuevas = dens.*

Inflamed, and by the mulled wine dark
Inebriated, take I, mark
   You, healing and heavenly balm.

Hid in the deepest delved earth
My loved one kept of wine no dearth,
   And there I drank my fill,
And when I drank, I knew no more;
I lost the flock I'd kept before
   And led o'er mead and hill.

There on his breast I lay reclined
And there I learnt the rarest kind
   Of a delicious science,
And holding nothing back, but all
Surrendering to his charm and thrall,
   I did my soul affiance.

All that I ever did or owned
Was freely to his service loaned
   In one bold enterprise.
I have no task: I guard no sheep,
I have no other prize to keep,
   Love's all my exercise.

And since upon the common ground
To-day I am no longer found,
   You'll deem that I was lost,—
That walking in a blissful trance
I into maze of love did dance,
   To Treasure Island crossed.

Of greenest emeralds, and of flowers
Gathered in freshest morning hours,
   We'll make our garlands rare,
That with the glint of brightest gems
Enmeshed, your love will find his petalled stems
   Inwoven with my hair.

And when you look upon my neck
And saw beneath the curls that deck
   My head, one hair escape and rest,
To see it there, and let my eye
Meet thine was all enough to tie
   Thee captive to my breast.

For when thou fixed upon my face
Thine eyes, they gave it wondrous grace,
   Till thou thyself wert captured
By thy reflected beauty.
And then my adoration duty
   Was, my *task* to be enraptured.

So dusky though my hue! Despise
Me not. For from thine eyes
　　Does come so rich a change
In all they look on, and thy gaze
Such fairness lends and favour as amaze
　　All, they're so wondrous strange.

And now we've seen the bride repair
Into the longed-for garden fair
　　Refreshed with scent and charm.
She there her bridegroom has divined
And clings to him, her neck reclined
　　On his embracing arm.

Beneath that selfsame apple-tree
My bride plighted her troth to me,
　　And there she took my ring—
There where her mother suffered wrong
Was ransom paid for all that long,
　　Long tale of suffering.

Ye birds that fly on wafting wings,
Ye mountains, valleys, rivers, springs,
　　And waters leaping from the height,
O lion that roars, O buck that springs,
Heats, breezes, winds and all the things
That terror from the darkness brings
When anxious thought our soul enrings
　　With prowling fears at night.

I charge you by the gentle lyre
That from henceforth ye cease your ire,
　　And by the siren's song,
I charge you not to touch the wall
Around her garden and her hall
Of sacred silences which all
　　Guard blissful sleep and long.[3]

And here, as he explains once more, reclining in intimate trust with her neck on the encircling arm of her lover, he leaves the bride resting, the bride who typified the contemplative soul united to the heavenly bridegroom.

But still the poet's fancies range; still the little bells of poetry ring through his mind. And in a moment he is away with the birds, birds coming from the Bible, birds flying through the air, birds jargoning their wedding songs, birds building their nests; since each had for the mystic its meaning:

[3] Pp. 225-7, st. 16-31.

The dove that flies with gleaming wings
The olive branch now homeward brings
    To Noah's teeming ark.
The bird who fain of love would teach
To him she loves on the green beach
    Is singing like the lark.

It was her lot to live alone,
Alone she through the air has flown
    At her adored's behest.
Because her painful loneliness
Knew only one to cure distress,
Alone with her alone, and bless
The lonely care she took to dress
    Her wild and waiting nest.[4]

When he explained these verses that surpassed all explanation, poetry and prose still mingled to make his mystical essay and to tell the story of his heart. For the saint was poet, the poet saint.

2

Nevertheless, there had been a stage in the process where San Juan had had to make the most determined effort to escape from images and even from thought. Santa Teresa never speaks of such an effort as this: the reason was that she was more a woman than an intellectual; and more a woman of affairs than a poet. Her whole nature gave itself to God in great harmonies of love and charity, harmonies which perfected her relations to all around her, and—though they aroused opposition—aroused also admiration and enthusiasm. She was, as it were, the perfect type of a religious Spanish lady; but San Juan was not a typical hidalgo who had become a mystic. He was first of all intensely intellectual. He was a combination of a theologian and a poet. It was, therefore, easy for his imagination to keep him back in the ravishing pictures it put before him: to stop in an imagination of some human love or some created beauty, and drink his joy from that. To be freed from his own passion and imagination, that was the problem—and he could be so to some extent by his theology. But were he to think hard, an equivalent problem would arise: his intense energy would be absorbed in the travail of the mind. His was a nature phenomenally intense; thought and imagination fascinated him in turn, each with its own exclusiveness. Some-

[4] P. 228, st. 34-5.

times he felt all thought, sometimes all heart; [5] therefore he had the subtle and arduous task of transcending both to give himself to that intense, concentrated, yet complete, love of God which by occupying all his faculties taught him what contemplation meant.

Teresa needed to refine and train her intellect: she needed more study of the Bible. She loved and acted simply as a woman. Only by the most heroic effort could Juan attain to what had become habitual to Teresa. He felt he must on the one hand escape from the little tracasseries of administration to keep his whole psychology calm and whole: "to detach itself from things, to flee from business; to live with measureless tranquillity." [6]

That is the first theme of *The Song of the Spirit*. Let the soul seek God in His own temple, which is no other than the seeker's soul. Always realize that God is in His hiding-place, and He must be served hidden within it. He has placed darkness in His hiding-place. "You do well then at all times, now by adversity, now by prosperity, whether of inward or outward things to keep God hidden." *For He is a God that hideth himself*.[7] He lives hidden in every soul, even in souls of grievous sin. And since He is hidden in humanity, so men are hidden in Him, and the souls of the faithful are especially hidden, hidden—with Christ—in God; and it is direct from God Himself that they learn all the secrets of the world He has created, and this hiding-place of the soul is the citadel of mysticism, the citadel from which He makes victorious forays in the environs of created life.

That, therefore, was the first truth to grasp: "the kingdom of God is within you." [8] You must be a Nicodemus, and come to Jesus through the night. The way from the house of bondage to the promised land is through the desert by the miraculous guidance of cloud and fire.

> Round each habitation hovering
> See the cloud and fire appear,
> For a glory and a covering
> Showing that the Lord is near.

[5] *Living Flame*, III, 3. "Sometimes all intelligence with hardly any love: sometimes all love without any intelligence." Cf. Baruzi, p. 708.

[6] *Ibid.*, verse 3 of strophe 4. Cf. Baruzi, p. 695.

[7] Isa. xlv, 15: "Verily thou art a God that hidest Thyself." C.E., I, 3.

[8] Luke xvii, 21.

Thus they march (the pillar leading
  Light by night and shade by day),
Daily on the manna feeding
  Which he gives them when they pray.[9]

3

Yet all the while San Juan was the son of the Church; and the Church was the Body of Christ, living to continue His Incarnation, living as a witness of His Resurrection and Ascension, living as a great corporate institution centred on the Mass. And to that institution San Juan not merely lived as a Spanish Catholic, but as a priest, a confessor, and a friar. He never showed the slightest inclination to depart from it: on the contrary, his whole aim was to live within it more strictly. The background of his life was the Mass, with the whole liturgy and the whole sacramental system of the Catholic Church. If he writes poems like a profane lover, or prose like a Quaker who cares nothing for forms, it was because in writing his spirit found freedom for its originality.

The Church had no quarrel with him. His writings were never under suspicion: in spite of the antipathy of Doria, he was generally recognized as the ornament of his order. His authority had been vindicated through the long succession of years. Beatified in 1675, he was canonized in 1726; and two hundred years later, in 1926, declared a Doctor of the Universal Church. Rome, in fact, set up this extraordinarily free mystic, this poet of love, this man who never said a word about her religious practices, whose works could have been written—in almost every paragraph—by a Protestant—Rome set him up as the supreme authority on the profoundest religious experience, him who, following Francisco de Ossuna, wrote of a contemplation that beyond all forms and images and the perceptions of outward things, even of the Incarnation and the Passion of Christ,[10] sought to worship the Invisible alone, the substantial mystery—the being of God.

Nor was this all. When he wrote in verse his essential meaning,

9 John Newton, *Olney Hymns.*
10 Let us remember, however, his devotion to the Incarnation and Passion in his poems: *Un pastorcico solo,* and not least in the *Romances:* and, if he wrote them, the poems *Ajeno de dolor, Aquas puras cristalinas.*

he went to laymen and romances for his model and wrote in the style of a pastoral poet in love.

His treatises on asceticism and mysticism—brilliant as they are—have neither the popularity, the intensity, nor the beauty of the poems which charm the man of letters as much by their passion, their imagery, and their music as they edify the spiritual man by all that they convey of the mysteries of the highest communions of the soul. Never since *The Song of Songs* had the poetry of passionate love been more eloquent. Thus the poet shows how in the most secret depths of heart and soul, the mystic consummates love. Here, then, is the essence, the truth, the finest and the purest part, of love.

"The characteristic ineffability of mystical experiences has obliged the mystical writers to employ allegories and metaphors," says Professor Sainz Rodríguez, "as in a certain way the whole spiritual life is a manifestation of love between God and man, metaphors referring to passion and the Christian idea of marriage predominate." [11]

For the Holy Spirit, working through human instruments, reveals to those whom He has chosen a vast range and mystery of meaning as to the life of Christ in God and of the Church in Christ, and the life of men in the Church both here and hereafter. It is this process of revelation which explains the use of symbolism both in *The Song of Songs,* and in *The Song of the Spirit,* since the Holy Spirit is super-essential love.

4

Love, said the Platonist Dionysius, is *unitiva virtus,* the power which joins two natures into one. It is a personal magnetism which blends two separate hearts. The agencies in the blood, which in the Middle Ages were called "spirits," and identified with the instruments of generation; the subtler power which resides in the eye, and speaks, if not to the soul, to the heart, which, as a vital magnetism, lives also in the understanding; the intuitive sympathies which, like music, pass in vibrant rhythm from one nature to the other: give a knowledge which is itself union, and which St. Thomas Aquinas compared to a fire; for when it is applied it consumes into itself the nature it touches. What, therefore, does the Church mean when she

[11] *Introducción a la Historia de la Literatura Mística,* p. 50.

says that God is love, or that where love and charity are, there is
Christ? She means, according to St. Thomas, that the knowledge
which God has of Himself is so spontaneous, so complete, so perfect
that what is known is a Perfection as distinct and vital as that which
knows, and that this knowledge is itself so perfect and so vital that
it, too, is without difference in degree or nature, so that here is a
triply perfect unity. It is this which, by sovereign choice, by impress-
ing form on nothingness created "Nature's living images"; for then
(we return to Dante's phrase)

S'aperse in nuove amor l'Eterno Amore.[12]

It is in this triple agency which is mirrored not only in the generation
of life, but in all act and in all thought, for each is a communion in
which there is a vital intercourse between a mind and that which is
outside it.

This intercourse finds expression in a creative concept. Knowledge
is nothing other than conception or generation: so the Church, to
express the relation of the Second Person of the Trinity to the First,
speaks of Him now as the Word, and now as the Son. We can attain
by an overflow of the Divine gifts within us to a unifying knowledge,
which is the intellectual love of God. It is on this faculty which San
Juan de la Cruz speaks with magisterial precision, and which he relates by a clearly reasoned system not only of theology and philosophy
but of æsthetics.

Though this mystic intercourse can be attained only by a peculiar
mental aptitude for divine love, and a gift of divine grace, much
of its psychology and its nature can be understood from analogies of
human love. We all know of men devoted to their wives, and to their
families, who have no taste for dreaming about them: there are others
who can busy themselves rapturously for hours in the memory or
imagination of some particular delight. So there are some who find in
prayer itself a form of doing good; while in prayer itself there is a
sharp distinction between those whose minds are busy and those who
remain poised over one consideration or one image in a happy repose.
Again, human love can become an experience so deep and so profound that not only does it make scenes of the outward world swarm

[12] Cf. p. 89.

with enchantment, but the realization of requited feeling seems to un-
veil the mystery of the universe. "My life, my All, my more," said
Sappho to Philaenis. To natures like Donne's, like Browning's, or
like Meredith's, or even like Wordsworth's, capable of intense rapture
in human love, to have the heart and mind absorbed in their love
seems to bring them to the core of all reality: the temporal things
pass away into a communion with a grandeur beyond: the poet holds

> unconscious intercourse
> With beauty old as creation.

It is, in fact, the distinction and the function of great literature to
keep suggesting a sense of universal and sublime things stretching
away illimitably from, and yet vitally connected with, a particular
scene or event. Wordsworth has expressed this with great precision in
relation to woods and streams, to

> The silence that is in the starry sky,
> The sleep that is among the lonely hills.

Meredith combined it by forever thinking of nature and of human
love in terms of one another, till he tells us that

> have we knelt, or never knelt
> And eyed as kine the springs
> Of radiance, the radiance enrings
> And this is the soul's haven to have felt.[13]

But it is when we get beyond this sense of mystery and beauty to that
of another mode of being where the body and its images are laid
asleep, when we are

> Rapt into still communion which transcends
> The imperfect offices of prayer and praise,

when, like Browning, looking at the other soul side of his moon of
poets, I see

> all the novel,
> Silent, silver lights and darks undreamed of
> Where I hush and bless myself with silence,[14]

[13] Meredith, *Winter Heavens.*
[14] *One Word More.*

THE CHARACTER OF OLD CASTILE, ILLUSTRATED BY A VIEW OF A CITY AND MOUNTAINS

it is at such times that human joys reach out towards and touch the joys of religious mysticism.

For Dom Bede Frost is right in his own way when he says that valid mystical experience is given to others than the conscious and deliberate contemplative Christian. Where the things of nature end and those of grace begin, who can say? Creation is irradiated with gleams of the Divine.

"Those who have set their eyes upon truth itself," he writes, "whether they be philosophers, seeking the inner and ultimate truth of things: or poets and musicians, translating ineffable mysteries into words and harmonies, which touch with magic fingers the inmost chords of our hearts: or scientists pursuing truth along the ways of experience: or the contemplatives, rising to the contemplation of Supreme Truth, God Himself, each have, in their own manner and degree, touched and tasted of the very source of life, of truth, of goodness and of beauty; they in doing so enrich their fellows with that which neither barbarian hordes, nor exploiters of men, no less barbarian in nature, can destroy. For different as are the mirrors into which they gaze, that which they look upon is the same image in which they were created and seeing in some manner they must reflect." [15] Nevertheless there is still a distinction between the natural experience and the supernatural contemplation of those who live in Christ for the ends of Christ.

For there the heart leads up to a life of the soul so far transcending human things that it can remain poised in contemplation without any imagery whatever; and beginning in this immediacy where the only speech is that of heart to heart, where pictures and emotions both are laid aside, the mystic, enveloped as it were in darkness, and yet holding an unseen hand, enters into the labours, the agony, the weariness, and the bliss of a life in immediate communion with the love and beauty of which the sublimest things of nature and of human kind were but transient and dim suggestions. For who can count the blessings of those who, leaving the ways of nature for ways sacred and all divine, learn the deep things of God and the mysteries of His Trinity?

[15] B. Frost, *In His Image*, pp. 223, 224.

5

The life of perfection, as we saw, requires a double action, one the negation of desires, the other one of loving union. With the annihilation of desire for created things must go the prayer of the heart—with, or without words.

The first great step in prayer is meditation in which reason and imagination are at work, but in which each attains nothing unless informed by love. Love, and not speculation, is the essence of prayer. When this loving consideration finds discursive thought impossible, when the imagination can no longer rest on particular things, when it rejoices in loving attention to God, the soul rests in the higher state of contemplation.

An English mystic, Walter Hilton, in *The Scale of Perfection,* traces the mystic life from the study of divinity to a "living love in devotion," and "a tasting of the sweetness of the love of God," which comes for a short time, and thence to a higher form for those who by the grace of Jesus and long travail, corporal and spiritual, have arrived at a rest and quietness of heart and purity of conscience so that nothing is more pleasing to them than to sit still in quiet of body and to pray always to God and to think on our Lord, until finally in true contemplation a man's soul is first reformed by perfection of virtues to the image of Jesus; and afterwards, when it pleases God to visit him, he is taken in from all earthly and fleshly affections, from vain thoughts and imaginings of all bodily creatures, and as it were much ravished and taken up from his bodily senses; by the grace of the Holy Ghost he is enlightened to see by his understanding truth itself, which is God, and spiritual things with a soft, sweet, burning love in God; then he becomes ravished with His love, and so the soul for the time is become one with God and conformed to the blessedness of the Trinity.

His contemplation has two forms: loving attention and simple recollection. The first is an attachment of the will and soul, without images or passions; the other is a regard from the depths of the soul, a quiet but steady gaze, a mild but intense ardour.

The touchstone of progress is the test of works. If ardent prayer (even though it should attain to rapture) does not show the result of an unselfish sacrifice in life, of detachment and of humility, unless above all it issues in faith, in hope and in charity, it is highly dangerous. Faith unites the understanding with God, hope turns the memory towards Him above all images of pleasure, charity burns as a living flame in the depths of the soul's heart to consume all into unity with the sovereign good.

Seeking, therefore, everything in God, who never fails and who is sufficient, the mystic has, indeed, placed his hope upon a rock. His is the strongest and most courageous love: it asks for neither sweetness nor savour. It prefers the difficult to the easy, work to repose, lowliness and contempt to height and praise. It finds the perfection of holiness in one thing only, an entire surrender of self to God, so proving that

> *Il ben nostro in questo ben s'affina*
> *Che quel che vuole Iddio e noi volemo.*[16]

This is the heroic venture on which San Juan de la Cruz was engaged.

6

Although he had explained the development of the Catholic mystic both with more scholarly precision and with more lyrical exuberance than any other, he makes it plain that it is yet a track which is different for every individual. He and Teresa were in intimate agreement: and they instructed one another. But their work is different. Both illuminated brilliantly the caverns of the soul. Neither insisted on a scheme. To each, in fact, had been given an individual nature to attain a new freedom under the guidance of the mysterious and infinite Wisdom. For contemplation gives each soul a separate and private ascent of the heights; [17] and the ascent is also largely independent of the sequence of time; for so high is its narrow, winding track, that it gives, at every turn, gigantic views, both forward and backward into the mountainous scenery through which it passes. The higher and more bracing the air, so much clearer is the sky, but

[16] Our own good with this good has one end,
   That what our Lord desires, desire we also.
                        Dante, *Paradiso*, XX, 137-8.
[17] Devout souls run in many ways and various directions, each according to the spirit which God bestows. C.E. XXV, 4. Cf. *Works*, E. Allison Peers, II, 322; and E. I. Watkin, *The Philosophy of Mysticism*, p. 131.

fiercer, when they come, are the ice and blizzard. At last the exercise
is so tense, the spectacle so sublime as sun and dark alternate over
the snow, and irradiate the immediate scene—the gulfs below, the
crags above—with the colours which flash upon the silvered earth in
the fires of cloud and ether, that the climber can distinguish no more
between effort and attainment. Joy is so poignant, pain so rapturous;
and though he is steeped in a bliss which exceeds all that he could
ask or think, the spectacle of his universe becomes sublimer in a flash
of "wild lightnings from the heaven of pain"; and his content is
transmuted to a yearning to contain more and to be less unworthy.

How is it, one might ask, that so much tension comes into a
mystic's life?

In the first place, it is after the aches, the weariness, the sleepless-
ness or vigil, the fasting, sometimes the illness, sometimes even the
scourging, by which the nerves in the flesh cease to provide for the
soul the sense of ease, that the edge and zest of exhilaration come.

Secondly, the soul will know the envy, the hatred, the intrigue,
the unfaithfulness, the suspicion and the calumny with which by a
natural reaction the ordinary man visits those living by a principle he
does not understand. Since the mystic is passionate, he will be accused
of disordered and unhealthy passions: since he is living by a higher
energy, he will be suspected of both superiority and uselessness: since
he shares much with poets and with those other contemplatives who
worship in other ways, he will be called a pagan; and since form is
less to him than spirit, he will be under suspicion of heresy. The
mystic must not marvel, therefore, if he is hated by the world, or by
a certain kind of churchman.

And, thirdly, he will suffer from subtle and insidious temptations,
from the crafts and assaults of the devil attacking him in dangerous
thoughts, and in forms so peculiar, that few can tell whether they
are sins or not.

But apart from all these he will suffer most of all from his love:
for his ardour for perfection will see in each flitting occasion of an
ordinary day the crisis of success or failure in what he cares for most.
He will be sensitive to the views and life of others: his nerves will
vibrate in felicity or depression to every spell of sunshine or cloud,
every breath of warm or cold air, in the atmosphere either of weather
or companionship. But more than all these, he is so attached to each

object of his love that it is torment to give any up. Yet he must one by one surrender them all. For his real joy is dependent not on these, but on a presence of which he is aware in the innermost self of self. The Divine Incarnation finds an abiding place, says another Spanish Carmelite, Madre Cecilia del Nacimiento, in the heart, by which she means "the intimate part of the will or the essence of the soul, where she has a life grounded in the very life and essence of her Creator, an immensity so profound that it is like a bottomless well or rather an ocean, since it was created by God after His own image or likeness." [18] Here the life of the contemplative is so intense and poignant that he has sharp foretastes of the life of sheer soul beyond death.

Yet, since in all these he must be patient, seeking the Divine Will, he will accept them with a resignation which means peace; and peace shines with a cloudless joy—a serenity of rest arising out of thankfulness and praise. As in time he keeps a sense of timeless being, so his grace has the richness and strangeness of the glory which invests, transforms, and perfects grace [19] by gleams which at last flow in noonday radiance on that depth which is the true place of understanding, which Hopkins called

> The selfless self of self most strange, most still
> Fast furled and all foredrawn to no or yes.[20]

Madre Cecilia called it the heart. The contemplative therefore holds in his heart a stillness which is alive like the heart of a rose.[21] Others know before they love: he loves at sight, and through loving knows by the knowledge given to his heart.[22]

Of such was the Carmelite and poet, Juan de la Cruz. Of such was not less Teresa who lived in the name of Jesus.

7

The characteristics that mark the contrast between San Juan and Santa Teresa are also the reasons for the harmony between them. Both

[18] Madre Cecilia, *Transformación*, quoted by E. I. Watkin in *The Philosophy of Mysticism*, p. 98.

[19] Terrien, *La Grace et la Gloire*, I, 99-101.

[20] Hopkins, poem 54.

[21] I owe this phrase to the Revd. George Seaver, who took it in turn from an anonymous essay written by Evelyn Underhill.

[22] Pascal.

had gifts which suited them to be placed in administrative positions, and both were advanced contemplatives: both knew that mystical theology by which the soul enters into intuitive communion with God and drinks from His grace and glory as the babe drinks from its mother's breast. But the result of this inflow of life and nourishment differed, as their gifts were different. Those of Teresa were very little in the world of philosophy or theology; but she shared with the great women of Spain a sovereign knowledge of life and men; and her every word and gesture show her power in managing them, a power which was strengthened, unified and perfected by her gift of contemplation. But San Juan was an intellectual; and when he had risen above the finest things of the intellect to contemplation, the abounding life, which he drank into the depths of the soul, enriched and illumined his philosophical faculties, and made him an expert in the psychology of mysticism. Many a navigator can by instinct manage a ship in a storm; but only he with a mathematical knowledge can chart the voyage. The light came direct from on high to enrich the particular gifts of San Juan; it made his psychological analysis extraordinarily subtle and precise.

What light does this throw on the relation of mysticism to poetry? Both Santa Teresa and San Juan were poets; she because without any close study of the Bible or her contemporary Spaniards she lived among people who had the gift and habit of making verses, and he because he had a refined and educated literary taste. Both then turned naturally to verse and its symbolism to express the gaiety and vitality which their mystical experience brought into their lives, or the passion with which they longed for its returns. Beauty was their delight, and poetry the language of their lives. But just as she was greater in the creative work of founding Carmelite Convents and building up the reform, so he, though not without administrative gifts, was greater than she as writer and incomparably greater as poet. The reason was not that he was necessarily a more advanced mystic or a greater saint. We cannot in our comparisons of such souls speak of such measures as less or more. But their gifts were complementary: she had the courage, strength and determination of a conquistador; he the sensitiveness, passivity and intuition of an enraptured bride. He was the less striking person in the eyes of men, and, though his elevation was admired, came far more slowly to influence and fame. Yet, in the realm of the lyric, he shone more and more eminent; it was because the passion of his nature, his intense susceptibility to the music and beauty of words, and his creative gift were both psychological and artistic, till finally his contemplative genius gave him a distaste for administration. So it is that in him both poetry and mysticism reach their culmination, that he is the prince of the frontier region where their territories interpenetrate, and their adherents rejoice over the conquests of one another.

8

He was capable of the hard work of thinking to apply it in the matters of faith. He was trained in the school of theological logicians. But it was not their language which he chose, or commended. His method was firstly that of the poet, and then of the Platonic interpreter of poetry, for, according to a saying in the Vedas, *"Poetry is a word the savour of which is its essence."* [23]

This led Réné Daumal to compare poetry with *Sapientia,* in which mystics delight to see a thing which is closely connected with *Sapor.* For them the gift of wisdom is, as we saw in the case of Denys the Carthusian, that which gives them a taste for love, and for the love of what is best. And since this taste is a thing of delight, it is also perceived and enjoyed as beauty, or again as music. And from these it leads to a balance of composition, to a choice and arrangement of words which not only by their meaning but also by their sound have a charm of suggestiveness which is all their own. "The functions of the poetical faculty are twofold," says Shelley; "by one it creates new materials of knowledge, power and pleasure; by the other it engenders in the mind a desire to reproduce and arrange them according to a certain rhythm and order." [24] By their freshness and surprise verses ring little bells of change from word to word till they wake the mystery of which their creator has seen the flashes as he looked on "love and joy and this delightful world." And this is poetry.

"In it," says Jacques Maritain, "we find indissolubly active, the reality and the personal experience, the world and all the soul. In its creation, feeling and meaning are led back to the heart."

[23] Jacques et Raissa Maritain: *Situation de la Poesie,* p. 34.
[24] Shelley, *A Defence of Poetry,* edn. 1880, vol. III, p. 131.

"Poetry is religious," says Jean Royère. "It is the history of a soul: it seeks to scrutinize the soul's mystery," [25] and, adds Raissa Maritain: "The source of poetry and of all creative intuition is in a certain experience which one may call a knowledge." [26] Not ordinary knowledge, but a knowledge which is intuitive, which is a thing of taste and savour in those inner faculties where "soul and heart and sense in concert move." And since sense is in concert with heart, and heart with soul, he who has this inner knowledge enjoys the soul's experience of harmony, beauty, joy or peace, realised or longed for. Therefore the imagination has a sense of order, and words a rhythm, and poetry chooses symbols which both please the lover's senses and transcend them. In poetry, says Jacques Maritain, we find indissolubly active the reality and the personal experience, the world and all the soul in its creation, feeling and meaning are led back to the heart, the blood to the mind, and passion to intuition. And through the vital activity of the intellect, all the faculties spring from their root and source into activity. It is the soul which is known in the experience of the exterior world, and it is the exterior world which is known in the experience of the soul in a knowledge which is not knowledge, for where is the concept in which it should take form? What it knows it knows as unknown—for its object is not to know but to create.[27]

Its instinct is to connect a mystical experience both with the created world and also with its own art of words. For "sounds as well as thoughts have relations both between each other and towards that which they represent, and a perception of the order of those relations has always been found connected with a perception of the relations of thought. Hence the language of poets has ever affected a sort of uniform and harmonious recurrence of sound, without which it were not poetry and which is scarcely less indispensable to the communication of its influence than the words themselves without reference to their peculiar order." [28]

Why then is this Carmelite a poet? It is because in his life of contemplation effort was rewarded by a flight of the soul into a breathless and rapturous calm. In this heavenly air, his whole being lived by an

[25] *La Phalange*, 1909.
[26] J. and R. Maritain: *Situation de la Poesie*, p. 34.
[27] *Ibid.*, pp. 154, 155.
[28] Shelley: *A Defence of Poetry* (1880), Vol. III, p. 106. The whole of this famous essay could have been cited in this connection.

intense life. His imagination caught fire, especially that subtle and suggestive sphere of the imagination which lives in the evocative power of words; but, with this excitement, there was always the calming sense of order which demanded a rhythm and an order in the words, while, at the same time, the symbols they suggested were chosen and arranged also for delight. Each must be fresh, yet each must fit its place. In each word aptness competed with surprise, and yet among them all was pattern and measure. And finally, the whole is a symbol of the end attained, for "the peculiar quality of love is to desire to be united and bound together with the beloved object to attain to perfection in the blessing of love." [29] "In one single glance, the soul sees that which God is in Himself and that which He is in the creatures." [30]

Therefore the Prince of Spanish mystics opened his secret in poetry like that of the *Song of Songs:*

> O night which was my guide,
> O night fairer than dawn,
> O night which to the side
> Of lover brought his bride
> And then didst make them one!
>
> . . . .
>
> I stayed: he let me rest
> My cheek upon his breast . . .[31]

And the contemplative blessed himself in the silence of his oblivion.

"The picture is consistent throughout, perfect and flawless. And what a picture it is! It is a warm summer night of the south, fragrant with the rich scent of the cedar-wood and the lilies. The vast boughs of the cedars sway through the gloom as the breeze moves gently among them. Beneath all is blackness save for the white gleam of the lilies. Through the trees looms the turret of some fantastic Oriental building—reminiscent of the Alhambra or the Alcazar of Seville. But this is but the external setting, an atmosphere plenteously charged with suggestion of passionate love in which the meeting and embrace of the lovers is placed. There is the bride, who has escaped the would-be hindrance of her household by the secret ladder and in disguise,

[29] Cf. p. 87.
[30] Cf. p. 139.
[31] Cf. p. 120.

while all are asleep. There is He who awaits in the darkness, the lover undescribed, because He is indescribable, Himself. The transformation follows, the embrace and the sleep of the Divine Lover. It is impossible to say these things in other words. Only the words of the saint are able to unite so intimately the earthly type and the spiritual antitype, to fuse so completely intensest passion with perfect purity. For the power and the life of the poem are a white heat of spiritual passion. That heat moulds the imagery and burns through it. Every detail is aglow with it, even the turret, the cedars and the lilies. In every supreme work of art the feeling of the artist thus moulds and penetrates the material embodiment, as life moulds and penetrates every limb of the human body." [32]

"The poetry of San Juan de la Cruz is metaphysical fire, a sort of white heat in which the abstract, the almost negative becomes ecstatically realized by the senses. . . . There is an abandonment to all the sensations of love, which seems to me to exceed, on their own ground, in directness and intensity of spiritual longing, most of what has been written by the love poets of all ages. These lines so full of rich and strange beauty ache with desire, and with all the subtlety of desire. They analyse the sensations of the soul, as lovers do, that they may draw out their sweetness more luxuriantly." [33]

Here then remains an impression which words can convey, but which is as much devoid of the definite and palpable, as music without words transcends logical thought. The harmonies convey their own meaning, and for the musician it is enough. It was in such a world as this that San Juan connected his mysticism with his expression—preferring poetry to prose. He connected his patterned word not merely with his admiration of love and beauty, but with the words which turned the key of the door into Christ's mysteries.

For Christ was the Word of the Father; and as such He had the words of eternal life, not only in the truth which He revealed, but in all words which prepared for Him, all which fulfilled His truth. Who could set limits to the power of such words? Well might he say, "I am as glad of thy word as one that findeth great spoils: the words of thy mouth are dearer to me than thousands of gold and silver." A kindred mystery was in the *works* of God. All were made in wisdom:

[32] E. I. Watkin: *The Philosophy of Mysticism*, p. 398.
[33] Arthur Symons, *Cities, Sea Coasts and Islands*, pp. 66, 67.

all had been raised in Christ into the heaven of heavens; nature, too, therefore, even though at times the prince of the air exerted power over it, had received a consecration and shone with what Wordsworth was to call the *gleam*.

9

If it is odd that he should be commended as a substitute for Buddhism, it may well seem puzzling that the name of so austere a master should be on the lips of many when godlessness stales the air. Yet, in the face of all surprises, he comes again to us in his four hundredth year with providential instancy. For still, while strident aeroplanes profane the sky, though the whirr and disturbance of ubiquitous machines come between the ploughman and the soil, to many the Redeemer returns. Above their din "He calls thee full oft with His sweet secret voice and stirreth thy heart full stilly"; but just because the call is still and draws me away from the traffic of the world, I hesitate to follow, lest I should be shirking; and yet, the greater the uproar and crash of the world, the more the need for me to put aside the stifling blackout of a war world and open my window to the night's freshness and its stars.

There are souls who are drawn to recollection: but still they are impeded, because, just as in the days of Santa Teresa, others accuse them of "a quietist tendency," as though loose impulse and slackness could not be distinguished from the urgency of contemplation, as San Juan distinguished them.

And others have thought that the mystic life was lived in temporal stages, each distinct, of first purgation, then illumination, then unity. But San Juan shows how often they intermingle, how early one may drink deep of bliss, how constantly one must run for betterment to the Cross, as love presses upward and inward.

And yet again many draw the inner wisdom of mysticism from poetry, including the poetry of the Bible, and San Juan shows them how in faith in the Word and in the Spirit this becomes the way of Holiness: and thus he reminds us that to those who love and learn the Bible comes what Coleridge called "the sense of wings uplifting" which makes them mount up as eagles when they pray.

And others, some of them within the Catholic Church and others outside it, see in its system a sumptuous array, or, at worst, a farrago of forms and observances, not realizing that its counsel is to ascend from these to a closer and more exact communion.

Others, again, having been given in the peace and bloom of their garden, or in the alternation of poetry with the wild, the still communion with the Sustaining Spirit, and then been told that this was a shoddy fake for mysticism, may learn how to make it real and perfect by seeing creation through the Divine Word and then through His Incarnation and Ascension.

But there are others who, enjoying transcendental favours, fail to realise that without self-denial, order and graciousness, these make life dangerous; for when personal opportunities are great, despotic powers of darkness will work their malign craft, even at the gates of heaven. And those who pray must watch—lest they enter into temptation.

And lastly we must know that when the turbine of the world is jarred and jammed neither production, nor economic security, nor yet wholesale ruin and destruction—will overhaul it. Each material remedy will bring a new disease and a new problem for man till his soul is redeemed. And to be redeemed is to reorganize the ways of memory and expectation: it is to enjoy and admire love and beauty: it is to complete faith by the elevation, the eagerness and the dream of hope.

10

But one would be doing an injustice to the poet of the soul as well as to the art of portraiture if one appeared, while insisting on his immediacy, to make him text for a moral.

He is too keen, too high, too prodigal, too much the artist, too much the Carmelite, too much the seer, for any portrait to be more than an interpretation, and no interpretation should be exclusive. But few can do justice to a portrait till it is appropriately framed.

This man's frame is in the gorgeous style of Spanish baroque. He burst into poetry at Toledo at the time when Cervantes and El Greco nurtured their genius in its streets. Spain's finest sculptor, Montañes, was born at Alcala-la-Real when at Granada Fray Juan de la Cruz was writing The Living Flame of Love. He was not only a writer on asceticism, but a troubadour singing to taut strings a song for Old

Castile. He is as much a trophy of its romance as the contemporary Escorial, as the baroque sanctuary of San Isidro in Madrid, or those bartisan turrets which point upwards from the Alcázar of Segovia like lances set towards the invisible Jerusalem to capture it by violent assault.

Spanish laymen admire the poet, while Carmelites venerate a friar who was a master and a saint. All are the single man who climbed from the plains by steep ascents to the crags among which lie the deepest caverns of our nature. There, pressing in further where the denseness deepened, he found their remotest corners lit with flame.

SAN JUAN DE LA CRUZ

POESÍAS

I

The Dark Night

1   En una noche obscura,
Con ansias en amores inflamada,
¡Oh dichosa ventura!
Salí sin ser notada,
Estando ya mi casa sosegada.

2   A escuras, y segura,
Por la secreta escala disfrazada,
¡Oh dichosa ventura!
A escuras, y en celada,
Estando ya mi casa sosegada.

3   En la noche dichosa,
En secreto, que nadie me veía,
Ni yo miraba cosa,
Sin otra luz y guía,
Sino la que en el corazón ardía.

4   Aquesta me guiaba
Más cierto que la luz del mediodía,
A donde me esperaba,
Quien yo bien me sabía,
En parte donde nadie parecía.

5   ¡Oh noche, que guiaste,
Oh noche amable más que el alborada:
Oh noche, que juntaste
Amado con amada,
Amada en el Amado transformada!

6   En mi pecho florido,
Que entero para él sólo se guardaba,
Allí quedó dormido,
Y yo le regalaba,
Y el ventalle de cedros aire daba.

7   El aire de la almena,
Cuando yo sus cabellos esparcía,
Con su mano serena
En mi cuello hería,
Y todos mis sentidos suspendía.

8   Quedéme, y olvidéme,
El rostro recliné sobre el Amado,
Cesó todo, y dejéme,
Dejando mi cuidado
Entre las azucenas olvidado.

II

Song of the Spirit

ESPOSA

1   ¿A dónde te escondiste,
Amado, y me dejaste con gemido?
Como el ciervo huiste,
Habiéndome herido;
Salí tras ti clamando, y eras ido.

2   Pastores, los que fuerdes
Allá por las majadas al Otero,
Si por ventura vierdes
Aquel que yo más quiero,
Decidle que adolezco, peno y muero.

3 Buscando mis amores,
Iré por esos montes y riberas,
Ni cogeré las flores,
Ni temeré las fieras,
Y pasaré los fuertes y fronteras.

PREGUNTA A LAS CRIATURAS

4 Oh bosques y espesuras,
Plantadas por la mano del Amado,
Oh prado de verduras,
De flores esmaltado,
Decid si por vosotros ha pasado.

RESPUESTA DE LAS CRIATURAS

5 Mil gracias derramando,
Pasó por estos sotos con presura,
Y yéndolos mirando,
Con sola su figura
Vestidos los dejó de hermosura.

ESPOSA

6 ¡Ay, quién podrá sanarme!
Acaba de entregarte ya de vero,
No quieras enviarme
De hoy más ya mensajero,
Que no saben decirme lo que quiero.

7 Y todos cuantos vagan,
De ti me van mil gracias refiriendo
Y todos más me llagan,
Y déjame muriendo
Un no sé qué que quedan balbuciendo.

8 Mas, ¿cómo perseveras,
Oh vida, no viviendo donde vives,
Y haciendo porque mueras,
Las flechas que recibes,
De lo que del Amado en ti concibes?

9   ¿Por qué, pues, has llagado
A aqueste corazón, no le sanaste?
Y pues me le has robado,
¿Por qué así le dejaste,
Y no tomas el robo que robaste?

10   Apaga mis enojos,
Pues que ninguno basta a deshacellos,
Y véante mis ojos,
Pues eres lumbre dellos,
Y sólo para ti quiero tenellos.

11   Descubre tu presencia,
Y máteme tu vista y hermosura;
Mira que la dolencia
De amor, que no se cura
Sino con la presencia y la figura.

12   ¡Oh cristalina fuente,
Si en esos tus semblantes plateados,
Formases de repente
Los ojos deseados,
Que tengo en mis entrañas dibujados!

13   Apártalos, Amado,
Que voy de vuelo.

ESPOSO

Vuélvete, paloma,
Que el ciervo vulnerado
Por el otero asoma,
Al aire de tu vuelo, y fresco toma.

ESPOSA

14   Mi Amado, las montañas,
Los valles solitarios nemorosos,
Las ínsulas extrañas,
Los ríos sonorosos,
El silbo de los aires amorosos.

15   La noche sosegada
En par de los levantes de la aurora,
La música callada,
La soledad sonora,
La cena, que recrea y enamora.

16   Nuestro lecho florido,
De cuevas de leones enlazado,
En púrpura tendido,
De paz edificado,
De mil escudos de oro coronado.

17   A zaga de tu huella
Las jóvenes discurren al camino
Al toque de centella,
Al adobado vino,
Emisiones de bálsamo Divino.

18   En la interior bodega
De mi amado bebí, y cuando salía
Por toda aquesta vega,
Ya cosa no sabía,
Y el ganado perdí, que antes seguía.

19   Allí me dió su pecho,
Allí me enseñó ciencia muy sabrosa.
Y yo le dí de hecho
A mí, sin dejar cosa;
Allí le prometí de ser su esposa.

20   Mi alma se ha empleado,
Y todo mi caudal en su servicio:
Ya no guardo ganado,
Ni ya tengo otro oficio;
Que ya sólo en amar es mi ejercicio.

21   Pues ya si en el ejido,
De hoy más no fuere vista ni hallada,
Diréis que me he perdido,
Que andando enamorada,
Me hice perdidiza, y fuí ganada.

22   De flores y esmeraldas
En las frescas mañanas escogidas,
Haremos las guirnaldas,
En tu amor florecidas,
Y en un cabello mío entretejidas.

23   En solo aquel cabello,
Que en mi cuello volar consideraste,
Mirástele en mi cuello,
Y en él preso quedaste,
Y en uno de mis ojos te llagaste.

24   Cuando tú me mirabas,
Tu gracia en mí tus ojos imprimían:
Por eso me adamabas,
Y en eso merecían
Los míos adorar lo que en ti vían.

25   No quieras despreciarme,
Que si color moreno en mí hallaste,
Ya bien puedes mirarme,
Después que me miraste,
Que gracia y hermosura en mí dejaste.

26   Cogednos las raposas,
Que está ya florecida nuestra viña,
En tanto que de rosas
Hacemos una piña,
Y no parezca en la montiña.

27   Detente, Cierzo muerto;
Ven, Austro, que recuerdas los amores,
Aspira por mi huerto,
Y corran sus olores,
Y pacerá el Amado entre las flores.

ESPOSO

28 Entrádose ha la Esposa
En el ameno huerto deseado,
Y a su sabor reposa,
El cuello reclinado
Sobre los dulces brazos del Amado.

29 Debajo del manzano,
Allí conmigo fuiste desposada,
Allí te dí la mano,
Y fuiste reparada,
Donde tu madre fuera violada.

30 A las aves ligeras,
Leones, ciervos, gamos saltadores,
Montes, valles, riberas,
Aguas, aires, ardores,
Y miedos de las noches veladores:

31 Por las amenas liras
Y canto de serenas os conjuro
Que cesen vuestras iras,
Y no toquéis al muro,
Porque la Esposa duerma más seguro.

ESPOSA

32 Oh ninfas de Judea,
En tanto que en las flores y rosales
El ámbar perfumea,
Mora en los arrabales,
Y no queráis tocar nuestros umbrales.

33 Escóndete, Carillo,
Y mira con tu haz a las montañas,
Y no quieras decillo:
Mas mira las compañas
De la que va por ínsulas extrañas.

ESPOSO

34   La blanca palomica
Al Arca con el ramo se ha tornado,
Y ya la tortolica
Al socio deseado
En las riberas verdes ha hallado.

35   En soledad vivía,
Y en soledad ha puesto ya su nido,
Y en soledad la guía
A solas su querido,
También ensoledad de amor herido.

ESPOSA

36   Gocémonos, Amado,
Y vámonos a ver en tu hermosura
Al monte u al collado,
Do mana el agua pura;
Entremos más adentro en la espesura.

37   Y luego a las subidas
Cavernas de la piedra nos iremos,
Que están bien escondidas,
Y allí nos entraremos,
Y el mosto de granadas gustaremos.

38   Allí me mostrarías
Aquello que mi alma pretendía,
Y luego me darías
Allí tú, vida mía,
Aquello que me diste el otro día.

39   El aspirar del aire,
El canto de la dulce Filomena,
El soto y su donaire,
En la noche serena
Con llama que consume y no da pena.

40   Que nadie lo miraba,
Aminadab tampoco parecía,
Y el cerco sosegaba,
Y la caballería
A vista de las aguas descendía.

III

The Living Flame of Love.

1   ¡Oh llama de amor viva,
Que tiernamente hieres
De mi alma en el más profundo centro!
Pues ya no eres esquiva,
Acaba ya si quieres,
Rompe la tela deste dulce encuentro.

2   ¡Oh cauterio suave!
¡Oh regalada llaga!
¡Oh mano blanda! ¡Oh toque delicado,
Que a vida eterna sabe,
Y toda deuda paga!
Matando, muerte en vida la has trocado.

3   ¡Oh lámparas de fuego,
En cuyos resplandores
Las profundas cavernas del sentido,
Que estaba obscuro y ciego,
Con extraños primores
Calor y luz dan junto a su querido!

4   ¡Cuán manso y amoroso
Recuerdas en mi seno,
Donde secretamente solo moras:
Y en tu aspirar sabroso
De bien y gloria lleno
¡Cuán delicadamente me enamoras!

IV

Ecstasy of Contemplation: I entered in.

> Entréme donde no supe,
> Y quedéme no sabiendo,
> Toda sciencia trascendiendo.

1   Yo no supe dónde entraba,
Pero, cuando allí me ví,
Sin saber dónde me estaba,
Grandes cosas entendí;
No diré lo que sentí,
Que me quedé no sabiendo,
Toda sciencia trascendiendo.

2   De paz y de piedad
Era la sciencia perfecta,
En profunda soledad,
Entendida vía recta;
Era cosa tan secreta,
Que me quedé balbuciendo,
Toda sciencia trascendiendo.

3   Estaba tan embebido,
Tan absorto y ajenado,
Que se quedó mi sentido
De todo sentir privado;
Y el espíritu dotado
De un entender no entendiendo,
Toda sciencia trascendiendo.

4   El que allí llega de vero,
De sí mismo desfallesce;
Cuanto sabía primero
Mucho bajo le paresce;
Y su sciencia tanto cresce,
Que se queda no sabiendo,
Toda sciencia trascendiendo.

5   Cuanto más alto se sube,
Tanto menos entendía
Qué es la tenebrosa nube
Que a la noche esclarecía;
Por eso quien la sabía
Queda siempre no sabiendo
Toda sciencia trascendiendo.

6   Este saber no sabiendo
Es de tan alto poder,
Que los sabios arguyendo
Jamás le pueden vencer;
Que no llega su saber
A no entender entendiendo,
Toda sciencia trascendiendo.

7   Y es de tan alta excelencia
Aqueste sumo saber,
Que no hay facultad ni sciencia
Que le puedan emprender;
Quien se supiere vencer
Con un no saber sabiendo,
Irá siempre trascendiendo.

8   Y si lo queréis oír,
Consiste esta suma sciencia
En un subido sentir
De la divinal Esencia;
Es obra de su clemencia
Hacer quedar no entendiendo
Toda sciencia trascendiendo.

V

Longing for the Divine.

Vivo sin vivir en mí,
Y de tal manera espero,
Que muero porque no muero.

1   En mí yo no vivo ya,
Y sin Dios vivir no puedo;
Pues sin él y sin mí quedo,
Este vivir ¿ qué será?
Mil muertes se me hará,
Pues mi misma vida espero,
Muriendo porque no muero.

2   Esta vida que yo vivo
Es privación de vivir;
Y así, es contino morir
Hasta que viva contigo;
Oye, mi Dios, lo que digo,
Que esta vida no la quiero;
Que muero porque no muero.

3   Estando absente de ti,
¿ Qué vida puedo tener,
Sino muerte padescer,
La mayor que nunca ví?
Lástima tengo de mí,
Pues de suerte persevero,
Que muero porque no muero.

4   El pez que del agua sale,
Aun de alivio no caresce,
Que en la muerte que padesce,
Al fin la muerte le vale;
¿ Qué muerte habrá que se iguale
A mi vivir lastimero,
Pues si más vivo más muero?

5   Cuando me pienso aliviar
De verte en el Sacramento,
Háceme más sentimiento
El no te poder gozar;
Todo es para más penar,
Por no verte como quiero,
Y muero porque no muero.

6 Y si me gozo, Señor,
Con esperanza de verte,
En ver que puedo perderte
Se me dobla mi dolor:
Viviendo en tanto pavor,
Y esperando como espero,
Muérome porque no muero.

7 Sácame de aquesta muerte,
Mi Dios, y dame la vida;
No me tengas impedida
En este lazo tan fuerte;
Mira que peno por verte,
Y mi mal es tan entero,
Que muero porque no muero.

8 Lloraré mi muerte ya,
Y lamentaré mi vida
En tanto que detenida
Por mis pecados está.
¡Oh mi Dios! ¿cuándo será?
Cuando yo diga de vero:
Vivo ya porque no muero.

VI

The Same.

Tras de un amoroso lance,
Y no de esperanza falto,
Volé tan alto, tan alto,
Que le dí a la caza alcance.

1 Para que yo alcance diese
A aqueste lance divino,
Tanto volar me convino,
Que de vista me perdiese;

Y con todo, en este trance
En el vuelo quedé falto;
Mas el amor fué tan alto,
Que le dí a la caza alcance.

2   Cuando más alto subía,
Deslumbróseme la vista,
Y la más fuerte conquista
En escuro se hacía;
Mas por ser de amor el lance
Dí un ciego y oscuro salto,
Y fuí tan alto, tan alto,
Que le dí a la caza alcance.

3   Cuanto más alto llegaba
De este lance tan subido,
Tanto más bajo y rendido
Y abatido me hallaba;
Dije: No habrá quien alcance;
Y abatíme tanto, tanto,
Que fuí tan alto, tan alto,
Que le dí a la caza alcance.

4   Por una extraña manera
Mil vuelos pasé de un vuelo,
Porque esperanza de cielo
Tanto alcanza cuanto espera;
Esperé sólo este lance,
Y en esperar no fuí falto,
Pues fuí tan alto, tan alto,
Que le dí a la caza alcance.

VII

The Christ Compared to a Young Shepherd.

1   Un pastorcico solo está penado,
Ajeno de placer y de contento,
Y en su pastora puesto el pensamiento,
Y el pecho del amor muy lastimado.

2   No llora por haberle amor llagado,
  Que no le pena verse así afligido,
  Aunque en el corazón está herido;
  Mas llora por pensar que está olvidado.

3   Que sólo de pensar que está olvidado
  De su bella pastora, con gran pena
  Se deja maltratar en tierra ajena,
  El pecho del amor muy lastimado.

4   Y dice el Pastorcico: ¡Ay, desdichado
  De aquel que de mi amor ha hecho ausencia,
  Y no quiere gozar la mi presencia,
  Y el pecho por su amor muy lastimado!

5   Y a cabo de un gran rato se ha encumbrado
  Sobre un árbol do abrió sus brazos bellos,
  Y muerto se ha quedado, asido de ellos,
  El pecho del amor muy lastimado.

VIII

Contemplation of the Blessed Trinity.

Que bien sé yo la fonte que mana y corre,
  Aunque es de noche.

1   Aquella eterna fonte está ascondida,
  Que bien sé yo do tiene su manida,
    Aunque es de noche.

2   Su origen no lo sé, pues no le tiene,
  Mas sé que todo origen de ella viene,
    Aunque es de noche.

3   Sé que no puede ser cosa tan bella,
  Y que cielos y tierra beben de ella,
    Aunque es de noche.

4   Bien sé que suelo en ella no se halla,
Y que ninguno puede vadealla,
    Aunque es de noche.

5   Su claridad nunca es escurecida,
Y sé que toda luz de ella es venida,
    Aunque es de noche.

6   Sé ser tan caudalosas sus corrientes,
Que infiernos, cielos riegan, y las gentes,
    Aunque es de noche.

7   El corriente que nace de esta fuente,
Bien sé que es tan capaz y omnipotente,
    Aunque es de noche.

8   El corriente que de estas dos procede
Sé que ninguna de ellas le precede,
    Aunque es de noche.

9   Aquesta eterna fonte está escondida
En este vivo pan por darnos vida,
    Aunque es de noche.

10   Aquí se está llamando a las criaturas,
Y de esta agua se hartan, aunque a escuras,
    Porque es de noche.

11   Aquesta viva fuente, que deseo,
En este pan de vida yo la veo,
    Aunque de noche.

IX

ROMANCE 1

Sobre el Evangelio "in principio erat Verbum" acerca de la
Santísima Trinidad.

En el principio moraba
El Verbo, y en Dios vivía,
En quien su felicidad
Infinita poseía.

El mismo Verbo Dios era,
Que el principio se decía;
Él moraba en el principio,
Y principio no tenía.

Él era el mesmo principio;
Por eso de él carecía;
El Verbo se llama Hijo
Que del principio nacía.

Hale siempre concebido,
Y siempre le concebía,
Dale siempre su substancia,
Y siempre se la tenía.

Y así, la gloria del Hijo
Es la que en el Padre había,
Y toda su gloria el Padre
En el Hijo poseía.

Como amado en el amante
Uno en otro residía,
Y aquese amor que los une,
En lo mismo convenía.

Con el uno y con el otro
En igualdad y valía:
Tres Personas y un amado
Entre todos tres había.

Y un amor en todas ellas
Y un amante las hacía;

Y el amante es el amado
En que cada cual vivía;
   Que el ser que los tres poseen,
Cada cual le poseía,
Y cada cual de ellos ama
A la que este ser tenía.

   Este ser es cada una,
Y éste sólo las unía
En un inefable nudo
Que decir no se sabía.

   Por lo cual era infinito
El amor que las unía,
Porque un solo amor tres tienen,
Que su esencia se decía;
Que el amor, cuanto más uno,
Tanto más amor hacía.

X

ROMANCE 2

De la comunicación de las tres Personas.

   En aquel amor inmenso
Que de los dos procedía,
Palabras de gran regalo
El Padre al Hijo decía,
   De tan profundo deleite,
Que nadie las entendía;
Sólo el Hijo lo gozaba,
Que es a quien pertenecía.
   Pero aquello que se entiende
De esta manera decía:
Nada me contenta, Hijo,
Fuera de tu compañía.
   Y si algo me contenta,
En ti mismo lo quería;
El que a ti más se parece,
A mí más satisfacía.

Y el que nada te semeja,
En mí nada hallaría;
En ti sólo me he agradado,
¡Oh vida de vida mía!

Eres lumbre de mi lumbre,
Eres mi sabiduría,
Figura de mi substancia,
En quien bien me complacía.

Al que a ti te amare, Hijo,
A mí mismo le daría,
Y el amor que yo en ti tengo,
Ese mismo en él pondría,
En razón de haber amado
A quien yo tanto quería.

XI

ROMANCE 3

De la creación.

Una esposa que te ame,
Mi Hijo, darte quería,
Que por tu valor merezca
Tener nuestra compañía.

Y comer pan a una mesa,
Del mismo que yo comía;
Porque conozca los bienes
Que en tal Hijo yo tenía.
Y se congracie conmigo
De tu gracia y lozanía.

Mucho lo agradezco, Padre,
El Hijo le respondía;
A la esposa que me dieres,
Yo mi claridad daría,
Para que por ella vea
Cuánto mi Padre valía,
Y cómo el ser que poseo,
De su ser le recibía.

Reclinarla he yo en mi brazo,
Y en tu amor se abrasaría,
Y con eterno deleite
Tu bondad sublimaría.

XII

FINAL VERSES ON THE CREATION 4

Hágase, pues, dijo el Padre,
Que tu amor lo merecía:
Y en este dicho que dijo,
El mundo criado había.

Palacio para la esposa,
Hecho en gran sabiduría;
El cual, en dos aposentos,
Alto y bajo, dividía.

El bajo de diferencias
Infinitas componía;
Mas el alto hermoseaba
De admirable pedrería.

Porque conozca la esposa
El Esposo que tenía,
En el alto colocaba
La angélica jerarquía;

Pero la natura humana
En el bajo la ponía,
Por ser en su compostura
Algo de menor valía.

Y aunque el ser y los lugares
De esta suerte los partía,
Pero todos son un cuerpo
De la esposa que decía:

Que el amor de un mismo Esposo
Una Esposa los hacía:
Los de arriba poseían
El Esposo en alegría;

Los de abajo en esperanza
De fe que les infundía,

Diciéndoles que algún tiempo
Él los engrandecería.

   Y que aquella su bajeza
Él se la levantaría,
De manera que ninguno
Ya la vituperaría.

   Porque en todo semejante
Él a ellos se haría,
Y se vendría con ellos,
Y con ellos moraría.

   Y que Dios sería hombre,
Y que el hombre Dios sería,
Y trataría con ellos,
Comería y bebería.

   Y que con ellos continuo
Él mismo se quedaría,
Hasta que se consumase
Este siglo que corría.

   Cuando se gozaran juntos
En eterna melodía;
Porque él era la cabeza
De la esposa que tenía.

   A la cual todos los miembros
De los justos juntaría,
Que son cuerpo de la esposa,
A la cual él tomaría

   En sus brazos tiernamente,
Y allí su amor la daría;
Y que así juntos en uno
Al Padre la llevaría.

   Donde del mismo deleite
Que Dios goza, gozaría;
Que, como el Padre y el Hijo,
Y el que de ellos procedía,

   El uno vive en el otro;
Así la esposa sería,
Que, dentro de Dios absorta,
Vida de Dios viviría.

INDEX